PATH TO GRACE

PATH TO GRACE

Reimagining the
Civil Rights Movement

ETHEL MORGAN SMITH

University Press of Mississippi / Jackson

The University Press of Mississippi is the scholarly publishing agency
of the Mississippi Institutions of Higher Learning: Alcorn State University,
Delta State University, Jackson State University, Mississippi State University,
Mississippi University for Women, Mississippi Valley State University,
University of Mississippi, and University of Southern Mississippi.

www.upress.state.ms.us

The University Press of Mississippi is a member
of the Association of University Presses.

Illustrations courtesy the author unless otherwise noted

First printing 2023
∞

Library of Congress Cataloging-in-Publication Data

Names: Smith, Ethel Morgan, 1952– author.
Title: Path to grace : reimagining the civil rights movement / Ethel Morgan Smith.
Other titles: Margaret Walker Alexander series in African American studies.

Description: Jackson : University Press of Mississippi, 2023. | Series:
Margaret Walker Alexander series in African Amercian studies | Includes
bibliographical references
Identifiers: LCCN 2023015019 (print) | LCCN 2023015020 (ebook) | ISBN
9781496846419 (hardback) | ISBN 9781496846426 (epub) | ISBN
9781496846433 (epub) | ISBN 9781496846440 (pdf) | ISBN 9781496846402 (pdf)
Subjects: LCSH: African American civil rights workers—United
States—Interviews. | African American civil rights workers—United
States—Biography. | Civil rights workers—United States—Interviews. |
Civil rights workers—United States—Biography. | Civil rights
movements—United States—History—20th century. | United States—Race
relations—20th century.
Classification: LCC E185.61 .S624 2023 (print) | LCC E185.61 (ebook) |
DDC 323.1196/073—dc23/eng/20230405
LC record available at https://lccn.loc.gov/2023015019
LC ebook record available at https://lccn.loc.gov/2023015020

British Library Cataloging-in-Publication Data available

For Marcus Bernard Smith, my favorite son.

CONTENTS

Book Notes   3

CHAPTER 1. An Army of God: Do What You Can Do   7
Dr. Sandra Mathews Ford (1953–) and Henry Michael Ford (1953–)

We Ready   23

CHAPTER 2. A View of Grace from the Top   27
John Canty (1925–2019)

Discerning Dreams   41

CHAPTER 3. An Unyielding Feminist: Shirley Chisholm   45
Susan Perry Cole (1948–)

Spelling Bee   57

CHAPTER 4. The Art of Activism   61
Constance Curry (1933–2020)

The Prell Sisters of Alabama   79

CHAPTER 5. What Color Is the World?   85
Blanche Virginia Franklin Moore (1917–2016)

Meteor   101

CHAPTER 6. Designing Dreams   107
Ann Cole Lowe (1898–1981)

Contents

Sam 121

CHAPTER 7. Walking Is Like a Prayer 127
Louise Bruyn (1931–)

The Conspiracy of Grandmothers 149
CHAPTER 8. Drinking from the Cup of Equality 155
Dr. Mary Emma Bruce (1910–2010)

The Problem with Evolving 175
CHAPTER 9. Another Other: White Negroes 183
Andrea Lee (1953–)

Deferred Dreams 197
CHAPTER 10. Two Ways of Seeing the World 201
Gloria Naylor (1950–2016)

Mother 211
CHAPTER 11. We Reached out to the Arts and the Arts Said Yes 215
Nikki Giovanni (1943–)

Acknowledgments 239

Notes 241

PATH TO GRACE

BOOK NOTES

The church ladies' cars were parked in our front yard. They must have come over to help Big Mama quilt, or there could be trouble. I stepped out of the school bus.

Big Mama, Miss Pearl, Miss Carrie Mae, and Miss Merle sat around our kitchen table, cleaning up our schoolbooks for our next term.

"How come dey can't just put de books outside de door?" Big Mama asked. They used rags and soapy water, sometimes a little spray bottle of bleach and water to clean the books, trying to get rid of the "Good Luck Niggers" written all through them. Big Mama and the church ladies had to fish them out of the trash first.

"No, dey just showin' how dey have power over us." Miss Pearl pulled another stack of books toward her from the table. Her arms are almost long enough to reach across the whole table.

"Dey think dis scare us." Miss Carrie Mae shook her head. "Lord, have mercy."

"Dey gonna have to do better dan dis to scare us." They laughed.

"Change clothes, get your food, and eat in de front room," Big Mama ordered my sister and me.

"Yes, ma'am," we said in unison.

Boxes of schoolbooks took up most of the space on the kitchen floor. Stacks of old newspapers blocked the door to the outside.

"Don't be messin' up nothin'. No crumbs on de floor either," Big Mama yelled.

"Yes, ma'am."

"By de time dey finish eatin, de books be cleaned up," Miss Carrie Mae tried to whisper. "Dey can wait to know dis cruel world."

We heard her. But what I couldn't understand was why did the white folks hate us so much. All of the colored folks were hard-working Christians.

"Look what I found." Miss Merle snatched a small bag from her huge purse with different colored inkpads and stencil stamps of roses. She used to teach home economics in Clayton until she retired. She knew how to make everything look pretty.

When my sister and I finished eating, we would wrap the books with newspapers that Little Mama got from the white woman's house, in the front room. Miss Merle stamped different colored flowers with her stencil and inkpads; the books were better than they'd ever been. The covers looked like flowered newspapers. Red roses were for science books, blue for English, green for math, and yellow for history. The algebra book was so big and heavy. I couldn't wait for the school term. I loved all of the books and couldn't wait to dive into them. I knew I'd make excellent grades since I had the highest-grade average than any other student in the whole school. Whenever I would show my report card with an A in every subject to Little Mama, she just shook her head and say, "Daisy would've made A pluses." Big Mama would say, "Dat's good. Don't be lettin' it go to yor head, you hear."

"Yes, ma'am."

Daisy was our oldest sister; I only knew her from the sad photograph hanging on the wall in the front room. The picture was taken two weeks before she died. Her hands, folded across her lap, looked like fragile flowers. Big Mama told us that Dr. Faircloth had said they had better get a picture made before it was too late. They scraped together $5.00 for a white man from Clayton to come and take the photograph.

<hr>

This was my last year at the Bethel School. Everybody was talking about what life was going to be like in high school in Clayton. Our teachers reminded us every day that we were worthy and could compete with any student in Barbour County, Alabama.

Miss Carrie Mae was going to make me three new dresses. She even bought a new zigzag sewing machine that could do all kinds of fancy stitches with buttons and hems. That made me happy. I wouldn't look country.

I wasn't concerned about my schoolwork. So what if I have to work a little harder? I will learn a lot more. Stacy Mae Williams was stuck up because she wore store-bought clothes, and boys thought she was cute. She never spoke to me unless she had to. Yesterday on the school bus she had to. "Mama said if you help me with my homework, she'll pay you a dollar." It was as though everybody stopped and listened. We had a math test last week. I bet she failed it. "Sure," I smiled.

—◆— —◆—

"Dis part ain't dat bad. De insultin' part is diggin' dem outta de trash cans. Is dat necessary? Power to de polls," Miss Pearl raised her pecan-colored fisted hands above her head. Miss Pearl didn't play, and everybody knew it. When I was six, I had to go to Clayton to get my shots; I rode the school bus with her. After she dropped the students off at school, we got in her new shiny car and drove to the clinic. I was a little scared, but she assured me it was no big deal. Riding in Miss Pearl's luxury car made me feel like I was on a TV show.

She was right. Afterward, we went to the mall and ate lunch at Shoney's. It was the first time I'd ever been in any kind of restaurant. I ordered a Big Boy because Miss Pearl said that was what she always ordered. Then we went into the Lerner's Shop, where she bought me a blue and white seersucker dress. That was the best day of my life.

But coming home on the school bus, students could be a little rowdy. Miss Pearl wasn't going to have any of it, and she lit into them. She didn't allow fooling around or talking. She kept order like the law. Folks in the community thought she was the best driver in the county. "She ain't never had nothin' close to no accident," the church ladies always said with pride.

Miss Pearl was always the first driver to get her contract renewed every year. Her clothes were starched and ironed. No matter how warm or wet the weather, Miss Pearl never wore a wrinkle. Her crisp light-colored blouses always matched her pleated skirts. Sometimes she wore pastel-colored shirt-waist dresses. She owned every color and even had penny loafers to match. Folks said she had to go to Montgomery to buy her shoes. She wore a new hairstyle and a new pair of glasses every school year.

To keep order, she assigned two students to take the names of trouble-makers, one in the front and one in the back. Another student opened and closed the door of the school bus for her. If your name ended up on either list, she'd stop by your house and have a chat with whoever was in charge. That meant real trouble for any student who disrespected authority from a God-fearing southern, colored woman in a high position.

Whenever Miss Pearl had trouble getting students to settle down, she just started in on her favorite sermon: "White folks is probably right in thinkin' de coloreds is crazy and dumb. Here I got yore no good lives in de palm of my hand. Lord, Lord, I just don't know. Any given second, all dat racket could make me so nervous, dat I could run off de road and kill everybody in less than one minute flat." She snapped her fingers high above her head when she got to that part. "My question is: do you ever use dem big heads for thinkin'? You in school to get a education, and here you not usin' dem big heads." She pointed to her head with her finger like it was a gun. "I just wish when I was growin' up, I had opportunity like yawl. You don't have to work in the fields. You eat three squares ever day. I know 'cause I know your folks. Most of you don't even have to work, nowhere 'cept 'round yore houses a little. Lord. Lord. Just once, prove de white folks wrong. Think! Think!" She pointed her right hand to her head again. She kept her left hand squeezed on the steering wheel. But she never took her eyes off of the graveled road. "One of dese days, I'm gonna write a book and call it *Niggers Is Crazy*. I bet I'll make so much money dat I won't ever have to thank 'bout drivin' dis here bus again. De white folks will buy it just to say, 'see, I told you the niggers is crazy!'" Her sermon always worked. Most students were asleep by the time she got to the 'provin' de white folks wrong' part.

CHAPTER 1

An Army of God: Do What You Can Do

Dr. Sandra Mathews Ford (1953–) and Henry Michael Ford (1953–)

Be mindful of the words of the Lord Jesus, how He himself
said, it is more blessed—make one happier and more
to be envied—to give than to receive.
—Acts 20:35

The mobile medical center pulled into Gee's Bend, Alabama, followed by a long caravan of cars. All sorts of people answered the call to bring medical supplies and treatment to poor people in this remote western Alabama town of some three hundred residents. A young doctor from Cuba, a ninety-nine-year-old couple, techies from Miami, a pastor from South America. The husband-wife team who set this in motion counted among their Army of God of diverse faiths, races, and ethnicities reached by email, word-of-mouth, and miracles. "That first caravan . . . it was like a train," recalled Dr. Ford, who, along with her husband, Henry Ford, leads the army. "When we turned the corner, it looked like it was never going to end."

The Fords and other volunteers have worked in the crook of the Alabama River for nearly twenty years, serving one of the most neglected populations in the country. Poor, Black people, who remained in the storied Gee's Bend, largely cut off from the world in the state's Black Belt. That name used to refer to the most fertile, dark, rich soil in the country, but now it's a poverty trap. Dr. Ford read an article in 2002 that referred to the Black Belt as "Alabama's

Dr. Sandra Ford and Mr. Henry Ford, founders of the Spirit of
St. Luke.

Third World," which was why they chose Gee's Bend as their first mission.
The article connected to what Dr. Ford experienced as a child in the Black
Belt and the abysmal medical treatment available to poor Black people. She
remembered watching an old woman die waiting to see a white doctor after
being ignored by the nurse in favor of white patients. "I think God has just
created us for this time and for this purpose . . . but one of the things that
we identify as a turning point is when I read that article."

Dr. Ford said the article led to some deep reflection and prayer. She and
her husband fasted for forty days along with their church looking for divine
guidance on just how they were supposed to help. She said, like Martin Luther
King Jr. and his wife Coretta, she and Henry were married to a cause that
demanded action. They fasted and prayed for vision. "We were married to
each other and it gave our marriage a bigger purpose," she said. "The fast hit
our spirits so that we could be in agreement about doing something for this
cause." They found the Book of Esther was calling to them, Dr. Ford said. He
is working behind the scenes, "opening doors and relationships."

And the path opened to Gee's Bend, and the army went forth.

Dr. Ford and I go way back to Bethel Elementary School in Louisville,
Alabama. We reconnected in college at Alabama A&M University. Her husband, Henry Ford, is a certified medical manager and owns a real estate
management company. They wear many robes. He also manages his wife's
medical practice, is the executive director of the Spirit of St. Luke Charitable
Foundation, and they sponsor A Promise to Help, where they take physicians,

nurses, health care professionals, lay people, ministers, and town people to volunteer to help others. Once a month, they travel to the most uninsured, underserved, underprivileged communities in Alabama and set up a mobile clinic to give free medical care. They run a clothing ministry and deliver free clothes—and they also feed everybody. Recently they've added a mentoring component for the youth. After I reconnected with Dr. Ford in 2006, I started supporting their cause, which became my cause.

"We just try to institute a sense of hope in these areas," Henry Ford flashed a big smile. "Every community has different needs; we try to identify those needs and use our influence in the communities to bring the type of help and assistance to those citizens. That is what we do."

He was the first person in his family to graduate from college with a degree in psychology from Auburn University, where he also played football. Dr. Ford wasn't even aware of the fact that her husband was the first African American to receive a degree in psychology. "There are so many Blacks, who's the first. I hadn't even thought about it until now," he said. That was so true. I was the first African American to receive tenure in the Department of English at West Virginia University. And I can keep adding to that list of *firsts*.

The Fords met at the gym after college. They'd been dating a while when one night, he shocked her by asking if she knew anyone who would kill a Klan member for him. He'd been beaten by them and nearly died. This happened when he was younger, but he still carried the internal pain with him. "This is not a way to build a life," he recalled his wife-to-be calmly saying.

After praying about what had happened to him, they became ordained ministers and asked God to use them. That's how they started to heal from the horrific beating he suffered from the Klan.

I am bowled over, first, that I know these people and grew up with Dr. Ford. Folks often throw their religion around like Sunday hats. But these folks, the Fords, live their cause; their commitment and spirit embrace family, community, and their belief in God's plan for them. They have managed to stay motivated after starting their journey nearly twenty years ago.

"Well, it's a combination of things," Dr. Ford said. "I think God has just created us for this time and for this purpose, but one of the things that we identify as a turning point is when I read an article in the local newspaper when I was doing my residency at the University of Tennessee in Chattanooga. 'The Black Belt: Alabama's Third World.'"

She remembered the horror of medical services in rural Alabama, especially for African Americans. She recalled being sick with bronchitis when she was eight years old and needing to see a doctor. There were two doctors who served that part of the county where we lived.

I, too, remembered that doctor's office in Clayton, over by the post office. Our school bus used to pass by it. Dr. Jackson had a Black nurse for the "coloreds." It made his white patients feel more comfortable, we heard. The colored nurse also sold Avon. "Even sick folks wanna smell good," was her sales pitch. Most folks agreed with her. She sold more Avon than any colored woman in the county.

Big Mama said, "she oughta be shame of herself, takin''vantage of sick folks like dat." Later we heard that the Dr. Jacksons were actually veterinarians. Dr. Ford didn't know about the veterinarian part.

"My dad would take me over there after he finished his work at school; we'd leave in the afternoon and stay until almost eleven o'clock at night. There was certainly a need for physicians because the healthcare load was so heavy. An ordinary visit would mean that you sat there for that long. Since it was segregated, Blacks were over here, and the whites were over here." She pointed. Ford looks more like her mother's side of the family, same light skin coloring, petite, but she also has a sense of humor.

When her father took her to the doctor, she watched a steady flow of white patients enter the doctor's office to every one Black patient. "An elderly Black lady was just moaning and rocking back and forward. She sat across from me. It was clear that she was in pain. I'll always remember that. It just stuck out so strongly in my mind. I remember that it was as if nobody cared. The nurse would come out and ignore her. (This was before the *colored* nurse.) And she sat there, and she sat there, and all of a sudden, she died." Dr. Ford teared up.

Even though I knew that story before interviewing her, it still shocked and saddened me. I had to keep myself from weeping. I am sure it affected her in a much deeper way. She was actually there bearing witness to such deep-rooted racism. What hatred one must own to allow a poor woman to die, and not be bothered by it. I bet that nurse went to church every Sunday and praised God. We were quiet for a few minutes.

"She just . . . she was in the chair, and she went down and collapsed. It touched me as a young girl to such an extent that I said, 'Lord, if you enable me to become a physician, I promise to help.'" Her father had wanted to be a dentist; since he didn't have the opportunity or the money to go to dental school, he did everything to put her on that path. "He was sitting there when that poor woman died . . . he was part of my dream and was my first encouragement to go to medical school."

I sat around their grand and colorful dining room, fighting back tears at such a sad and wonderful story. Their living and dining rooms are open to each other. The rooms are painted purple and gold, representing Henry Ford's beloved fraternity Omega Psi Phi. Dr. Ford is a member of Delta Sigma Theta sorority. Even though the space is grand, it still felt warm and comfortable.

We took a bathroom break and sipped a glass of lemonade. We needed it; this information was hard and painful.

As Ford pursued her career, her father would take her to visit different physicians. One of them was the first Black woman to practice not just in Montgomery but in the state of Alabama from the College of Philadelphia. Dr. Dorothy Seay Wilson graduated from the Medical College of Philadelphia. She became an important role model for Ford. Later, when she went to UAB [University of Alabama at Birmingham] as one of the few Blacks in the program, she was subjected to racial discrimination. But through her role model and family, she saw and felt encouragement. Her friends told her, "It was like God was giving her all sides. You can come back 'cause you were *affected*, but you weren't *infected*."

"So it hadn't really turned me off from helping people. I wasn't *infected*; I was just *affected*, so there was hope, and I was thankful. There's God . . . His hand is in every move. When I was in college, I was saying I don't think I want to do that. I actually tried to major in special education. I think I was just scared."

In the 1970s, when we were in college, we always knew Ford was going to be a doctor. In biology class, when it was time to dissect the rats, she would walk around and ask, "When are the cats coming?" Her determination and passion were equal to the character Beneatha Younger in the stage play *A Raisin in the Sun*, where Beneatha kept reminding her family, friends, and potential beaus that she was going to be a doctor, and they better get used to it. Her narrative revolved around a classmate named Rufus, whose head burst open after a fall. And a doctor made it better, put it together again. Beneatha Younger dreamed of doing the same thing as Dr. Sandra Mathews Ford, "fixing folks."

Dr. Ford had no idea she was one of the first five Black females in medical school and, subsequently, the first Black internist to practice here in Birmingham.

"I remember being the only doctor on call in the emergency room," she recounted. "A white man was brought in. He had cut himself with a saw or something. When I went to help him, he screamed, 'Don't want no nigger touchin' me.'"

"Oh my god, what did you do?" I asked.

It was a busy Saturday night, and one of the nurses told him that Dr. Ford was the only doctor on call. He just sat there bleeding and swearing. Finally, the nurse came to her. "After he apologized, I treated him. So it's been a long, hard road, but when God has His hand on you, it's got to be for you. Against all the odds and so forth, you just keep moving forward." Even though I am used to these kinds of stories that too many Black folks in America often encounter, not just in African American literature that I teach, but also in real life. I had to close my eyes. I dropped my tape recorder.

Gee's Bend

Everything came out of the fast. Dr. Ford remembered the article associating the Black Belt with a Third World country. She remembered the old lady who died waiting for treatment and her husband's assault by the Klan. They had reached out to people doing missionary work. They wrote down ideas that popped into their heads—they had visions. "God was giving us things every day," she said. "We heard Him speaking to us . . . so we had a bunch of sheets of paper, and we put it together at the end of the fast, and we came up with this pamphlet here. This is our vision; it has our mission statement: 'Do What You Can Do.'"

"That's why we chose to have our first mission in Gee's Bend," Henry Ford added. "We knew very little about the western part of the state when our mission launched. We did our research and found some things about it that spoke to us, telling us it was the ideal place."

"Let me tell you how it happened," Dr. Ford sat back in her comfortable leather chair, dressed in casual light blue-cropped pants and a matching blouse. The room was quiet; even the early spring noises of chirping birds and crickets were silent. "God led us to one of my patients, who was in the ICU and subsequently died. I was telling his wife about our work, and she said, 'Oh, [my husband] has a cousin that is down in Wilcox, Alabama, in Camden. Cheryl will be the contact for you. And she can help you . . . really help you.'"

12

Henry Ford described the meeting in Wilcox as "really something." The mayor was there, and other higher-up government officials. People came from the city council, judges. "There's a Black doctor and a white doctor." He laughed. "The Black doctor's name was White, and the white doctor's name was Black."

"That's a sign!" We laughed.

"People from all around heard about the fact that we were interested in the Black Belt, and it was just a huge congregation of people. We took a group of people from our church . . . people who were interested, just a big think tank. Cheryl put all this together. That's how we decided to go to Gee's Bend first."

The Fords paint a big and bright picture, though not without struggles, but their faith in these communities, in each other, and in God is second to none. I feel honored to be in their presence. My life was in need of a spiritual lift; I couldn't have found a better place to start.

Henry Ford continued, "God gave us a roadmap during that fast, and that's what we're doing today . . . In Gee's Bend, most of the Black people who live there are named Pettway. But if they left Gee's Bend, they are called Pettaways, like runaways."

Black people are tied to the land as their enslaved ancestors had been. The Alabama River has its curves and bends, and Gee's Bend is surrounded on three sides by water. There's one way in and one way out. In 1816, Joseph Gee marched seventeen enslaved people from North Carolina and began cotton production. Next to arrive was Pettway, and he bought enslaved people from Gee. "He, supposedly, was a pretty good enslaver, as far as slave owners go."

After the Civil War, a lot of the enslaved people took his name and began sharecropping. It solved the transition where people could work the land and earn a living. Farmers borrowed from the landowners to buy seeds, equipment, and other things needed to work their share. They put food and clothing on their tabs to the owners too. If they made enough money, they could survive. But when Pettway died, his wife wanted to leave. After a really tough winter, she did not want to live in the countryside anymore. So she called in all the debts.

The farmers had no money to pay; the wife summoned the sheriff and townspeople to strip the farmers of everything of value, everything they needed to make a living. The people had nowhere to go; they had no money, no real skills, and faced roving bands of white vigilantes.

Gee's Bend Citizens early 1900.

I found a similar pattern when researching my first book *From Whence Cometh My Help: The African American Community at Hollins College.* African Americans who came to the college in 1842 as enslaved stayed on after the Emancipation as servants. Men left if they could and changed their names with hopes of sending for their families later. Often that did not happen. The level of racism and hostility made it impossible to find decent work. Who could have been prepared for that? African Americans, including those in Gee's Bend, thought their newfound freedom was an asset. But they were left behind to die.

"And the story goes that one guy in Birmingham heard about what was happening, and he got supplies together and went down to Gee's Bend," Henry Ford said. "He may have gotten other people to raise money to help get supplies. They just talk about this one guy who spearheaded it. And so, literally saved the lives of all those people. No one remembered his name."

The Gee's Bend story of grim survival continued into the 1930s when a merchant who had given credit to the farmers died. His family collected the debts in a most inhumane way. The poor families witnessed as their food, animals, tools, and seeds were taken away again. This time the community survived with the help of Red Cross rations. Most of the land was then sold to the federal government and the Farm Security Administration. Those organizations set up Gee's Bend Farm, Inc., a pilot project intended to help sustain the citizens. The government sold tracts of land to the families, giving African American families control over their land—a rarity for the times. But, in the latter part of The Great Depression, the citizens of the area faced difficult challenges as farming practices became mechanized, and consequently, many left the community, seeking better employment opportunities.

Today Gee's Bend is known for its quilts. Historian and curator William Arnett brought attention to their artistic production with his Souls Grown Deep Foundation in Atlanta, Georgia, as he helped organize exhibits that featured the quilts.

In 2002, while I was on sabbatical on a research fellowship at Brandeis University, I had the pleasure of witnessing one of the exhibits at the Museum of Fine Arts in Boston. School buses were transporting students to the museum from all over the city. Lines were blocks long. It was a marvelous moment. The quilts are special, with patterns that are influenced by African textiles. Women pieced together the strips of cloth to make bedcovers. Of course, the Gee's Bend women, like my mother and grandmother, made quilts to keep themselves and their children warm in unheated shacks that lacked running water and electricity. They developed a distinctive style of quilting, noted for its lively improvisations and geometric simplicity.

Gee's Bend was also a critical part of the civil rights struggle in the 1960s. It was an all-Black town with the strategic advantage of being peninsular with one way in and out, offering a kind of protection from white terrorism. It was near the hotbed of violence and resistance, Selma!

From Gee's Bend to Camden, the county seat where people voted was forty miles of road and a bridge crossing. Many in the community couldn't afford a car. But by ferry over the Alabama River was affordable and it only took seven minutes. In 1962, during a voting rights campaign, the ferry was destroyed by the Klan, which was a major impediment for would-be Black voters.

"Martin Luther King would stay there," Henry Ford said. "The civil rights leaders who would come and stay because . . . the civil right workers felt safe there. But the Klan got pissed off because the civil rights workers would come over during the day and protest in Selma; and then they could go and be safe. The Klan burned the ferry down. The citizens of Gee's Bend tried to rebuild a ferry for forty years. Forty years!"

I was in disbelief for about forty years. It sounded more like a developing nation rather than the United States. In fact, King used the divide between Gee's Bend Black citizens and the white county courthouse to illustrate the rift in America's racial policies.

"Then they had all kinds of folks who came down there trying to get the ferry back up. We went to Gee's Bend with intentions of praying that God would break the gridlock that was keeping the Gee's Bend people from having a ferry open. So we took our group down to the site where the ferry used to be, and we prayed." They later returned with the mobile clinic and caravan of volunteers. The ferry resumed service in 2006. Their prayers had been answered.

"You are the miracle that you've been waiting for," I said.

An Eye Foundation doctor believed that God had sent her to give help. And she talked about the Fords coming to Gee's Bend, and she told another person, and that person told another person, and so on. The eye doctor didn't even think about who was going to be there. She got all of her supplies together. "I feel like I shouldn't go because I don't have anything but me," she worried. "And I don't have a lot of supplies."

"I told her that God just wants her to show up and don't worry about it. Do What You Can Do," Dr. Ford remembered. "That's our motto. Do What You Can Do."

The eye doctor showed up with nothing but her lens to look into the eyes of patients. But the Eye Foundation and Lions Club had a big surprise, a mobile clinic.

"Million dollar, maybe multi-million, for a mobile clinic," Dr. Ford said and opened her hands like blooming flowers. It was parked just south of Gee's Bend and contained "all kinds of high-tech stuff. The eye doctor . . . started jumping and shouting. 'Oh God, I know you sent that for me because I showed up.'"

"That was just the start of it." Dr. Ford took off her tennis shoes. "It was like, one of our church members said, 'we touched the very heart of God.' . . . If you want to see the power of God, you fast and pray. And you'll see just the miraculous and the unbelievable heavenly possibilities."

There were miracles that even rendered them speechless, like the flat tire emergency late one night on a rural road. Dr. Ford nodded toward her husband.

"It's got those dual wheels on them." He twisted his hands like the wheels. "We couldn't get them off. We needed professionals to do it."

"It was black dark," Dr. Ford said. "We pulled off on this country road in front of this old service station, and they went in. The man said there was nothing he could do to help. The group went back to work on loosening the lug, and it still wouldn't budge."

"And we have some big guys, and nobody could break the lug. And then, out of nowhere, an old man appeared in a beat-up truck. 'How can I help you?' he asked."

"We told him what had happened."

"'I can help you,' he said."

"He had the exact perfect equipment." Henry Ford jumped up out of his seat like a preacher shouting. "'How much do we owe you?' And he said, 'Nothing.' And then he was gone as suddenly as he had appeared."

I bet they had told this story many times, but their energy and passion were like it had just happened, and I was the first person hearing the story.

"And not only did he have the tools, but he actually knew how to do it. He changed these tires by himself. All we could do was stand there looking with our mouths open," Henry Ford said. "We were scared to do anything because he had to be an angel."

"It was an angelic visitation," Dr. Ford said with a deep smile.

"What a miracle," I said.

"A miracle in Greentown," Henry Ford said. "It's just miraculous things that happened. And He still has His hand on this. I'm telling you."

Another miracle was about a woman named Angela Jackson. This year was the Fords' tenth anniversary working with Jackson, a pharmaceutical representative. She sends and gets medication from a global organization that does international ministry. They send medicine to foreign countries but agreed to do that for people in the States too. "So she got some medicine called Brilinta, and it is something like Clavix, a blood thinner, works like a sophisticated aspirin, but it's a new medicine and extremely expensive," Dr. Ford said.

"Jackson sent some, but she had it for two years before dispensing any. Why are we bringing this? But we get to Fort Deposit, and this lady comes up. Do you know what she asked me for? 'Do you have Brilinta?' . . . I asked her to spell it because I wasn't sure what she was saying. She had a few samples in her bag, and it was Brilinta."

The woman had stents; her arteries were clogged. She told Dr. Ford this was the only drug that kept her stents open, and she didn't have anymore because it was expensive; it cost her $250 for thirty pills. "I just wanted to

Gee's Bend Quilt. Photo courtesy of Gala Farley.

shout." Dr. Ford clapped her hands. "I had it that day. I had two years of the medicine. I gave her over $2,000 worth of medicine."

"And this lady said—oh, you should have seen her—she said, 'that's God who came here! He came here just for me!'" Ford laughed. "She broke down. We have a picture of her. And this lady was just testifying, and it was just such an encouragement of my spirit to know that God's hand was still on this project."

Dr. Ford's family has a long history of service in the Black Belt communities of Alabama. And even a longer history in the civil rights movement. They supported Dr. King and encouraged people to register to vote and helped to prepare them for the tests that were imposed on African Americans. They drove folks to voting polls. Her family didn't just teach us, but they were committed to the education of poor Black children in the tiny towns of

Gee's Bend Quilter. Photo courtesy of Gala Farley.

Barbour County, also the home of white supremacist, George C. Wallace. Dr. Ford's father, George F. Mathews, was the principal of our elementary school—the Bethel School, a poorly structured wooden building with three main rooms next door to the New Bethel Baptist church where my sisters and I were baptized.

On the small stage, the first-grade class was taught next to a coal-burning heater. The boys had to go outside to get coal; the girls had to sweep the floor. We took turns with the chores based on our seating in the classroom. The second and third grades lessons were taught in the auditorium; they could spread out since it was the biggest classroom in the school. The second-grade class sat by the door; and the third grade clustered by the huge window in the back. They couldn't even hear each other. The fifth and sixth were stuffed into a room with a makeshift patrician to separate them from the sixth and seventh grades. Those classes were smaller than the lower classes.

Daily devotion was conducted by singing "The Star-Spangled Banner," repeating the Pledge of Allegiance with our right hands spread over our hearts, and we concluded with the Lord's Prayer. We sang spirituals like "Down by the Riverside" or "Amazing Grace." Mr. Mathews taught us French and science in the sixth and seventh grades. I never got in trouble in his classroom. Boys got in more trouble than we girls. He was heavy-handed with that gray leather and rawhide strap. Our parents approved; they knew our teachers had our best interests at heart.

⊱ — ⊰

To my surprise and delight, when I arrived at Alabama A&M a few years later, there she was, a student, just like me. We were thrilled to see each other again. I especially remembered our biology class; Dr. Alice Jenkins was considered a very tough professor. She was known for failing her own brother. But she was better known as one of the best mentors at the university. I liked her, but Dr. Ford adored her. Even then, Ford was already walking around wearing white jackets, looking like a doctor.

After we graduated from college, Ford went to medical school at the University of Alabama at Birmingham. I moved to Atlanta and worked in marketing with a degree in Business Administration. After my son grew up, I was awarded a full fellowship to graduate school at Hollins University in Roanoke, Virginia, and became a writer and a professor of English. Dr. Ford is a distinguished internist in the Southeast United States. We reconnected when I lectured at our alma mater in 2006.

Our successful lives were made possible because of the civil rights movement, for sure, but we also had caring and thoughtful teachers and supervised homes. There wasn't that much difference between my mother's and my grandmother's lives. It was the 1960s when change happened in huge numbers for educated Black folks, especially in the South. Although our success came with a price, it was still possible; and it was that movement that laid the foundation for all of the social movements to come.

Our parents and teacher always told us that the work they were doing was to make the world better for us. And the world would continue to get better for our people as long as we picked up the torch and passed it to the next generation. "The struggle will always continue," they preached. "For Black folks, a win is never a win without a continuous fight."

Dr. Ford looks pretty much the same as she did in school, petite and pretty. Her hair is different. She used to wear a short afro, but now it's twisted like small braids, and it looks stunning. She has spent forty years in private practice and has worked with the state, teaching with the residency program at

Traditional Counties of the
Alabama Black Belt

Source: Center for Business and Economic Research,
The University of Alabama

Map of Alabama showing the Black Belt where the Spirit of Luke do most
of their work.

the Princeton Baptist Medical Center in Birmingham. I was anxious to hear
what she had to say about the newly passed Affordable Care Act since it was
the law of the land. The Patient Protection and Affordable Care Act, often
shortened to ACA or Obamacare, is a United States federal statute enacted
by Congress in 2010 and signed into law by President Barack Obama.

"I think that we really need it. I'm hoping that Alabama will change its
position on extending Medicare," she said. "In my travels throughout the
Black Belt, we encounter so many underserved, unprivileged, uninsured
people, and it's just a *must*. I think we're really going to have to push for that
... But I think, for the most part, it's a very positive thing. I think that it's a

right to have health care in a developed country like this, and to have people who are sick and just can't have access to medical care is not acceptable."

━━   ━━

I have witnessed some of the power of A Promise to Help. We served an old sawmill town called Vredenburgh in Monroe County; about three hundred citizens live there. In 2017, nearly ninety percent of the people were unemployed. Every year the town puts on a Christmas parade for A Promise to Help. Last year, the sun was bright, and everyone was singing Christmas carols. Henry Ford played Santa. Each child received a coat, shoes, hat, and gloves, along with a wrapped gift from Santa. And each household received a turkey. We all left feeling the real spirit of Christmas. As the sun was setting, we headed back to Birmingham. Looking back, we saw a sea of *Doug Jones for Senator* signs. The community was excited about voting, some of them for the first time.

"There is just . . . all of these stories," Henry Ford said. "They are such miracle stories."

WE READY

Big Mama and Little Mama dressed in their Sunday-go-to-meeting clothes on a Tuesday was a sight my sisters and I had never seen. Not only that, we didn't have to go to school that day. Big Mama fixed fried bologna sandwiches and wrapped them in wax paper. She pushed apples and red tomatoes into another brown paper bag. Along with that, she poured a pitcher of lemonade into a gallon jug and placed it in a cooler surrounded by ice. Little Mama put paper plates and cups in another bag.

"What she say 'bout you not comin' to work?" Big Mama asked.

"I told her, didn't axe," Little Mama answered.

"She decent 'nough, I reckon."

"Never had no trouble wit dem."

Ruby and I cleaned the kitchen as they continued packing their lunch on the table in the middle of the room. Our sister, Ida, sat at the other end of the table with her coloring book and crayons. Of course, we didn't ask questions. Children were to be seen and not heard was the law of our house rules. Ruby and I would commiserate once they left.

The church ladies rolled up in a new silver 1964 Chevy Impala. Not only did Miss Pearl drive her own car, but she also drove the county school bus for the colored high school students. And she was the first and only woman we had ever seen who smoked three packs of Camels a day.

Big Mama told me that I was in charge since I was the oldest. If we need something, see Mr. Gus Eustey, two houses down. Otherwise, we were to stay inside. Since we lived in the country, we weren't afraid. But I wondered how

Mr. Gus Eustey could help us since he was in a wheelchair and only had one leg. "Got dem sugars bad," one of the church ladies said.

They dashed in to show off their flowing fall outfits. Everybody was happy, wearing their lightweight autumn wools and matching hats tilted to the side or back out of their faces. I'd never seen the women so excited; they were giggling like schoolgirls. Even Big Mama was laughing and talking.

Our teachers had been giddy, too, about voting for the first time. Change had come to our little town of Louisville, Alabama, where fewer than one thousand citizens lived. In 1965, the Voting Rights Act was signed into law, and most Black folks of legal voting age were heading to the polls for the first time. During most of American history Black citizens have been prevented from voting for some reason or another—poll taxes, literacy tests. . . i.e., white poll workers asked Black citizens questions like, "How many bubbles in a bar of soap? How many words in the Bible?" All of those wounded and dead bodies long ago paid for that right.

We were taught about our rights under US law in our civics class. Signed into law by President Lyndon Johnson, Congress would amend the Act five times to expand its protections guaranteed by the Fourteenth and Fifteenth Amendments to the Constitution. The most important law for Black folks since the Thirteenth Amendment to the Constitution had passed: Thirteenth-Section 1: Neither slavery nor involuntary servitude, except as a punishment for crime whereof the party shall have been duly convicted, shall exist within the United States, or any place subject to their jurisdiction. Section 2: Congress shall have power to enforce this article by appropriate legislation. Mrs. Knox, our civics teacher, stressed sections of the Fifteenth the most: Section 1. The right of citizens of the United States to vote shall not be denied or abridged by the United States or by any State on account of race, color, or previous condition of servitude. 2. The Congress shall have the power to enforce this article by appropriate legislation. She always read this one three times and banged her fist on the desk at the end. I never knew a time when civil rights weren't a part of my life. Although I didn't understand all of the language, we knew times were getting better for us coloreds.

Watching my mother, I wasn't sure how things were getting better. I never understood why Little Mama had to go to work every day except a few Sundays a month. We wanted her to stay home with us. My sisters and I knew our mother through work, not words, by touch and silence.

When Little Mama would get home from work bone-tired, we soaked her feet in an old tin blue wash pan with hot water and Epsom salt. Ruby poured the hot water; I massaged her feet, my younger sister Ida patted them dry with a towel. Little Mama slept through these sessions. She knew how to lay her head just right on the sofa so we could condition her scalp with Dixie Peach and brush her hair—her long dark curly hair that neither of my sisters or myself inherited.

Helping my mother included sprinkling the starched clothes she took in to iron from another white family; she was paid a dollar per laundry basket. After the clothes were sprinkled, we put them in a plastic bag and placed them in the bottom of the refrigerator, where the moist clothes waited for our tired mother.

Afterward, we fixed her a plate of whatever Big Mama had cooked. Sometimes we gave her updates on *The Perry Mason Show* from television. Often she fell asleep before we completed the updates.

When they got back from voting, they still were happy and chatty. They saw folks they hadn't seen in years. And there was no trouble with the white folks at the polls. It seemed as though the world had tilted toward the right side of history. I had no other memory of our house feeling joyful. Big Mama ordered us around with chores and homework. We helped Little Mama out as much as we could after she got home from work. She was often sad because of the loss of her firstborn, Daisy, at age seven; she died from hookworms. My sisters and I never knew the perfect child. By the time we came along, she had been dead for more than ten years.

Big Mama moved in with us after Grandpa Alex died. I was four, and Ruby was two. I only saw Grandpa Alex once or twice; he was tall and lanky. I remember him kissing Ruby and me. His face felt scratchy, and he smelled like cigars. While Little Mama cleaned the white woman's house, Big Mama supervised the assembly line of domestic relations in our house. An ideal set-up since Little Mama showed no interest in nothing except cleaning the white woman's house.

With Big Mama in charge at our house, delicious scents always wafted through the air. I loved leaping off of the school bus and running into our warm and cozy house. Our yard bloomed, too, just not like the white woman's.

Our flowers were more like splashes of yellows and whites here and there. But we kept our dirt yard swept with a homemade straw broom.

Soon after Big Mama moved in with us, Little Mama mustered up enough courage to kick Mr. Tex out of our house and out of our lives. He was her third husband, my sisters' daddy, and everybody's disappointment. A tiny man with processed hair and copper-colored skin that shaded more red in the summer; he never had much to say except on the weekends when he had been drinking; although he was never violent. After Friday's payday, we often didn't see him again until late Sunday night when he'd stumble home without money or food, and the bickering would begin. Sometimes Little Mama would go to the sawmill on payday to try and catch him before he got away with his paycheck. Finally, she put Mr. Tex's clothes on our front porch in five brown paper bags from the Winn Dixie. She told Mr. Pig Walker, a deacon in the church, to go by the sawmill to tell Mr. Tex that if he didn't come and pick up the clothes by Saturday, she was going to give them away.

My father was Little Mama's second husband. He had been killed in a truck accident when I was a baby. He and Mr. Johnny Lee drove a gas truck for the Cagney Brothers Gas Company; it exploded. Mr. Lee survived, but my father didn't. Since I never knew him, I never thought of him. What happened to him was like a dream that turned into a nightmare since we, his family, didn't receive one penny from the gas company. Mr. Tex, my stepfather, was such a poor example of a father; I never imagined what a good example looked like until more than fifty years later. That's when I met Mr. John Canty of South Carolina.

CHAPTER 2

A View of Grace from the Top

John Canty (1925-2019)

I lived in a country that made it hard to work, hard to make a
living because of race. You feel like you're less than a citizen.
But you've got to live.
—JOHN CANTY

Who among us has been at the epicenter of American history from the
time of the assassination of President John F. Kennedy to the fall of Berlin's
Wall? John Canty wasn't top-level staff, but he was there, seeing, hearing,
and bearing witness to the pulse of history for nearly a quarter of a century
as the White House mail router. He was the first Black person to hold the
position. I met him when he was ninety-two years old and had recently lost
his wife of more than sixty years. I was working on this book about unsung
witnesses to history, especially the civil rights movement. He was gracious
when he opened the door of his home in Summerton, South Carolina, in the
considered manner of a man who was at the elbow of five presidents sorting
mail and determining what was important enough to bother the president.

As he reclined his long body into his comfort chair, I looked quietly over
the collection of his White House years, and it looked in every way like a
museum. He displays his mementos in his small study and hallway from his
days at the White House—photos of former presidents: Johnson, Nixon, Ford,
Carter, and Reagan. Handwritten notes and cards grace his paneled walls

John Canty. Photo courtesy of the Canty family.

from Sammy Davis Jr., Pearl Bailey, and Michael Jackson. Canty described Michael Jackson as being "nice." I think he would describe everybody as "nice." When he smiles, everything around him lights up. He answered questions thoughtfully, honestly, and often with humor.

Everything is framed and properly arranged in chronological order. The glass case in his hallway holds sample gifts that were given to guests who visited the White House, a pack of Kent cigarettes, shot glasses, coasters, ballpoint pens, and matches.

He had never been interviewed about his work. He seemed a bit uneasy at first, but that soon disappeared. He waited patiently for my questions

The last photo of John Canty before he died in 2019. Photo courtesy of the Canty family.

before answering them. It was a skill that probably led to this long success in Washington.

He wasn't political, but he was well aware of the politics of his job. "I just wanted to work. That's all, no more, no less," he said. He paused before explaining that he knew what was happening in the world. As a Black man who grew up in South Carolina, served in the military, and was one of the few who worked the mailroom at NASA, he was well aware that the world was changing. He saw the struggle on the face of President Johnson as he pushed through the 1964 Civil Rights Act in Congress.

"He walked around with those beagles behind him, scratching his head with pencils behind both ears," Canty said. "He was always looking down. Sometimes shaking his head."

Although the passing of the Civil Rights Act was of monumental importance to the country, Canty maintained that "it sounded better than it actually was. Really nothing much changed." He looked down at this tan carpeted floor that matched his brown leather recliner. He only answered questions; he never volunteered information. I'm sure that was a useful characteristic to own if you worked in the White House that changed so much from president to president, the people behind the politics.

I met Canty through an old friend who's a historian and lives in Sumter, South Carolina. Deloris Pringle thought he'd been a White House butler like the character Forest Whitaker played in *Lee Daniels' The Butler*, but we learned he worked at NASA as a clerk and then at Pennsylvania Avenue. But now he's a retired ninety-two-year-old widower. His wife had recently passed; they didn't have any children.

At the White House, his job entailed managing incoming mail and checking to see whether the president should get the mail or what special government body should. When he was offered the position, he told them he would have to think about it. He was so calm when he talked about receiving a call from the White House. Canty didn't seem to get overly excited. He acted like getting a call from the White House was not that big of a deal.

Two or three weeks later, he hadn't called the White House. Canty wasn't sure he wanted to go there. He had heard it was a hot bed for politics. And he liked where he was. But he received another phone call from them inviting him to just come and have lunch with them again. He went and proposed that he would come over on detail, which meant, if he didn't like it, he could return to his present job at NASA. They agreed, and the secret service started their background check on him. He went to the White House on a short detail and stayed eighteen years. He was just a clerk (as he described himself) in the beginning, but after the Johnson administration, he was promoted to presidential personnel, where he managed the Document Section. All incoming mail, including the president's, came to his office, and he made decisions about where the mail was forwarded.

From 1964–69 he worked for President Johnson, earning $5,000 a year. He was a presidential personal mail router (assistant) for five American presidents: Lyndon Baines Johnson, Richard Milhous Nixon, Gerald Rudolph "Jerry" Ford Jr., James Earl "Jimmy" Carter Jr., and Ronald Wilson Reagan. I was bowled over when I learned that no one had ever interviewed or researched this living treasure.

Canty didn't know much about President Johnson, so he never got too close to him. The president would come around when the staff fellowshipped on the White House lawn. But Canty felt that the white folks thought Johnson was too good to be around Black folks. He frowned as he talked about the racism in the late 1960s. In spite of the racial climate, "President Johnson treated everyone equal as far as I could tell," he said. Everyone was grieving over the assassination of President Kennedy but, at the same time, trying to respect President Johnson. Although no one talked to Canty directly, it was clear that folks were very sad.

Johnson never talked to Canty personally about the Civil Rights Act, but Canty appreciated the work the president did for the country with the War on Poverty, Head Start, Medicaid, Medicare, and other programs to help the country heal and help folks in need. When the president talked to him, it was mostly about the grounds and gardens. "Whether you were a janitor, gardener, or a high-level staff member, President Johnson showed you respect," Canty said.

He remembered Johnson walking around the grounds with his famed beagles, often with pencils behind both ears. One time, Canty and his late wife were walking the White House grounds, one of her favorite things to do. She was eating a bag of potato chips. They ran into President Johnson. He reached his hand into his wife's bag of potato chips. She was so happy. "I am never going to wash my hands again," she said. That memory made Canty laugh.

One of Canty's most marvelous moments in the White House was when Johnson appointed Thurgood Marshall to the Supreme Court in 1967. "I'll never forget how much pride we [Black folks] felt."

Canty maintained that the Vietnam War had a lot to do with President Johnson's demise. Later, he realized how difficult it must have been for the president who witnessed the assassinations of President Kennedy, Malcolm X, Martin Luther King Jr., and Robert Kennedy. "It was too much." Canty hung his head. He was disappointed that he wasn't invited to President Johnson's funeral.

Unlike President Johnson, President Nixon was more personal and knew all of their names. He told the staff if they needed anything, they could come directly to him. He always showed high regard for their work and gave them the highest pay raises possible. Canty remembered his department having sofas, radios, televisions, and other items they hadn't had before. All of this was without being asked. Canty thought Nixon was too liberal to be a Republican, starting the EPA and giving Black folks the highest raises. "He wouldn't make it in the GOP today." We laughed.

With the arrival of Nixon, staff was nervous about their jobs. It was a changing of the guards from a Democratic to a Republican administration. Often new presidents brought their own staff, especially with a change in the parties. All Canty wanted to do was work. This is what he repeated throughout the interview. He thought President Nixon was "a very nice guy who got caught up in some stuff that wasn't altogether his fault. Nixon brought a whole lot of young people, right out law school, with him to the White House. They wanted to make a name for themselves, so they advised the president like he was above the law. They just went out and messed him up."

By the time Nixon came into Office, Canty had been promoted to presidential personnel, including the information center, which included getting FBI background reports assembled for perspective hires. He and his wife had also bought a house in DC. "President Nixon wasn't a bad guy, a good man actually. When the Watergate scandal happened, the mood around the White House was somber; it was terrible," Canty said, crossing his long legs. "Everybody hated to see Nixon go down. I don't think it was really his fault. He was a good president." When Canty teared up again, I didn't know if I were more touched or shocked.

Like most of the staff at the White House, Canty was surprised in 1974 when Nixon resigned.

I was finishing up college at Alabama A&M University in Huntsville. Sandra Mathews Ford and I, along with other students, crowded around a small black-and-white television in our dormitory lobby, not believing what we were witnessing and wondering how it would affect our lives. What would our hard-earned college degrees be worth in our new world?

Canty walked right behind Nixon when he came down the steps of the White House for the last time, but when the photo came out in the newspapers, he had been cut out. He shook his head. "Yes, I was cut out." Canty didn't have any other contact with the Nixon family after that last day.

Folks in the White House were whispering about the resignation, but not to him. The few Black folks working there were scattered about. Canty did more listening than talking. He didn't have much encounter with President Ford, the thirty-eighth president. He wasn't around that long, from August 1974–January 1977. But he did do his *Saturday Night Live* sketch by pretending to fall down. The staff always laughed politely.

So Mr. Jimmy and Miss Rosalyn arrived at the White House. Canty describes them as "nice people." Even though President Johnson was from Texas, the Carters were more southern (from the Deep South). But Canty didn't find comfort in the fact that the Carters were from Georgia. "Carter came in, he was nice, but he looked at DC like it was Georgia. For example, DC is much more expensive than Georgia, more people, more everything."

"More sophisticated?" I asked.

"Yeah. A lot of the folks who came in with President Carter had to go back to the Georgia woods. DC was too high for them, the cost of living and social class," Canty said and sat back in his easy chair, recounting memories of long ago. "If they didn't have family money, most were just country folks."

Unfortunately, when Carter and his family moved into the White House, the country was locked in an energy crisis, the inflation rate was as high as five percent, and there was the failed Iran Contra Rescue. "Carter cut back on everything. The heat was down so low sometimes we had to keep our coats on," Canty recalled. "Carter didn't come around and talk to the staff like Nixon had. He mostly took away what Nixon had given them. His wife seemed nice, though." I found it ironic that the Republican president was more liberal than the Democratic president.

"When President Carter came in, he cleaned house. Nothing unusual about that since that's what new administrations normally do, but not so much with the lower lever jobs," Canty said.

"He wanted to bring in his Georgia boys." We laughed.

Canty's department had to get rid of all the items that Nixon had given them. The sofa was the only thing that stayed; they took the radios and televisions. They were told that they didn't need those items in the workplace. Carter was acting like a Republican, and it was a Republican who had given them the televisions and radios.

Carter faced a massive energy crisis with long gas lines everywhere, especially with big American gas-guzzlers for cars. President Carter even appeared on television wearing a sweater, trying to convince Americans to turn their heaters down. My parents didn't buy the President's Roosevelt remix. They weren't turning the heat down since they didn't have heat growing up. Now that they had it, they were going to use it; it helped make up for being cold for most of their childhood in the winters. Canty agreed with their philosophy. He said they insisted on keeping the heater at sixty-eight degrees. "And you know, Black folks don't like to be cold." Canty hugged himself. "But

John Canty and President Jimmy Carter. Photo courtesy of the Canty family.

there was ways to get around that." He grinned. "President Carter was a nice president; and he had a nice wife. But a few things he wanted to cut back wasn't nice," Canty said.

I had just seen some Billy Carter beer on eBay. I laughed and wondered if it was authentic. Canty had seen Billy Carter a few times, "walking around the White House like a cowboy." He never saw Miss Lillian (the president's mother).

Canty didn't care if Carter won a second term or not. He didn't know "what was behind him." Even though he would have to go through the interviewing process again, which meant he wasn't sure he would have a job. If Carter stayed, he knew he would have a job. But most of the time during that administration, Canty was wishing for President Nixon.

Canty was a veteran on the job by the time the Reagans arrived. They were older with no children who lived with them in the White House. With the new regime came a new interview.

"Some *little girl* came in and wanted to interview all of us. So she interviewed me, and then she told me, 'I don't know what's gonna happen . . . I
don't know whether we're going to keep you or not, but we'll let you know.'"

"Where was Carter when you needed him? Come back, Jimmy." We laughed.

Canty met with ranking Republicans, and they liked him. One of them
went to the president on his behalf. "After this *little girl* interviewed me, she
told me that she'd let me know something," he said with the only bit of anger
I detected in his voice during the interview. "This guy had been there with
Nixon." He kept his job.

Canty thought Reagan was nice, but Nancy Reagan was kind of snooty.
In fact, he thought most of the presidents were nice, but some of their wives
were the bossiest women he'd ever seen. Nancy Reagan was one of them, and
the other one was Lady Bird Johnson.

I thought she was very protective of Johnson; he was another one of those
smart men who married up, self-made. According to him, he got kicked out
of Southwest Texas State Teacher's College. And he spent a few months at
Georgetown Law School. She would watch every speech he made. She gave
strong and stern critiques. "Well, Lyndon, I want you to look up more; and I
want you to say your words clear and say them like you mean them." She was
a good critic. But I think both she and Nancy Reagan were trying to protect
their men. Reagan was old, and his wife knew that he was slipping mentally,
which probably made her even more determined to protect him. But when
Donald Regan, President Reagan's chief of staff, hung up the telephone on
the first lady, he was fired in less than five minutes. Just when you thought
Reagan was close to death, he fired not just his chief of staff but one of his
oldest friends.

Canty didn't have any encounter with the Reagans. I asked him if there
was anything else that he wanted to add to the interview. He said no, not at
the time, but he would contact me if he thought of something else. That part
of the interview ended with him telling me that he adored the Obamas and
that he was sure that Hillary Clinton was going to run for president and win
because she had his vote and support.

Lee Daniels' The Butler was playing in theatres when I interviewed Canty.
He didn't like it that much; he said that it brought back too many bad
memories. And he didn't think that it captured what was really happening.
And finally, he thought it was too violent. After he teared up, I didn't ask
him any more questions about the film. He gave me a similar response

when I asked him about his late wife, Mary Tindal Canty. It had been nearly two years since she died. I decided to ask another question. How did you meet her?

Canty is a tall and gracious southern gentleman with the patience of a farmer. The memory of how he met his late wife spread a sparkle across his face. He leaned forward from his comfortable chair and grinned. "Well, she was from out of town. Everybody was talking about how pretty she was. Everywhere I went. I heard about this Mary Tindal," he said. They met finally at the Silver Café in Sumter, South Carolina. "We got married in 1947. Married for sixty-three years, eleven months, and eleven days." Canty laughed for a long time. They didn't have a wedding; he only had four dollars for the license.

Canty was living in DC when Rosa Parks refused to give up her seat on the bus in Montgomery, Alabama. He was also in DC when Emmett Till was brutally murdered. He said he thought it was "all of it was wrong . . . [Parks] was very brave and courageous for all of us." Canty then recounted a similar situation when he was in the service and returning to Tallahassee from Tampa on the bus with six other soldiers. "The driver wanted to seat seven of us on that back seat. We refused. We told him that we weren't going to sit no seven people on that seat."

"I'm trying to do y'all a favor," the driver said.

"You're not doing us no favor 'cause we don't care whether we get back down there. We're in the Army," Canty said. The driver got angry and called for the station manager, who approached them. "We told him, Mister, we're not going to fit no seven people on that seat. And so then he decided to give us two of the other seats in front of that long seat. That bus driver was mad; he took us back to Tampa. He was flying."

I had heard stories of Black soldiers who had to stand up on a long ride, maybe between two or three states, and they stood up on the train all the way. Even white women offered to give them their seats, but they wouldn't take them. Even baseball great Jackie Robinson refused a bus driver's order to get up and move to the back of the bus. It was 1944, and he was an Army lieutenant stationed in Texas. He was court-martialed over the incident but was later acquitted.

John and Mary Canty. Photo courtesy of the Canty family.

From Small Town to Seat of Power and Home Again

John Canty was born with no middle name in 1925 in Silver, South Carolina, the youngest of six children. Silver is a tiny town with a population of just a few hundred citizens. As a young man, he couldn't wait to get out. "Nothing much was going on in South Carolina," he smiled. He said his uncles had left for Virginia and Philadelphia and came back to visit sporting nice clothes, seeming happy.

Canty moved to DC in 1943 after he graduated from high school seeking opportunities for a better life. He joined the Great Migration that saw more than six million African Americans leave the rural South for cities in the North, Midwest, and West. Black people headed toward what writer Richard Wright called "the warmth of other suns." Other places had to be better than the cotton fields, sharecropping, and Jim Crow of the South. Pulitzer Prize–winning journalist, Isabel Wilkerson, uses the same title in her epic book about the history of the Great Migration. This was "a leaderless movement" guided only by hopes of a better life. Even though this was an important movement, the civil rights movement propelled the change in African American lives we recognize today.

Canty moved in with his older brother and found construction work at what would become Andrews Air Force Base, earning eighty-seven cents per hour.

John and Mary Canty. Photo courtesy of Ethel Morgan Smith.

After that job, he and his brother moved to Michigan to build hangars. Less than a year later, he was drafted into the Army and sent to a series of bases in the US, where racial segregation was the rule, and finally to Saipan Island in the Pacific Ocean. It was 1944, and he arrived just in time for the Battle of Saipan. He and his fellow Black soldiers were dumped on shore and couldn't pitch tents because they didn't know where the enemy was. They stayed overnight in the woods wishing they were back on the ship. But soon, they learned they'd been spared: The ship was bombed the same night.

After the service, Canty held a series of jobs trying to make ends meet. He cleaned planes and drove taxis. By 1958, he was married and was worried that he had no insurance or other benefits. "I lived in a country that made it hard to work, hard to make a living because of race," he said. "You feel like you're less than a citizen. But you've got to live." He applied and got his next job as a clerk at the Naval Ordnance Laboratory, which became NASA. When his supervisor went on to a White House job, Canty was promoted. From there, he was bound for the White House.

Canty retired when Reagan came into office. He and his wife moved back to Summerton, South Carolina, not far from where he was born.

They didn't sit around. I wanted to know more about his church and the work he was doing there. Deloris Pringle, the historian who introduced us, helped the church to secure a grant for an expansion of Taw Caw Missionary Baptist Church in 2006, where Canty has been a member for twenty-nine years. Before that, he was a member of Purity Baptist Church in Washington, DC.

"A man who lived in an old raggedy house was sick. The lady from the health department called around to see if they could get somebody to help fix his house." Canty said they didn't go in for fear the house would fall in. "So we got a group together. We called ourselves Christian Hands, Black and white. We decided that we were going out and ask some churches for money."

Canty and his wife were already volunteering with a Catholic church delivering food and other duties. They asked that church for a donation and were given $5,000. "We were happy because one of the guys found a used trailer in Sumter for $2,300. We had to put a well in and some other things . . . He was eighty years old and had never lived in a house with plumbing or running water or nothing." The man became a favorite of the women volunteers, including Canty's wife. "Two white ladies wanted to take him in while we were working on the house. That man was so scared. He said, 'No, I can't go home with yawl.'"

The man lived in the house for two years before he died. "At his funeral, the white women were weeping," Canty said. "They had gotten too attached to Mr. McBride. The house was returned to Christian Hands, and they could give it to somebody else in need." Canty did a lot of work like that until the money dried up.

Canty wanted to show me his beloved Taw Caw Baptist Church. After the Civil War, freed slaves began holding services under what was called a "Bush Arbor" until 1885. After that, the church was damaged by fire and in need of great repair. The white Baptist owners sold their church to the local African American Baptists for four hundred dollars. Taw Caw is the name of a well-known plantation that used to be in Summerton, SC. It was named for the stream that runs through the property.

Pringle, the historian, hadn't seen the church since the completion of the expansion. We were so excited. I will always carry a bit of that day with me. I wasn't worried if my project was worthy, I felt overjoyed and honored. I will always be in awe of a kind and gentle man who had lived through some of the darkest hours of America's history and radiated with gentleness and honesty.

At the church, I learned that a few of the ladies were interested in dating Mr. Canty. He said there was often some casserole or pie left at his front door, with a note, "Mary would want us to take care of you." Canty grunted. "Mary would want you to leave me alone."

He invited us for supper at Shoney's. Our conversation continued without the tapes. I was concerned about his little museum since he doesn't have any immediate heirs. We asked him if he had thought about where he wanted his papers to go. He didn't say right away.

We continued eating. I looked up at the television monitor and saw Serena Williams playing tennis. Since I am a big tennis fan, I excused myself and walked over to the television. Serena was serving for the match. I rejoined my group and apologized again.

"Did she win?" Canty asked. "Next stop Charleston."

"So you're a tennis fan?"

"Yeah." He laughed. "You know, I thought about what you ladies asked. I want my papers in South Carolina. All my people are here. This is home."

We drove away with full stomachs and overflowing hearts that Sunday evening. Mr. John Canty is a national treasure and should be preserved as one. He is a gentle gem of another era but fits in anywhere; he is kind and thoughtful. I had driven five hundred miles in the rain from Morgantown, West Virginia, to interview him. I would've driven five thousand miles to interview him. His life has been remarkable, straddling the eras of share-cropping, Jim Crow, the Great Migration, World War I, World War II, and Vietnam, but it was the civil rights movement that made it possible for him to serve at the White House. Mr. John Canty joined the ancestors in 2019.

DISCERNING DREAMS

I grew up believing it was my job to help Little Mama keep the memory of Daisy alive since I was the next oldest daughter; she shouldn't be forgotten. After all, God had honored our family with her presence, even if it had only been for seven short years. I often heard Little Mama say this to Big Mama. Daisy used to stand up in church and recite scripture better than any preacher. As far as Little Mama was concerned, Daisy was the *one*, and everybody else thought so too. I used to worry about my little dead sister up in that cemetery, especially in the wintertime with too many old folks for company.

I wish she were alive too. I would have a big sister to look up to. Since she was perfect in every way, I bet she'd have been kind too. We could've had long conversations about books and boys and everything. We'd have greased each other's scalps and "kitchens" with Dixie Peach. She would have taught me to make perfect piecrusts. Sometimes I wanted to scream to Little Mama; we all lost her. But God has blessed you with three other daughters, and we're here, and we're alive, begging for crumbs of affection or just attention. I don't remember a day passing when Daisy's name wasn't mentioned in our house.

One of the worst times was when we were spring cleaning; Little Mama found a blue comb with missing teeth behind the dresser. It was the last comb that she had used to comb Daisy's hair. She swore she could see strands of her hair. She was so distressed that Big Mama thought she was going to have to get Dr. Faircloth to come. Instead, two of the church ladies came. One was an usher at church; she brought some smelling salts that she used on the women in church when they shouted as the "spirit" of the Lord touched them. They finally got Little Mama to settle down. She slept a whole night and day. One of the church ladies went by the white woman's house and told her that Little Mama was sick. The white woman wanted to know when she was coming back; she didn't want her washing and ironing to pile up.

But now, I was going to high school; my world was growing. My sister had been dead longer than she had lived. She moved further and further from my heart, but not Little Mama's. The future was calling my name. High school in Clayton was real. I was prepared with three new dresses that Mrs. Carrie Mae made on her new zigzag sewing machine. We had ordered black Mary Jane shoes from the Sears & Roebuck catalog. Big Mama and Little Mama didn't allow us to go into stores that didn't let us try on clothes. I loved catalog ordering; I didn't have to be bothered by mean white folks. My writing tablets, pencils, and even a few Bic ballpoint pens felt like new beginnings.

Some students slept on the bus. I was too excited. The ten-mile drive was a world away from Louisville. We passed new and beautiful houses that I dreamed of living in one day. The houses were prettier than the white woman Little Mama worked for. And Miss Pearl, the bus driver, was so nice to me. Life was good. For the first time in our lives, we colored students of Barbour County, Alabama got brand-spanking new textbooks. I had never even seen a new book.

Big Mama and the church ladies didn't care that much about Governor George Wallace standing in the front door of the University of Alabama in 1963 to keep two scared and brave Black students, Vivian Malone Jones and James Hood, out. "He talk dat mess all de time," Big Mama said when she heard him on television.

"Wanna make sure he let de white folks think he as racist as dey thank he is," Little Mama said.

"We know his folks. Probably some of us 'round hare done spanked his ass, a time or two." They laughed.

Later we learned from our history teacher that Wallace had to give us *coloreds* something since we could vote now.

Big Mama despised him because he made his dying wife run for governor. "Poe Miss Lurleen." Big Mama would shake her head. The silver strands of her hair sparkled like she was standing in the sun as she sat around the kitchen doing chores. My sisters and I would be in the front room, a few steps away, doing our homework.

"What kind of man would keep it from her dat she was dyin'? She didn't git a chance." Little Mama shook the shirt she was ironing.

"Low down, dirty dog. His day will come, and it will come hard. And just think, white folks thank dey got de high hand with God." Big Mama wagged her finger toward the heavens after she took the pot roast out of the oven.

"Dat poe woman didn't know she dyin. De doctor told her husband, and he wouldn't let nobody tell her." Little Mama folded the white shirt like they looked in stores.

"Ump ump . . ." Big Mama said.

Lurleen Brigham Wallace was forty-one years old when she died from uterine cancer. Since the law prevented her husband, George Wallace, from running for governor for two consecutive terms, he wanted to run her. When the doctor told him about her cancer, he ordered the doctor not to tell her or anybody else. As a result, she went four years without treatment. She was shocked when she learned she not only had cancer, but her husband had concealed it from her for four years. She died after fifteen months in office. Schools and other state offices were closed; flags were lowered to half-staff.

Lurleen Wallace was the first female governor of the state of Alabama and the only governor to die in office. Outraged at her husband, she began radiation therapy in December 1965, followed by a hysterectomy in January 1966. By 1967, an abdominal growth was found. She endured at least five other major surgeries, but the cancer had spread. She was forty-one years old when she died.

George Wallace also lied to the press continuously about her condition by telling them she had "won the fight." After her funeral, George Wallace moved out of the governor's mansion and back to a home that they owned in Montgomery. He left his eighteen-, sixteen-, and six-year-old children. Their oldest daughter had married by then. The children were sent to live with family members and friends.

We were sad since she was so young and had left four children motherless. Big Mama and Little Mama were mad. "His day will come," Big Mama said to the television as we watched the funeral of Governor Lurleen Brigham Wallace.

CHAPTER 3

An Unyielding Feminist: Shirley Chisholm

Susan Perry Cole (1948-)

You don't make progress by standing on the sidelines, whimpering,
and complaining. You make progress by implementing ideas.
—SHIRLEY CHISHOLM

Susan Perry Cole was fresh out of law school in 1977 and found herself
smack in the middle of turbulent civil rights times as a congressional aide
to New York Congresswoman Shirley Chisholm. Cole described what it
was like to work for the first Black woman elected to Congress and who
would, among many other notables, be the first serious female candidate
for US president. She was a woman who challenged the Democratic Party
line if she thought it was wrong and championed the rights of women and
children. Cole described the office as broken up into little cubicles where
people shouted across the room and held animated meetings around their
desks. She talked about the energy Chisholm put in the air.

"Everything was party and leaders, and it is supposed to be, all top down,
all patriarchy, but Mrs. C. (as she was known to staff and friends) did not
follow it . . . You were expected to follow the party or pay a price," Cole
recalled. "She said she wanted to be remembered as 'having guts,' and I can
say without a doubt, she had guts."

Chisholm rose through New York politics from her Brooklyn base to
run for Congress in 1968. She beat out men with powerful backing, like

Susan Perry Cole, Chisholm's congressional aide.

James Farmer Jr., to become the first Black woman elected to Congress. She created a powerful coalition behind her campaign slogan, "Unbought and Unbossed," the title of both her autobiography and a documentary. Proud of her Caribbean and American heritage, she landed in DC, ready to fight for racial and gender rights. But when she threw her hat into the presidential ring, she found little support among key feminists or Black elected officials.

"Mrs. C. was right. We know if she had been a man, she would've received better treatment, especially by those old race organizations," Cole said. "The [Congressional] Black Caucus certainly should have supported her. Even though everybody knew she wasn't going to win. But they didn't have enough vision to understand that we had to start somewhere."

Cole worked as Chisholm's legislative staff director during her last years in Washington. Cole knew a few things about determination and guts from her own life. But it was under the Congresswoman's tutelage that Cole refined her purpose.

❧ ❧

By the time I met Cole through mutual friends, she had moved from Atlanta to Washington, DC, to work for Congresswoman Shirley Chisholm. Today, she heads the Legal Services Corporation in Rocky Mount, North Carolina. I felt fortunate to have mentors and friends in my life. I'd never known Black women attorneys. The only educated Black folks I knew in Alabama were teachers/professors and sometimes preachers. My new friends were sophisticated and informed; they dressed like they had stepped off the pages of fashion magazines. But more importantly, they were nice, funny, and full of ideas about changing the world. This was the life I had dreamed about and didn't even know it.

One year Cole invited me to Washington, DC for New Year's. We were going to cook a traditional Black Southern New Year's dinner, collard greens, black-eyed peas, potato salad, and chitterlings. Cole had never cooked chitterlings before, nor had I. But I was confident; I had seen Little Mama and Big Mama cook them. Surely we could cook some chitterlings. After spending all afternoon cleaning chitterlings in her bathtub, we finally cooked them with an onion like Little Mama said over the telephone. Our New Year's meal of cornbread, black-eyed peas, collard greens, potato salad, and chitterlings turned out well. But we were so exhausted I don't remember being awake to celebrate the beginning of 1980 when the new year finally arrived. But I do remember smelling like chitterlings for a long time. We invited friends over the next day to help us eat over the movable feast. They were impressed with our bravery.

When Cole was offered the job right out of law school as one of Congresswoman Shirley Chisholm's legislative aides, we friends stayed on the phones for hours with excitement. Even though I was far away from the government of Washington, DC, having Cole working for Congresswoman Chisholm, I felt engaged with the world. These new friends and mentors also encouraged me to get involved in civil and women's rights issues. I watched the news and read newspapers with great interest. The world was changing, and I wanted to be a part of it, and I wanted my son to be prepared for this new world.

Even though I didn't have a law degree, I was a college-educated Black woman, and the world seemed to be leaning toward us for once. It was an exciting time. For me to have these marvelous women in my life was a gift from the universe. This meant that since I had received, I had to give back, meaning I was seeking employment for the less fortunate. I worked for the Atlanta Legal Aid Society and the Law Student Research Council before I went to work in marketing for a Fortune 500 company. I was a single parent with no support other than my income to take care of my son.

It didn't matter if it was two months, two years, or five years since we'd spoken; we were always able to pick up where we left off. Cole's long straight black hair was cut in a sophisticated bob with sprinkles of gray. Her smile and beautiful teeth were the same. She spoke with a smile in her voice. "And you got to understand the southern ways if you are from New England," she said of her life and work in North Carolina. "You have to be aware that walking around wearing a Boston Red Sox baseball cap is not a good idea. And little nuances, like speaking to everybody and being friendly, are part of the southern charm."

That was the beginning of reconnecting with Cole for this interview. It had been more than forty years since I met her. We sat at her office in Rocky Mount, where she heads the North Carolina Legal Services Cooperation.

Destined for Justice

Susan Perry Cole was born in 1948 in Providence, Rhode Island. She grew up in a very ethnically diverse, poor neighborhood with Hasidic Jews, Italians, Irish, and Blacks. Cole described her home life as chaotic. Her father drank and sometimes turned violent toward her mother. He was also a hard worker, often working two jobs. Cole believed that he worked himself to death like so many other poor people. "There were a lot of things about him that weren't that good, like his violence towards my mother. But on the other hand, I had a relationship with him," Cole said.

She learned about sports from him. "My relationship with him helped me to realize now how important it is for girls to have relationships with their fathers, and it helped me to build my confidence."

Her mother showed her strength and emphasized education. She didn't join the PTA or visit the schools her children attended. "She communicated to us that school was important, and I loved it. Being good at it set the platform for how I was able to get out of Rhode Island."

Even though Cole's life was disrupted by poverty and alcohol, there seemed to be more of a balance. "But there were lots of happy times too." All of her family were around, and they fellowshipped together. Nobody was stretched out in different places. There were many cousins, and they played together and entertained themselves. Cole found reading a world that she could retreat into and lose herself. Her grandmother gave her the book *Fifty Famous Fairy Tales*. She read that book until the pages fell apart. She learned when she was in school she could succeed and she loved it. The positive reactions she received from teachers, even though her teachers were white, they realized that she wasn't stupid and treated her well, which motivated her.

Cole's grandmothers were major figures in her life. Her mother's mother was an elevator operator. That position wouldn't be considered that significant today, but during the 1940s, it was a great job with a steady paycheck and benefits. And the work wasn't nearly as hard as most designated work for Black women. "She wore a little uniform and stood on the elevator and threw that switch. We would go downtown to one of the big downtown buildings. She was a very stately woman with high standards; it was clear to me how important it was to please her."

But Cole was still motivated to get out of Rhode Island. To her, it was "too small, too square, too everything and not enough Black people. And, of course, I knew nothing and had no money." Her family couldn't help with college; they knew nothing about higher education. "I had taken a summer trip to New Jersey, so I decided to go to college in New Jersey." I had no idea Cole was a full-blooded Native American. Like most folks, I thought she was a light-skinned Black woman with shoulder-length black straight hair since that was how she described herself. She said both her parents and grandparents were descended from Native people and stressed that heritage. For years she had neglected it, but now she was interested in embracing it. "I realize that it is an important part of me, my children, and now grandchild," she said. Her parents and grandparents were proud of their heritage and attended Pow Wows and other Native events. One of her sisters had even visited a Native American community in Provincetown, Massachusetts, and said she was shocked that they all looked like their mother. "I remember seeing pictures of people in Indian clothes," she said. "Being young and ashamed, I didn't pay much attention. After I left Rhode Island, I dropped that part of my life."

Cole landed on Rutgers University's Newark campus in 1966 as an undergraduate student. A year later, the city erupted in a four-day riot triggered by police brutality. Twenty-six people were killed, and the city suffered massive destruction. "[It] was like getting a PhD in street life, equity, and social justice," she said. "That was an exciting time. It created my political development." Cole received her undergraduate and law degrees in 1970 and 1974, respectively. During her law school days, she was involved in the politics of the rural South. There was poverty law with different kinds of clinical programs where students worked on real-life issues. Students were being shaped

Shirley Chisholm and Rosa Parks.

and didn't know it. But it was a very male dominant, with Caribbean and other Black male intellectuals in the forefront. "It was all right for women to be in the background, copying, and typing, making phone calls, bringing coffee and food, but not in the front of the room," she said. Cole rejected this role and joined the woman's movement, which included bringing legal help to women in prisons.

Like Cole, many of her siblings went to college and moved on from Providence. Her sister Bobbi is nearby in Charlotte, North Carolina. "I always looked up to her. She has balls, you know," Cole said. We laughed. "Just like Mrs. C., who didn't look tough, dressed like a little school mom with that crazy accent (Chisholm said of herself). I never saw anything undone on her. And she walked fast but erect." But very important to Chisholm was her Caribbean background of knowing she was not one of the colonial powers. She was never confused about who she was, Cole said. She was confident and a great role model. "It's sad today that a lot of folks, even adults, don't know who she is. Never mind her role in modern history."

Chisholm Rising

Shirley Anita Chisholm began exploring her candidacy for president of the United States in 1971 and formally announced her bid a year later at a Baptist church in her district of Brooklyn. There she called for a "bloodless revolution" at the forthcoming Democratic nomination convention. She was the first African American major-party candidate to run for president, also making her the first woman ever to run for the Democratic Party's nomination. US Senator Margaret Chase Smith had run for the Republican presidential nomination in 1964.

But standing in that church, she was a long way from her roots on her grandmother's farm in Barbados, where she went to a one-room schoolhouse and learned self-pride. Although born in New York City in 1924 to immigrant parents—her father an unskilled laborer and her mother a seamstress and a domestic worker.

Chisholm was sent to Barbados when she was five. She didn't return to the US until 1934, and in her autobiography, she wrote: "Years later I would know what an important gift my parents had given me by seeing to it that I had my early education in the strict, traditional, British-style schools of Barbados. If I speak and write easily now, that early education is the main reason." She always considered herself a Barbadian American. "Granny gave me strength, dignity, and love. I learned from an early age that I was somebody. I didn't need the Black revolution to tell me that."

She earned her BA degree from Brooklyn College in 1946, where she won prizes for her debating skills. She was a member of the Delta Sigma Theta sorority. She taught in a nursery school while earning her master's degree in elementary education from Teachers College at Columbia University in 1952. She ran a daycare center until politics caught her interest. Her timing was right too. After a stint in the New York State Assembly, in 1968, she was elected as the Democratic national committeewoman. The same year she ran for the US House of Representatives from New York's 12th Congressional District, which as part of a court-mandated reapportionment plan, had been significantly redrawn to focus on Bedford-Stuyvesant and was thus expected to result in Brooklyn's first Black member of Congress.

Chisholm's presidential campaign was underfunded, and she struggled to be regarded as a serious candidate instead of a symbol. She was ignored by much of the Democratic political establishment and received little support from her Black male colleagues. She did enter several Democratic presidential primaries and gained 151 delegates. She later said, "When I ran for Congress, and when I ran for president, I met more discrimination as a woman than for being Black; men are men."

Her husband, Conrad Chisholm, supported her candidacy. But as a security guard he was concerned for her safety. During the campaign, three confirmed threats were made against her life. Her husband served as her bodyguard until the US Secret Service gave her protection in 1972. She finished the primary in seventh place. "I ran for office in spite of hopeless odds . . . to demonstrate the sheer will and refusal to accept the status quo."

Cole learned much about political dealings under Chisholm. "I got exposed to some of the top leaders in the Congress, and I learned how to be politically astute," she said. "Parties really dominated. You did what the party told you to do. You did what the leadership told you to do. I understand [House Speaker] Nancy Pelosi. In order to get that healthcare bill through, she had to crack heads."

Chisholm reached across the aisle and racial divide. Cole remembered one Congressman, John Buchanan, a Republican from Alabama whom Chisholm worked with. "She would have relationships with these whites," she said. "She would influence him, and he would influence her; they were buds. She had those kinds of relationships across different kinds of *isms* that folks didn't expect. She was full of surprises."

But the mighty force was Chisholm, who could take speeches written for her and make them "ring." She was afraid of one thing: The "well." She was afraid to speak on the floor of the House. Apparently, she got confused one time, and something went out of sync while she was on the floor. It was embarrassing. "You have to know your parliamentary procedure and when you are supposed to yield. They were going to be looking at her with a magnifying glass, every little thing . . . What would you do if you were thrust in the limelight like that? I would probably be crushed . . . But she refused to let them break her. That's what she meant by saying she had guts."

Cole recalls when they wanted to put her on the Agriculture Committee, knowing that her constituent was urban. She surprised them when she took it and mandated the present-day food stamps program by providing food for women and children, known later as WIC. That's when they understood whom they were dealing with.

The congresswoman was very proud of her Black heritage and very attentive to her appearance. "She was kind of vain. She kept a big mirror on her
desk and didn't seem to tire of looking at herself. You've got to have that kind
of ego in order to take on a platform. I learned that these people are different
but are alike in certain ways. They tend to need for this constant attention
for everything to revolve around them."

Looking back, Cole remembers working with Chisholm meant you were
on the streets at all hours of the day and night, but it put stress on family
life. But Cole was young and knew she was helping to make history. She was
proud to have had "the experience in the end with somebody, the first Black
woman to actually run for the president of these United States, who was not
an idiot or a bimbo, a dignified, abled and confident Black woman."

Chisholm talked about the stress in her personal life, too, in her book and
the documentary, as well. She even talked about her nineteen-year-old self,
being young, innocent, and in love with a man she became engaged to, but
it turned out that he had another wife in Jamaica. That was a heartbreak for
her; she cried on camera even at the end of her life.

Later in 1949, she married Conrad Chisholm, a private detective. I think
she wanted a family; she said in the end that she didn't have time for a personal life. That marriage ended in divorce in February 1977.

Later that year, she married Arthur Hardwick Jr., a former New York
state assemblyman. He was subsequently injured in an automobile accident.
Chisholm was dissatisfied with the course of liberal politics in the wake of
the Reagan Revolution, and she wanted to take care of her husband. She
announced her retirement from Congress in 1982. Chisholm resumed her
work in education, giving speeches and teaching classes at Mount Holyoke
College in Massachusetts. She also picked up honors like being inducted into
the National Women's Hall of Fame in 1993.

Cole continued, "I like the fact that Mrs. C. was involved in education. We
didn't understand the significance of good early childhood education. She
asked the question, are we politically sophisticated enough when she was
running? That was an interesting question. I don't think we were."

"But who was? I am sure she was as sophisticated as any of the men."

"Uh-huh. Black women are not valued. That was one of the points made
from the film, *Unbought and Unbossed*. Black women were (and still are)
marginalized. Let me say this too, Mrs. C. let the Black Panthers be a part of

Shirley Chisholm's wedding.

her campaign. Black politicians today who would still run away from them
. . . She was honest, decent, and wasn't afraid. When I say decent, I mean
nobody ever heard her say a mean word about anybody. That is very rare,
especially for politicians."

Cole had no further contact with Chisholm after the congresswoman
retired. "She was probably exhausted and was content having a little time
to herself."

After Chisholm retired in 1991, Cole found it impossible to stay on Capitol
Hill. She cited Reagan and the inability to get things done on the progressive,
liberal agenda. People were afraid. "It was the beginning of this extreme right-
wing agenda that was beginning to frame out this, really virulent opposition
to abortion rights," she said. "Mrs. C. had a womanliness agenda; she had
a Black people's agenda . . . Her main interests were women, children, and
education, those kinds of bread and butter issues."

Chisholm again showed a singular vision when she tried to bring women
of color into the Woman's Movement. "Black women were very standoffish
. . . they did not trust white women. Chisholm was way ahead of her time.

She was trying to be a bridge builder; she didn't want to run just on Black or woman's issues. Everybody was shooting bullets because everybody wanted her to address their issues . . . Why not do both? Chisholm often asked that question . . . I saw her as a bridge, but people often stepped on her," Cole continued. "I don't know if they really walked across, maybe to a certain extent, because she did do something."

Making the Next Move

At the time Chisholm retired, Cole was unmarried. She wasn't sure she wanted to get married, but she was sure she didn't want to come home to an empty house. "I started to ask myself, what was I doing?"

Cole's boyfriend left his job at the *Washington Post* for a job in Detroit. She did not follow him. He was there about eighteen months because he didn't like it that much either. She took the job in Rocky Mount. She turned it down at first, but they put a lot of pressure on her to take it by appealing to her liberal-leaning. Running a brand-new legal aid office in a community she had never lived in, the rural South, was quite a challenge for her.

"After I came here, a lot of people seemed concerned. I mean, it was not exactly realistic to go from legislative staff director to a rural legal service in a place like North Carolina; I mean, who does that?" She laughed. Her boyfriend joined her, and they've been married for thirty-four years.

About 57,000 citizens live in Rocky Mount. Legal aid, in a place like Newark, is just part of the fabric. Cole found that legal aid in North Carolina put you on center stage; every move you made was monitored. And the legal system didn't want anything changed. If Cole had understood all of the dynamics of what she was getting into, she said she'd never have had the balls to come to eastern North Carolina. If she had understood the history of the state and how racist this part of the state was, she might have made a different decision.

"And thinking that I wasn't really making a big difference over in Congress, maybe there is something that can be done, so I came down here."

Dave Cole, her husband, gave up a lot too. It was either move or breakup. He never got his journalism career back on track and ended up working at a Black radio station in Rocky Mount. "It was a hard thing to do, one of the hardest things I have ever done was to come here and try to fit in," she said.

Everything was a surprise to Cole, from the smallness of it, the intimate questions like: Who is your father? What church do you go to? Or you don't come from here? Cole learned how dominant the church was in the culture and what it's like to grow up rural and poor and on a farm. The male patriarchy was all tied up in the culture. People on her board surprised her when they thought her brand of legal aid would be divorces and other common family matters. But Cole did voting rights ligation, which they thought was too controversial. She did not understand them; they did not understand her. She was regarded as a Northerner even though she was coming from DC but still a northerner to them.

"Soon after she got there, a Black voter registration drive took off. She called it 'an uprising.' A real Black voter engagement uprising in this state happened. We got Black elected officials starting to take all seats at all levels, state, local, all of that. To live through that period was really a privilege for me. It dovetailed with this background of Mrs. C." Cole thought back to her early days in Rocky Mount and the pressure she had felt from the Black male leadership not to rock the boat. "I don't know what they expected, but they didn't expect systems change work. I felt the spirit and energy of Mrs. C. was with me . . . I loved it at the end of the film when she said, 'I want to be remembered as a woman who was a catalyst for change in the twentieth century.'"

In 2005, Chisholm died in Florida. She is buried in the Oakwood Mausoleum at Forest Lawn Cemetery in Buffalo, New York. Her vault inscription reads: "Unbought and Unbossed." Cole and I thought it should also say: "Here lies a woman who had guts."

Dave Cole, husband of Susan Cole Perry, joined the ancestors in 2019.

THE SPELLING BEE

Big Mama and Miss Carrie Mae stitched me a pumpkin-colored jumper to wear to the spelling bee. A small row of daisies dancing around the hemline. A smaller row of daises sprouted around the collar of my light blue blouse.

"Stand still," Big Mama ordered as she pinned the jumper on me for fitting. We got the material from the rolling store, which was a shop on a truck that brought goods to rural America since so many people lacked transportation to shop in regular stores. We weren't allowed to go into the stores in town since they wouldn't let us try on clothes and often wanted us to go to the back door where the delivery folks came in. "De rollin' store ain't got but one door," the church ladies said.

Miss Carrie Mae had cut the pattern from newspapers that Little Mama brought home from the white woman's house. Miss Carrie Mae was a stout, dark-skinned woman with gold-trimmed front teeth; one even had a gold star on it. Her sewing had improved since she bought a new zigzag sewing machine from Sears on time payments. She started sewing when her three daughters were young. Her dream was for them to marry well. "De nicer dey dress de better chance dey have of snatchin' a good one." She asserted as she snapped thread threw her gold teeth. When her daughters took home economics and learned to sew, they increased their chances of marrying well.

Little Mama didn't say a word to me about winning the county spelling bee contest. I was glad, in a way. All she would do was tell me how Dead Daisy would've won everything. At least she bought the cloth for my new jumper. All the church ladies congratulated me and knew I would make the race proud. Even Big Mama said, "That's nice." She didn't even say, "don't let it go to your head," like she usually did.

To get to the spelling bee contest by 7:00 p.m., I had to spend the night with Mrs. Lindsey, my math teacher. She didn't talk much, just smiled a lot. Her front teeth were like Peter Rabbit's. She was knock-kneed with thin shoulder-length hair, and she always smelled like Evening in Paris perfume.

"You've done very well, Ethel. Try and not get too nervous. You have a good chance of winning. And if you do, you'll be on the front page of the newspaper."

"Yes, ma'am; I'll try my hardest."

Mr. Lindsey, the principal at the Mt. Zion School three towns over, arrived home two hours later.

"You have time to take a bath and relax a little before supper." Mrs. Lindsey smiled.

Their bathroom was roomy with wallpaper that was splashed with tiny pink and blue flowers. The towels were different shades of pink. A giant cookie jar on the back of the toilet was filled with pink bars of Dove soap. A basket of *Jet* and *Ebony* magazines was on the left side of the toilet seat. The church ladies and our teachers said those magazines carried the real news about our people. A small space heater stood in the other corner. White cotton throw rugs covered most of the cold floor. I took a bath and pretended I was getting ready to be on television.

My jumper was a perfect fit. With my penny loafers spit-shined, a generous layer of Vaseline on my legs, and knots in my stomach, I was ready for the spelling bee contest.

For supper, we ate meatloaf with Cheese Wiz on top, lumpy mashed potatoes, canned green beans, and two slices of toasted Wonder bread. I guess Mrs. Lindsey didn't know how to cook since she didn't have any children. We drank a glass of milk to wash the supper down. Mr. Lindsey said grace and asked God to remember their contestant in the spelling bee. I wondered how God would know which contestant to bless since Mr. Lindsey didn't mention my name. The food made the knots already in my stomach churn like making fresh buttermilk.

Mr. Lindsey was a rotund red-brown man who walked with a cane. He didn't talk much, either. We quietly drove to the white school for the spelling bee contest.

Twelve of us had spelled our way to the state championship. I didn't know any of them. Mr. Knight, our principal, and his family were there, along with several white folks, which made me even more nervous.

I thought that if I didn't win, maybe I could get a boyfriend since all of the boys were taller than me. There was a refreshment line with cherry Kool-Aid in a clear punch bowl and store-bought chocolate chip cookies. A huge bulletin board at the front door said: GOOD LUCK FROM THE RED DEVILS! I guess they couldn't write what they usually wrote in our used schoolbooks GOOD LUCK NIGGERS since so many officials, Black and white, were present.

"Good evening, everyone. It's time to get started. This is an occasion we can all be proud of. These young people have worked so very hard. I would like to congratulate each of the twelve finalists; you're already winners," glowed Mr. Knight. "Without further ado, I would like to introduce our narrator for the evening, our very own Mrs. Opal Britt." Everybody clapped.

Mrs. Britt was considered the hardest English teacher in Barbour County. Students could tell her mood by the shade of red of the wig she sported on a particular day. If it were deep red, they were in real trouble. Her daughter was going to 'Bama, home of the "Crimson Tide" to study engineering; she had made the highest score ever recorded in the state of Alabama. "Now that's 'Roll Tide,'" Mrs. Britt had said. "Roll Tide" is the rally cry for the Alabama Crimson Tide athletic teams.

When the spelling bee came down to the wire, I felt the sweat on my waist where the rubber of my half-slip was. I was scared to look down; my socks had slipped down into my penny loafers. And the Vaseline felt like lead on my legs. Three contestants were left: Nathaniel Thornton from Riverview, Josephine Haynes from Dillon County Training, and me.

The next thing I remembered was being on the floor and people standing around me. ETHEL, ETHEL, I heard.

"Ethel, E-T-H-E-L," I spelled. With a hit of smelling salts and the spelling of the word Xenophobia, I won second place. Nathaniel Thornton won first place and my heart. We three finalists were supposed to appear on the front page of the *Montgomery Advertiser* the next day, but it never happened.

CHAPTER 4

The Art of Activism

Constance Curry (1933-2020)

The civil right movement didn't begin in Montgomery, and it didn't end in the 1960s. It continues on to this very minute.
—Julian Bond

I hardly remember a time when Constance Curry wasn't in my life, and many other people feel the same way. She was at the epicenter of the civil rights movement in Mississippi during the violent days of the 1960s. Today she exposes how that state's education system is mostly a pipeline to prison for Black boys. A second-generation Irish immigrant who was raised in the South, she's connected to big names like Julian Bond and African drummer Babatunde Olatunji; but she has spent her life writing about heroes in the margins of the struggle. She gives a voice to folks whose words are muffled or lost in the noise of history.

"She's damn funny, too," is how Julian Bond described his best friend. Not only did Curry go to law school at age fifty, but she also went to comedy school at the same time. Julian Bond, the civil rights icon and her lifelong friend, was living in Charlottesville, Virginia, called Connie on his birthday. She told him she was going to pay his way to comedy school for his birthday. He said he would only go if they went together. After they completed the class, Julian declared them officially funny.

"When I met Julian, he was nineteen, I was twenty-five, and we started telling each other jokes." They remained lifetime friends until he died in 2015. Julian Bond was the first African American to have his name placed in the nomination for vice president of the United States. He could not accept since he was only twenty-eight years old, under the age of eligibility according to the Constitution, which is thirty-five years old.

"I've been telling jokes all my life since I was little. Folks have always known about my filthy mouth." Curry and I laughed. I, too, remembered some of her joke-telling skills. I also remember spending many lovely days and nights at her beloved beach house on Hunting Island, South Carolina, a draw for writers and social activists—from Pat Conroy, John Lewis, Julian Bond, Andy Young, Maynard Jackson, Letia Fitzgerald, Vivian Malone Jones, Dorothy Boden, and other dignitaries and artists. There was always some activity happening at her house, a cookout, potluck supper, or an ad-hoc committee meeting about some urgent issue having to do with civil rights. She kept a log where you not just signed in but wrote about your experience on the Island. Just reading the log was entertaining.

The brisk autumn day I interviewed Curry at her house on Myrtle Street, it looked the same as I remembered more than forty years ago. I choked up a bit with gratitude for the memories. She was mourning the loss of her beloved beach house, artist and activist colony during a hurricane. She was also organizing her files to begin writing her memoir. Her story is remarkable.

The Student Nonviolent Coordinating Committee was one of the major civil rights organizations of the 1960s, and Curry was the first white woman appointed to the executive board. Founded by Bond, it emerged from the first wave of student sit-ins and formed at an April 1960 meeting organized by Ella Baker at Shaw University in Raleigh, North Carolina. After its involvement with the Voter Education Project, SNCC grew into a large organization with many supporters in the North who helped raise funds to support its work in the South, allowing full-time organizers to have small stipends. Often becoming targets of racial violence and police brutality, SNCC played a seminal role in the freedom rides, the March on Washington, Mississippi Freedom Summer, the Selma Campaigns, the March Against Fear, and other historic events. SNCC's major contribution was in its fieldwork, organizing voter registration, freedom schools, and direct action all over the country, especially in Georgia, Alabama, and Mississippi.

Constance Curry. Photo courtesy of Billy Howard.

Curry left SNCC in 1964 for the American Friends Service Committee, a Quaker organization. Her first assignment as a fieldworker was to go to Jackson, Mississippi, and help a group of white women monitor the public school desegregation to try and have a peaceful transition. Jean Fairfax was working as a field secretary; she reached out to Curry since she was already in Jackson working with the Black community. During that time, she discovered white women who were working toward the same goal. They did not want another New Orleans or another Little Rock.

Curry went to Mississippi in the summer of 1964 with SNCC workers. It was called "Freedom Summer" or the Mississippi Summer Project, where volunteers attempted to register as many African American voters as possible in the state. The bodies of civil rights workers James Chaney, Andrew Goodman, and Michael Schwerner were found that August. "The violence that summer was horrifying. We were all scared but knew we had to continue our work," she said.

Four years later, Curry still received threatening phone calls. After one meeting, she returned to her Atlanta apartment to find her Volkswagen with

"KKK" painted all over it. She was afraid that school desegregation would blow their work apart.

That is how Curry started traveling as the southern field secretary. This was after the 1964 decision that mandated if the organization was going to receive federal funds under Title VI, it had to come up with a desegregation plan. Many school districts came up with "Freedom of Choice," which stated that students could choose to go to any school in their district, but those Deep South districts knew that the sharecroppers were dependent on those white plantation owners; and they weren't going to deviate.

In 1965 Curry met May Bertha Carter, her husband Matthew, and a few folks in the community. Their organization helped them to survive. Fifty-three families had signed up to integrate schools. But by the opening of school, they all had withdrawn because they were threatened with evictions, job losses, and bodily harm, and the Klan had shot into the Carters' house.

When Curry and another fieldworker learned that May Bertha and Matthew had enrolled eight of their children in the white schools, they went to visit them immediately. Curry and the other fieldworkers were there to make sure the transition was as smooth as possible. All of the fieldworkers were white women because they posed less of a threat to the lawmakers. By then, May Bertha had left her husband Matthew in Jackson with the children and had moved to Atlanta to try and earn a better living. She was working for the Georgia Council & Human Relations. Then she came to work at the America Friends' Service Committee where Curry worked.

Curry worked for the AFSC for ten years until they lost their grant. She then returned to Atlanta and started working for the city government under Mayor Maynard Jackson, the city's first African American mayor. She received a call about a conference called "Women in the Civil Rights Movement," sponsored by Georgia State University and the Martin Luther King Jr. Center. There she saw May Bertha across the room. It had been thirteen years. Her husband Matthew had passed. Curry described him "as a wonderful man; he sewed and made underpants for his little girls. He would help bathe all of them."

"May Bertha told me all of their children had graduated from the white high school, and seven had graduated from Ole Miss. I've got to write this amazing story," Curry told herself.

That's how her first book, *Silver Rights*, started. Later it influenced a documentary, *The Intolerable Burden*, which Curry researched and produced. The

Map of Mississippi.

Carters used the Freedom of Choice Plan to enroll the youngest eight of their thirteen children in the public school in Sunflower County, nine miles from Drew, Mississippi, population 1,700, in the fall of 1965. Even though the Carter family lived closer to Drew, they had done most of their shopping and church going in Merigold and Cleveland, Mississippi, like other Black citizens in the area. The Drew school board designated the plan to put districts in compliance with the Civil Rights Act of 1964. Given the racist attitudes, Blacks were not expected to choose white schools.

The Carter family saw it differently. Curry's moving documentary shows the Carter family's commitment to obtaining a quality education in context by examining the conditions of segregation prior to 1965. The family faced many hardships—getting fired from jobs, bodily harm, and anything that could be taken from them—"white resistance" was massive, which led to resegregation. In the epilogue, the film poses the dilemma of "education v. incarceration," a particular threat to Black youth. While the town of Drew is geographically isolated, the patterns of segregation, desegregation, and resegregation are increasingly apparent not just in Mississippi but throughout the public education systems in the United States.

On that first day of school in 1965, the Carter family's dreams of getting freedom seemed to be coming true. But they were not ready for the consequences. "We witnessed the family's struggle against society and the conflicts that resulted from the choice to go against society by doing what was right. The Carter family did get support from many organizations that were trying to promote racial equality."

The Carter family ran into many conflicts and challenges, but they overcame them all by stepping over the color lines that many others refused to cross because they were afraid. They and their children could've been killed, and nothing would've happened to the terrorists. After Matthew Carter regained his job, he became ill again and died a few years later due to blood clotting and a heart attack.

Aaron Henry was the head of the NAACP in Mississippi for about thirty-five years. Curry knew him from the time she was an AFSC fieldworker in Clarksdale. She frequented his drugstore, and they became friends. "One day, he called me and said a lot of people have wanted to write his memoir, but he wanted me to do it," Curry said. "I was so flattered."

Henry was born in Dublin, Mississippi, on July 2, 1922. His parents, Ed and Mattie Henry, were sharecroppers. While growing up, he worked on the Flowers Brothers' plantation in Coahoma County, twenty miles east of Clarksdale. He hated everything about growing cotton because of the hardships that it had on African Americans working on the plantations. His parents, like the Carter family, believed education was essential for the future of Henry and his family and other African Americans. He attended the all-Black Coahoma County Agricultural High School. After that, Henry worked at a motel as a night clerk to earn enough money for college. But instead of going to college, he enlisted in the Army. Those three years taught him that racial discrimination and segregation were common all over. He described his experience in Robert Penn Warren's book, *Who Speaks for the Negro?* But at the same time, it confirmed his feelings that segregation was worse in his home state. He decided that he would work for equality and justice for Black Americans. When he returned home after World War II in 1946, he found a Progressive Voters' League had been formed to work for the implementation of the 1944 Supreme Court decision abolishing white primacy.

As a veteran, Henry was interested in the Mississippi legislation that exempted returning veterans from paying the poll tax. Under the poll tax laws, a person had to have paid his poll taxes for two years prior to the time he or she voted. He tried to get Black Mississippians to go down to the courthouse to register to vote. When Henry went to the circuit clerk's office to register, he was rejected, as other Blacks had been. The clerk asked him to bring a certificate. After he brought the certificate, the clerk informed him that he still needed to pass various tests to show that he was qualified to vote. He finally registered to vote after he read several sections of the state constitution and went satisfactorily through more tests. He used his G.I. Bill to enroll in the pharmacy school at Xavier University in New Orleans. After graduating in 1950 with a pharmaceutical degree, he married Noelle Michael and went into his own pharmacy business.

As a businessman in Clarksdale, he became involved in local and state activities, especially events around African American voter registration. He organized an NAACP branch in Clarksdale mainly because of the incident where two white men, who were subsequently found not guilty, raped two Black girls.

In 1959 Henry was elected president of the NACCP and served for decades. He became a close friend of Medgar Evers, who worked as an NAACP secretary in 1950. On June 12, 1963, Mr. Evers was assassinated in his driveway in Jackson, Mississippi. This had a great impact on Henry.

Aaron Henry: The Fire Ever Burning was written by Constance Curry from Henry's papers. The book was published three years after he died in 1997. The book is an important contribution to the civil rights movement and Americans everywhere. Henry helped to secure the head start program for Mississippi and risked his life so that all Mississippians could enjoy the rights guaranteed under the US Constitution. Although his name is not familiar as Martin Luther King Jr., Malcolm X, Medgar Evers, or other icons of the civil rights movement, his role was just as important. He did a lot of behindthe-scenes work and also helped financially.

Curry continued her work on how the Mississippi education system for Black children, especially Black boys, was a pipeline to the prison system. For someone who never set foot in a courthouse, her impact on giving voices to folks whose voices were muffled and lost in the noise of whitewashing history with racism. Her contribution to the cause of civil rights is monumental.

Her next book, *Mississippi Harmony: Memoirs of a Freedom Fight*, combines her historical analysis and the proud voice of the Hudson sisters. They are among the unsung women of the civil rights movement. The lives of Winson and Dovie Hudson, fearless sisters, were finally able to register to vote in 1962, which inspired other Blacks in violence-prone Leake County, Mississippi, as well as those who gave support from the outside like Vernon Jordan, former director of the Voter Education Project of the Southern Regional Council, the Urban League, and civil rights icon.

On the back cover of the book, Pulitzer Prize author and civil rights activist Alice Walker wrote: "How is the tender unshakeable love that we have for our people kept alive in us? Through the music, yes, and even more profoundly, I believe through the stories. Stories of real heroic lives lived full tilt into the face of some of the worst times human beings have ever known. Lives like those of Winson Hudson and her equally indomitable sister, Dovie. This precious book reveals some of whom we mean when we so proudly and so humbly."

Winson Hudson's story is about her struggle for racial justice in the cradle of segregated Mississippi; it is also inspiring, riveting and important. Constance Curry allows Hudson to speak in her own voice and take center stage. With her sister Dovie as her partner in the struggle, the two Black women defied the racial rules and charted their own half-century fight against the Ku Klux Klan, the voting registrar who refused to certify Hudson as literate to vote, and all other obstacles that were put in their paths.

With Curry's editing, Hudson's life becomes a template for the broad-scale social change in the Deep South. I am sure there are countless Winson and Dovie Hudsons who werenever sought to share the national spotlight. But it was through women like these that the day-to-day, incremental change was achieved.

Path of Grace tells real stories about how the segregationist policies of Strom Thurmond, Trent Locke, and Jim Crow were more than "a set of annoying rules," as Trent Locke describes. For the Black community of Harmony, Mississippi, to simply survive these noxious injustices would be an admirable story itself. Winson and Dovie Hudson were able to rise above and end many of the wrongs. These women are some of the unheralded heroes who literally risked their lives, jobs, and homes to fight the national civil rights effort on a local level. The book shows us that segregation is like pernicious smog that chokes the most mundane of human efforts—feeding your family, educating your children, and worshipping your God.

◆——◆

When I received an autographed copy of *Deep in Our Hearts: Nine White Women in the Freedom Movement*, edited by Constance Curry, my first book, *From Whence Cometh My Help: The African American Community at Hollins College*, had recently been published. Curry wrote: "For Ethel—Who would have dreamed we'd do books. Congratulations. Love Connie-October 2000." Those were my sentiments exactly. It took me back to all of those years ago when "us doing books" wasn't even on our dream radar.

Curry's work and belief will always make my heart sing. She has no idea how she had maintained the light in a state that is so riddled with racism and hate. This country owes her gratitude, respect, and appreciation. She has always been instrumental in my life as a friend and a mentor. As I interviewed her, I saw the parallel in our lives.

◆——◆

"We are all very different: southern and northern; rural and urban; state university and Ivy League, middle class, working class, and poor. We were moved to our radical activities in various ways: by Marxism, Christian existentialism, and immigrant folk wisdom; by our grandmothers and the Constitution; by Thoreau and Dumas; by living on a kibbutz; by African freedom fighters; and by a Deep South upbringing. Our book *Deep in Our Hearts* is about girls growing up in a revolutionary time and place. It is about love and politics and the transcendence of racial barriers. We offer this work to enrich the chronicle of a social movement that forever changed the country and our lives." Barbara Ransby wrote this moving foreword.

These first-person accounts by white women activists represent a critical voice, yet one that has not been often heard. This book breaks that silence. *Deep in Our Hearts* gives us another lens through which to view the politics of race and gender in the civil rights movement [and] probes the themes of growth, discovery, friendship, and courage . . . The real gift of these stories is a more optimistic legacy for a new generation of Blacks and whites as they navigate the ever-volatile path of racial relations into the twenty-first century and, hopefully, take up the challenge that 1960s activists did of trying to make the world a better and more humane place.

——— ———

Curry didn't have the typical southern white upbringing. Her parents, Ernest and Hazel Curry, were born in Belfast, Northern Ireland. They came to the US and settled in Patterson, New Jersey, where Curry and her sister were born. The family moved to Greensboro, North Carolina, soon afterward, where Curry calls home. She started the third grade there. She recalls her mother being very independent and an avid reader. She even paid social security for the African American woman who worked as their housekeeper. Because of that, her mother didn't have many friends. The other white women resented her throwing money away on the maid. "My parents were wonderful on every level with both my sister and me, in terms of letting us be who we were and do what we wanted. They never encouraged anything about civil rights or the freedom movement or justice."

But segregation and injustice were clear in Greensboro, North Carolina. And having just come over from Ireland, they spent three or four years moving around trying to find their way in America, but they did not understand segregation at all. "I think being a child of immigrants makes the child more aware of the Bill of Rights and the Constitution. You become more aware too because you grow up reading about them. I always had the support of my family. I was always doing things out in the community, trying to make the world a more just place. I don't think they understood half of it, but they were always behind me."

Later Curry realized how fortunate she was. A lot of the white women who got involved in the Movement were thrown out of their homes and families. She was very close to her family. And they never objected to her work for social justice since they believed in the same cause. "Ireland was going to be a mess for years and years to come in the fight between the British trying to control Northern Ireland and Southern Ireland trying to be free," her father often said.

While going through her papers, Curry came across something she wrote titled "The Easter Rebellion," which was the Irish Easter Rebellion. The poet Patrick Pierce was always on her mind in her early days at Agnes Scott College. He warned, "Beware masters when the people shall rise . . ."

I knew that Agnes Scott College in Decatur (the Atlanta area) had been a major influence on Curry's social and intellectual development. I wanted to know what that experience was like. And how she ended up going to college there.

She planned to go to a woman's college and knew about Agnes Scott from her church, and a friend was already attending. She applied and got a full scholarship. "I was the Agnes Scott dream student, Phi Beta Kappa, student body president, had been a Fulbright scholar to France, and Mortar Board. So it wasn't like I was some kind of maverick," Curry remembered. "I think Agnes Scott has always had a tradition of good professors. I wouldn't call them liberal, but they certainly had an atmosphere of free thought."

Riding the MARTA bus in the 1970s passing Agnes Scott College, I thought it was a dream place for intellectualism with the most beautiful campus I had ever seen. Later I started attending evening programs there. They presented a program once a month called Travelogues. Watching and learning about places far from America was the beginning of my travel bug.

Curry attended Agnes Scott, and even though it was segregated, she said she loved her professors. She majored in English and history and had lots of friends. "But what was most important, they tolerated me being involved with the National Student Association. They were one of the only white colleges that didn't drop out of the NSA after *Brown v. Board of Education*," Curry said.

She has always felt fortunate in that she grew up in the 1940s, '50s, and '60s in a totally segregated society with all the usual prejudices of southern whites. She knew early and always asked the question, "why?" Why was there such a big gap between the reality of what she saw around her and what she read in school about the Constitution? "What I was learning in church about God, all of the goodness of loving everybody, and then in my daily life, even as a child, I could see disparities between the word and the reality."

"Were you discriminated against because of being Irish?"

"No, but we felt a lot of anti-Yankee sentiments. That hurt since we were from New Jersey. I remember my sister coming home from school saying someone's mother said she didn't care if Jesus Christ was running for president as long as he wasn't a Democrat. That was back before the great strangeness of the mix-up between Democrats and Republicans."

Curry said she had been thinking more about her Irish background lately as she was going through her papers preparing to write her memoir. "Even though we were from Northern Ireland, Protestant, and considered part of the Rebellion. My father left Ireland because of oppression. I've lived my whole life thinking about it, talking about it, and writing about it. And you sort of get it into your soul that oppression is oppression is oppression."

Curry learned early on that the English, the British Empire, had tried to control and treat the Irish the same way, as lower class, not humans. "I remember the 'pigs in the parlor' imagery. That is particular true of Southern Ireland, but a lot of prejudice. I don't think my mother and father believed that. It was the manifestation of the beginning of the battle that made them leave in 1925. They knew it was going to be a long hard battle. How much of that seeped through to me? I don't know, but it became clear when I was in college in the 1950s reading William Butler Yeats and Patrick Pearce, an Irish revolutionary, a lot of Irish radicals saying, 'Beware when ye masters, when the people rise up.' I always equated that to slavery, 'beware of the white masters.'" Curry continued, "The only difference here, of course, is we've got slavery and the legacy of slavery to make the racism and the intolerance so much harder and even more complicated. My main concern today is about the schools to the prison pipeline."

Curry believes this is the resegregation of the public-school systems.

"The schools are absolutely terrible, and white people are still sending their children to private schools that are segregated. I was just talking to a friend of mine who was on the NAACP board. At the Walnut Grove prison, a juvenile detention, privately owned in Mississippi, outside of Jackson, thirteen- to nineteen-year-olds, six hundred beds, and it's full."

"And probably stays full."

"When the warden went to the board of directors and asked could they get some educational programs. He was told, 'What do you want to educate them for? Half of them are in there for life.' These are thirteen- to nineteen-year-old children." She teared up.

"Clayola Brown, my friend, was there visiting, looking through the barbed wire fence, when she felt somebody tugging at her shirt; it was an eleven- to twelve-year-old Black child. 'You know, that's where I want to go. They got three hots and a cot in there, and they got books. And you warm in the winter, and it's cool in the summer. Since you're my color, maybe you can help me get in.' All I could think about was, is this what the civil rights movement was for? It's just too heartbreaking," Curry continued.

Curry's path to the resistance movement goes back to an incident in the fourth grade at a Greensboro lunch counter. "Douglas Gilly was standing next to me. He called one of the servers 'a nigger.' I turned around to him and said, that woman is as good as your mother. I learned quickly you don't talk about folks' mama in the South. Anyhow, I had on a new raincoat; he pushed me in the muddle puddle at play period. Even now, I can see the spattered mud on my new yellow coat," she recalled.

Curry didn't have any direct contact with African Americans until 1951, when she was a student at Agnes Scott College in Decatur, Georgia. She had the opportunity to go to a National Congress sponsored by the United State National Student Association. A lot of southern universities were members: Emory, Georgia Tech, Morehouse, Spelman, Clark, and all over the South. Delegations would send representatives up to this National Congress, which was always held in the middle of the US so that it could draw from all over the country.

At age eighteen, Curry went to Ames, Iowa, for her first National Student Congress. They debated political questions. She found it interesting, but more interesting was that she had a Black roommate from Xavier University in New Orleans. They got along well. At Agnes Scott, they didn't have Black students for a long time after Curry was a student.

At the National Conference meeting, Curry met some delegates, and she started going to meetings. She would take a taxi to Spelman or Morehouse or wherever the meeting was held. "I had to get permission from my mother and father, written permission, every time I went to an interracial meeting. Part of that was trying to protect the college. We're talking about integration, eating together, when segregation was the law of the land. My mother finally said, 'Can't I just write you blank permissions? Do I have to write a new one every time you go to a meeting?' But that was the way it was, so I did bit by bit."

Curry was elected chair of the National Congress, but by that time, it was called the Great Southern Region. It stretched from Texas to Georgia, all the way across the South.

After *Brown v. Board of Education,* southern white colleges and universities stopped participating in the National Congress. Agnes Scott has always stayed in since 1954; Curry was the chairperson. By that time, Babatunde Olatunji, the famous Nigeria drummer, was the president of the student body at Morehouse College and Curry was the president at Agnes Scott. They became good friends.

"I remember planning a meeting at the YMCA (known as the white Y) on Forsyth or Lucky Street in downtown Atlanta. We were allowed to have the meeting there, but we couldn't eat together. At lunchtime, when we came out, all of the Black students headed down toward Auburn Avenue. That's when I began to realize that it wasn't only religious, intellectual, and historical stirrings but that the law affected my life personally. It was against the law for me to eat with my friends. My passion and determination grew bigger."

Curry remembers another act of defiance; she was working for the city of Atlanta as the director of human services. A young Black man was accused of robbing a filling station. There was no eyewitness, and they didn't find anything on him. He said that he was jogging through the neighborhood and happened to cut through one of those filling stations. Something disappeared from the filling station, and he was arrested. Curry hung the jury by refusing to vote. She thought it was ridiculous that he was accused in the first place. But the all-white jury was willing to find him guilty because he was Black.

"After I hung the jury, I thought I could've done a better job at defending that young man. About the same time, I saw in the newspaper that Woodrow Wilson College was holding night law school. That's what motivated me to go to law school at age fifty."

In the late 1970s, I remember riding the MARTA bus passing through the lovely neighborhood around Agnes Scott College. I often wondered who went to college there. This was long before I knew I would end up in such a place as Hollins University, a similar place.

I remember thinking how wonderful it was that Curry went to law school at age forty. Later I learned she was fifty when she enrolled in law school. Maybe I could change my life too. It was the 1980s. I had worked as an investigator at EEOC and in marketing at Xerox. Neither was fulfilling in any way. At age thirty-seven, I applied and was awarded a full fellowship at Hollins University to study creative writing. Hollins, like Agnes Scott, is very southern, all female (with the exception of the very small graduate programs), mostly white, and a campus so stunning photographs cannot do it justice. At Hollins, I felt like I had been transported in some *Gone with the Wind* world.

Instead of practicing law, Curry used her law degree to get into prisons to interview inmates and write about their experiences. She loved law school, as she loved high school and college. Studying gave her a better idea of how the world worked. She even loved being fifty and being in law school. She was sure that students referred to her as "the old lady." But that changed; one day, in her constitution law class, they were discussing *Heart of Atlanta Motel, Inc. v. United States.*

The Supreme Court ruled on December 14, 1964, that in passing Title II of the Civil Rights Act, which prohibited segregation or discrimination in places of public accommodations involved interstate commerce. The important case presented an immediate challenge to the Civil Rights Act of 1964. For much of the one hundred years preceding 1964, race relations in the US had been dominated by the system of racial segregation that, while in name provided for "separate but equal" treatment of both Black and white Americans, perpetuated inferior accommodation, services, and treatment of Black American citizens.

The Heart of Atlanta Motel, a large motel in Midtown, was in violation of the terms of the Civil Rights Act of 1964 because it didn't allow African Americans to check into the motel. Owner Moreton Rolleston filed suit in federal court, arguing that the requirement of the Act exceeded the authority granted to Congress over interstate commerce. He maintained that it violated his Fifth Amendment right to choose customers and operate his business as he wished and resulted in the unjust deprivation of his property without due process of the law and just compensation. Finally, he contended that Congress had placed him in a position of involuntary servitude by forcing him to rent available rooms to Blacks, thereby violating his Thirteenth Amendment rights.

The United States countered that the restrictions requiring adequate accommodation for Black Americans were unquestionably related to interstate travel and that Congress, under the Constitution's Commerce Clause, had the power to address such a matter in law. It further argued that the Fifth Amendment did not forbid reasonable regulation of interstate commerce and asserted that the Thirteenth Amendment applied primarily to slavery and the removal of widespread disabilities associated with it. The US District Court for Northern Georgia issued a permanent injunction requiring the motel to stop discriminating based on race. In 1964, the motel closed.

When Curry told her classmates that she and some close friends were part of the group that helped to make that law possible, they began to look at her differently. She's sure they stopped calling her "the old lady." She went on to pass the Georgia Bar with no problems.

Not long after passing the bar, Curry took an early retirement from the city government for a fellowship at the Carter Woodson Center in Charlottesville, Virginia. She had access to her detailed AFSC Mississippi notes and spent a year interviewing all thirteen of the Carter children. She interviewed the mayor of Atlanta and lots of other governmental officials. "I just had so much, and the blessings kept coming; I also had a New York agent!"

"Now, that's a blessing for a southerner to get a New York agent," I said.

"What's weird, when I was up in Virginia, I wrote an article for the *Virginia Quarterly Review* about this family. I didn't know literary agents read literary magazines. He contacted me and said if you ever write a book, call me. Is that unbelievable?"

"Unbelievable and so wonderful." I agreed.

"There were so many rejections, and all of a sudden, Algonquin said, 'We want your book.' Shannon Ravenel taught me so much about writing from the very beginning."

"'Connie, life doesn't always have to be chronological.' So the first line in *Silver Rights* is, to go back to my own roots . . .'"

Silver Rights is an important book of its era. It was awarded the Lillian Smith prize for nonfiction in 1996. The book was also a finalist for the 1996 Robert F. Kennedy Book Award, was recommended by the *New York Times* for summer reading, and was named the Outstanding Book on the subject of human rights in North America by the Gustavus Myers Center for the Study of Human Rights. It was adapted into a documentary, *The Intolerable Burden*, in 2004, researched and produced by Curry.

From the depth of slavery and the civil rights movement came many broken families and hearts, bodies, and unforgettable painful memories. Curry portrays a family caught in the middle of the struggle for freedom of choice. Civil rights icon Vernon Jordan said this about the book, "We sometimes forget what prices were paid to defeat segregation in the Mississippi Delta and what courage it took. The book reminds us all of this moving account of the Carter family. It's an important document and an inspiring story."

The Carter family put their lives on the line from the time Mae Bertha signed the Freedom of Choice papers for the four younger children; the older children, Larry, Stanley, and Ruth, signed the papers for themselves.

In addition to her education at Agnes Scott College and the Woodrow Wilson Law School, Curry did graduate work in political science at Columbia University and was a Fulbright Scholar at the University of Bordeaux, France.

She was also awarded fellowships from the Institute for Women's Studies at Emory University and the Carter G. Woodson Institute Center for Civil Rights at the University of Virginia in Charlottesville.

Curry credits an important part of her education and experience to civil rights activist and icon Ella Baker. "I remember specifically Ella's speech because her whole talk was 'More Than a Hamburger.' She warned that work was just beginning: integrating lunch counters was one thing, breaking down barriers in areas as racially and culturally entrenched as voting rights, education, and the workplace was going to be much tougher than we could have imagined. And she further warned, 'don't let anyone, especially the older folks, tell you what to do.'"

A few months later, Baker wrote in the *Southern Patriot* that the students made it crystal clear that the current sit-ins and other demonstrations were concerned with something bigger than a hamburger: "The Negro and white students, north and south, are seeking to rid America of the scourge of racial segregation and discrimination—not only at the lunch counters but in every aspect of life." "She was such an eloquent and powerful speaker. The impact of that speech hit my spirit, and I began to realize that the sit-ins were more than the movement, and it was beginning to be much more than a demand for something to eat at a lunch counter. I was so overwhelmed at the breath of the representation there."

Ella Baker said, "Give light, and people will find the way." Constance Curry has always maintained that light.

THE PRELL SISTERS OF ALABAMA

Miss Winkie Prell, the oldest of the sisters, taught me how to read literature and type. She was stern, perfectly dressed in corduroy jackets and skirts of blues, browns, and greens, always with a light-colored or white starched and ironed cotton blouse and gold cuff links. Her suede shoes always matched her outfits. In the spring, she wore pastel-colored shirtwaist dresses with matching pumps. She didn't smile much like Miss Ella, who was the prettiest of the Prell sisters, but she pushed us to do better, "take notes as you read literature until you get used to the story." I learned to type 120 words per minute in her typing class. Another gift she gave me was diagraming sentences, which taught me to love words.

"And by all means, use the dictionary," she preached as she paced around the classroom in our four-roomed segregated school next to the church it was named for, Bethel. We read *Animal House, The Scarlet Letter, The Catcher in the Rye, Macbeth,* and other Shakespeare plays. I am sure I did not understand the total literary meaning of those classics, but it was the beginning of my journey toward critical thinking.

The summer I turned thirteen, I got my period and read *Gone with the Wind.* Pleased with myself that I had read such a big book, I told everybody; but I stopped when I figured out that most folks didn't know what I was talking about. Not only was it a big book, but the dialogue was harder than reading the Bible. But Miss Winkie Prell was very impressed. In fact, she sent me a handwritten letter in the mail. Her name and address were sprawled over the top of the baby blue stationery. The pretty paper sang a joyous song to heart. I felt like we were members of a secret club of admiration. She congratulated me on such a marvelous accomplishment. This was the beginning of me reading important books; she went on to write. I read the perfectly written letter every night before I went to sleep. Afterward, I prayed that I would one day write as beautifully.

Little Mama had a week off of work from cleaning the white woman's house. The white folks had to go to Florida to bury their aunt. Reading was one way to stay out of Little Mama's way. If she said anything, it was about dead Daisy. Never about us, even when she plaited our hair, it was never as good as our dead sister's. I didn't want to be anywhere near her.

The third and youngest Prell sister, Miss Bertha, taught my youngest sister at Shady Grove School. She loved to laugh and made everybody around her laugh too. She sported a huge afro and wore clothes made from African prints when she had lived in Ghana for the two years she was in the Peace Corps. She looked like Angela Davis wearing Dashikis. At the beginning of the school year, she presented a program with a projector showing us her Ghana pictures. The children looked so pitiful and raggedy. None of them smiled. I guess they didn't have much to smile about. We understood what our parents meant when they told us, "Eat your food, children in Africa starvin.'" Miss Bertha's main conversation was about power to the people. She called everybody my sister or my brother.

Miss Ella, the prettiest of the sisters, got along with everybody; Mr. Knight, our principal, was the only person who had any trouble with her. She taught math and science. Mr. Knight's booming voice sounded more like that of a country preacher than a school principal. He often used his voice to assure us we'd never amount to nothing. In fact, none of us would never set foot outside of Barbour County unless it was to prison, he often added. He wore blue and brown slick and shiny-looking suits, white shirts only with flowered matching ties. We heard he made his children shine his shoes before they went to bed every night. We thought his children also shinned his baldhead with a biscuit every morning before he came to school.

Katie Payne, one grade ahead of me, couldn't come back to school. She had to get married over the summer to Leroy Rumph. Everybody was talking about her pregnancy. My stomach cramped from my first period.

The next weekend I ran into Katie working at the Piggly Wiggly. I was happy to see her but didn't know what to say, but I tried to act natural.

"Me and Leroy was gonna get married anyway."

"I know. How you feelin'?" She looked the same, but she was gettin' plump, and her hair was longer and thicker.

"Get sick in the mornins' a lot, but that's easin' up now. My feet swell from standin' so much. Leroy soaks them in Epsom salt every night when he come home from workin' at the barbershop. He real sweet."

I was glad when other customers lined up. "That's nice. I have to go, but I see you later. I miss you."

"I miss y'all too. Can't wait for you to come and see me." We hugged.

"I will, soon."

That was the same summer that Big Mama told my sisters and me that when the ambulance came to the house to get dead Daisy, Little Mama ran behind it, and when she couldn't catch it, she rolled behind it like a log. She screamed so hard she lost her voice for a week. It took Mr. Gus Eustey (before he lost his leg) and two other men from the community to bring her home. Dr. Faircloth came and gave her a shot. Big Mama said she slept for two days.

One of the church ladies called the white woman and told her that Little Mama was sick. The white woman wanted to know when she was coming back. She didn't want her washing to pile up.

The week before our Thanksgiving break Miss Ella called a meeting with all the girls, fifth-seventh grades. Our Bethel School only went to the seventh grade. After the seventh grade, we rode the school bus about ten miles to attend the Barbour County Training School in Clayton; since there was no high school in Louisville for *us*, but there was a high school for white students.

Miss Winkie and Miss Ella seemed to show up out of nowhere for the meeting. We heard that Mr. Knight had told Miss Ella that she couldn't have *her* meeting on campus. She told him she could as long as she was conducting educational business. And what she was doing was called biology. Quietly, the Prell sisters ushered us girls into the small and smelly auditorium like soldiers. No men were allowed. Miss Maude guarded the front door of the room. And Miss Winkie stood at the back door.

I was nervous since I didn't know what to expect. My stomach ached even more. I bet Katie Payne's stomach hurt all the time with a baby growing in it like a balloon. Plus, her feet were swollen from working all day at the Piggly

Wiggly, and she had to get even fatter. Having babies didn't sound like a good deal for girls. Leroy got to stay in school. All he had to do was work more hours at his uncle's barbershop.

Miss Ella spoke first. She talked about the respect and responsibility that we owe to ourselves. "No one will respect you if you don't respect yourself." And it ended with the usual, "keep your skirt down and don't have sex until you're married; then you have to." That we heard from home, the church ladies, and other teachers. Afterward, we laughed; and I was able to relax some.

She passed out pamphlets called *Growing Up and Liking It.* I had never seen a book about how the female body works. We were told to wait until we took biology. I had just learned about periods last year, but not in detail. Just that our periods were something to fear because you bleed for about a week, and you could have a baby. Being a girl was complicated; there was so much to learn. She asked us if we knew what menstruation was. We all said yes, ma'am. That's good; first, we're going to dispel some of the myths and wise tales. We clapped and thanked her.

"Good afternoon, my sisters. We're going to talk about the beautiful human body. There is not a more powerful gift from the universe than having the ability to bring life into the world. No one else can do that; it is to be honored," Miss Maude said.

All I could think was, wow! She was the coolest and smartest person I've ever met; she wasn't just smart, but she was hip and cool. She sometimes called us baby, and she used words like groovy, and everything was beautiful. I'd never met a hip person in Alabama. We took a fifteen-minute break to read the pamphlet in groups and came up with questions or comments. Miss Maude told us this was a safe space and that the more education and information we had about our lives, especially our bodies, the better decisions we'll make, which meant we'd be happier and productive human beings.

Unlike the other Prell sisters, Miss Maude was a student at Alabama State during the 1960s. "Family legacy be damn," is how the other sisters described her decision to go to Alabama State rather than Alabama A&M like other members of their family. But every year, the sisters put that difference aside and checked into the Tutwiler Hotel in downtown Birmingham to enjoy the Magic City Classic football game between Alabama State and Alabama A&M.

Miss Maude had been part of a protest at Alabama State in 1960 when more than a dozen students marched to the Montgomery County Courthouse. The students decided to sit-in to protest the segregated dining rooms at the courthouse. Policemen met them at the door with aimed guns and forced them to leave. The students were called niggers and were pushed outside by the police. Folks were taking their pictures. The pictures were sent to the governor and posted in the *Montgomery Advertiser*. The white folks of Montgomery demanded that the college be shut down since it was state-funded.

When we came back together, Miss Ella talked about Katie Payne. "We should support Katie; I've already paid her a visit; and will continue to do so. Hopefully, you'll reach out to her too. This is a time when a person needs their friends. What happened to her could happen to any of us if we're exposed. That's all I am able to say about that." She paused before she continued. "But let me say this, please go to the clinic; it's free; see a doctor, a nurse, somebody if you need help in making major decisions in your life. And please, please, don't ever allow anyone to talk you into doing anything that is not in your best interest. You are our children with bright futures. Do you hear me?" Miss Ella wiped her teary eyes.

We knew she was serious. Our teachers didn't cry. After she composed herself, she finished her talk about good hygiene and how important it was to stay clean as possible. Nothing I had heard about my period was true except the cramping. Couldn't wash your hair, don't get caught in the rain, you could faint easily; wild animals might track you down since they smelled your blood.

"And if you ever need anything, we are right here without judgment," Miss Ella finished her talk. I felt more confident.

The next week a small cabinet was placed in the girl's coatroom with "Please take whatever you need. This is your private space." Inside of the cabinets were sanitary napkins and belts, toothbrushes and toothpaste, wash clothes, soap, and underwear.

Once a month, our school held a full devotion. All eighty-something students and seven teachers gathered in the auditorium. Usually, somebody who could actually sing would sing at least one song, always a spiritual, sometimes two if it was a holiday. "Take My Hand" or "Down by the River Side" were the most common. Sometimes we'd have a special guest to talk to us about the value of education. At the end, we would repeat the Lord's Prayer.

There didn't seem to be a special guest when Mr. Knight took the podium. I thought he was going to rant about how none of us Negroes would ever set foot out of Barbour County. Mr. Reed, our history teacher, told us it was his way of motivating us. Last year when the smartest student in the whole school had to get married, he was fired up. "You, see, I told you so." I never understood why he thought rooting against us was motivation.

But that day, Miss Ella and the other Prell sisters weren't having it. Miss Ella stood up straight as a pine tree and started clapping in the middle of Mr. Knight's talk. Soon Miss Emma and Miss Eleanor joined her. Everybody was looking around in disbelief. I felt like I was participating in a civil rights protest, not against evil white folks, but against evil Black folks. Just when I thought I couldn't be shocked anymore, everybody was standing and clapping. After the Prell sisters, other women teachers followed, and then all of the teachers, which gave the students courage to stand. By then, Mr. Knight had slipped out of the room. Miss Ella started singing "All of God's Children Got Shoes."

CHAPTER 5

What Color Is the World?

Blanche Virginia Franklin Moore (1917–2016)

I was born to be somebody!

—BLANCHE VIRGINIA FRANKLIN MOORE

Blanche Franklin Moore was thrown out of school for colored children when she was eight years old because she was too dark-skinned. It was 1925 in a West Virginia coal mine town. The teacher sent home several notes declaring the school was for *mulattos*, mixed-race children. Not for "regular Negroes." Moore remembered her grandfather took exception to this common tone-of-skin discrimination where Blacks who could pass for white received preferential treatment—and in Moore's case, an education. Her grandfather Henry Thaddeus Franklin asked his white mine supervisor to intercede. He did but to no avail. Little Blanche would not go back to school for another year.

But what the incident marked for the Franklin family was the beginning of decades of a long commitment to education for the Black working poor of the West Virginia coalfields. In tents and living rooms, log cabins and shacks, the family patriarch, Henry Thaddeus Franklin, found the space, the money, and the teachers to educate Black children. He would live long enough to see the highest court in the land order integration of public schools, but Franklin and those like him were the vanguards of the civil rights movement. In Franklin's case, working child by child.

Early photo of Virginia Blanche Franklin Moore.

Stories like the Franklin family are the heart and soul of the civil rights movement. Their narratives show the struggles that made possible Rosa Parks, Martin Luther King Jr., Fannie Lou Hamer, Fred Shuttlesworth, and many other names that have been buried in the whitewashing of American history. Henry Franklin was a minor protagonist in a major movement. He helped to navigate the present and the past of the civil rights movement.

Moore dreamed of being a teacher. Her grandchildren remember how she was always teaching them about nature, food, geography, and fashion. Moore didn't have the opportunity to get a proper education to teach, as was her dream. Even after *Brown v. Board of Education*, she and her family still weren't able to attend West Virginia State, which began as an HBCU (Historically Black Colleges and Universities). It was a state school established for Black students, like most states in the South especially.

"Black folks paid taxes for that College, believing that our children and surely our grandchildren would be able to go there. White folks took everything from us," Moore said. "Our way was paid in full by the blood, sweat, and tears by our ancestors, like Granddad." Moore is well-spoken and direct. She couldn't get an education; she educated herself through nature, cooking, and traveling.

In 1927, West Virginia State College, now West Virginia State University, was accredited by the North Central Association of Colleges and Schools, the first of seventeen original Black colleges to gain such status. What interested me most about the college was how it underwent a significant transformation following *Brown v. Board of Education* to desegregate public education. The college transformed from a Black college (HBCU) with a primarily residential population to a predominantly commuter school with mostly white students. The same thing happened at Bluefield State College in Bluefield, West Virginia. I think this is the most abusive interpretation of *Brown v. Board of Education* and Title VII of the Civil Rights Act. Moore agreed. "That's where I should've gone to school, along with other Black children whose folks worked in the mines. My children and grandchildren should've gone to school there. They stole it right from under us and had the nerve to be proud of the decision." Moore teared up. "It was a Black college, after all. Other states had colleges just for us. West Virginia State University, what a hot mess."

◆— —◆

I first met Moore on a snowy January morning in 2012 at a nursing home in Clarksburg, West Virginia, not far from where she grew up. I interviewed her three times, and we talked on the phone several times more. One of her relatives had contacted me when he learned I was working on a book about unsung civil rights heroes. He thought the Franklins would interest me. I found Moore, at age ninety-five, alert and eager to share her story.

"I was born to be somebody," she declared. I put flowers I bought for her in a vase. She sat back in her broken La-Z-Boy recliner. Her legs and feet were very swollen, so heavy they broke the footrest on the recliner; she was waiting for a new recliner. She suffered from diabetes and a heart condition. She reminded me of my own grandmother, with nutmeg brown, sparkling eyes and a clear voice. I knew we were going to get along. The first thing I noticed was her smartness. I wished I could teach her to use the computer, which would expand her world. She loved to learn.

It was the Galloway school that sent Moore home. She walked a mile and a half, over highways and hills, to the streetcar that took her to school. She remembered the *mulatto* teacher had blond hair and blue eyes. When her grandfather couldn't get the *mulattos* to take all the Black students, he went to the board of education. He was told, "they weren't gonna have two schools for nigger children," Moore remembered.

Her first school was Hepzibah, but it soon closed. Moore's mother was working in Galloway and thought it would be a good school for her daughter.

Although her grandfather worked long hours in the mines, he also was an inventor and ran a restaurant. He kept his eye on the prize: opening a school so Moore and other Black children could learn. He hoped to enrich their lives and send them beyond the isolated life of coal mining.

Her grandparents raised her. But her grandmother died when she was nine years old, which left her grandfather. They lived in small coal mining towns around Clarksburg. Henry Franklin worked with the Dawson Coal Company, which opened in 1917, the same year Moore was born. At the time, according to federal records, the mine employed one hundred men and operated two to three days a week, and sold coal to the NYC Railroad.

The white mine superintendent had gone to the school to find out why the third-grader was being kicked out of school since she was such a good student and not a troublemaker. During that time, there were two schools in Dawmont, a coal-mining village outside of Clarksburg, one for whites and one for Blacks. The schools were separated by one block. The superintendent was told that the child was too dark-skinned and wasn't wanted at the school.

That *mulatto* teacher, whom Moore remembers well, especially her blue eyes and blonde hair. Like the other mixed raced students, she didn't want anything to do with the "regular Negroes," as they were called. Early on, Moore was the only Black child in their compound comprised of shanties; the others were Italians. They only played outside during the summer because the winters were long and rough. But as the coal mining compound grew, other Black families came. Still no school for those who were dark-skinned.

Her grandfather rode a horse some ten miles to Philippi, the Barbour County seat, to meet with the mine supervisor. "Well, Henry, I know what you come for," Moore remembered her grandfather said of the meeting. "The teacher down in Galloway was here, just left. Tole her she had to teach all children. She said she wasn't gonna teach your granddaughter. Tole her I'd pay her out. She left and headed back to Ohio." Young Blanche didn't have a school to attend.

Henry Franklin.

"No school, no church, and hardly a place to live," she said sadly. But her grandfather was not giving up. "Granddad really wanted a school for me, and he kept after the superintendent."

Finally, in 1926 the superintendent told him, "Henry, I'll tell you what you can do. You get a building, I'll pay the rent and get a teacher, and I'll pay the wages."

Henry Franklin was widely regarded as a smart man with a good head for business and a generous heart. The Franklin family history starts with him. When he was twelve years old, he had to support his family by being a trapper in the mines, a person who opens and closes ventilation doors. It was not clear how he got to West Virginia from Christiansburg, Virginia, where he was born. His father had been killed trying to keep the peace between neighbors. Since Franklin was the oldest boy of seven children, he became the man of the house. After that, he found himself working the coalfields of West Virginia. He never went beyond sixth grade, but education became his passion. He understood its power, especially for poor Black children.

When his first mine job ended, he returned to Virginia and married Blanche Bain. They stayed in Christiansburg long enough for him to buy his mother a house. He, his wife Blanche, and her daughter Roberta moved to Cleveland, Ohio, seeking a better life, like so many African Americans during the Great Migration. But soon after that, he was back in West Virginia.

"He was hung up on the mines," Moore said of her grandfather. It was an opportunity many Blacks sought in the early twentieth century instead of farm work. He sent for his family. With his wife working as a maid in Clarksburg, they were able to buy a house. Blanche Franklin was a great cook and branched out into catering and, finally, her own restaurant. The bill of sale for the restaurant is dated in 1918; it was located across the street from the Waldo Hotel. Franklin paid $100 down for the $700 price of the restaurant.

Life was good until Franklin was fired from the mine for union activism. He was the president of his union and demanded union wages and equal pay for his Black members. They were all fired. But his family had to have food and shelter, so Franklin opened a small store in one room of his house. About that time, he received a patent for a "new and useful Invention in Coal Mining Machines." He designed and built a model of a coal-loading machine. He received a patent, and everybody knew about the machine. It was used in the mines all around West Virginia, even called "the Franklin machine." He hired Clarksburg attorneys Matt Hood and G. H. Duthie, but they stole the patent design, Franklin told his family. They never received any financial benefits.

"He took the loss hard. Never got over it," Moore said of the story passed down the generations. She teared up again. "I always felt I witnessed the incident, but I was a small child when it happened. They took it and never even looked back."

The family was forced to move to another nearby mining town, Galloway. This was near Moore's mother, who was unmarried when Moore was born. She allowed her parents to raise Little Blanche. But Moore saw her mother, who had married. Moore wasn't close to her; she considered her grandparents her parents.

Franklin was desperate to work and reluctantly took a job crossing a union picket line. He was a "scab," hauling coal from the mine by horse and wagon for the mine owners who wanted to break the union. Each afternoon the strikers would shoot at them with high-powered rifles. Not to kill but to shut down mine production. Still, Moore remembers bullets flying. "My grandmother, mother, and I would lie down on the floor every afternoon at two until the shooting stopped."

Other mining jobs followed until Franklin could move his family into a log cabin in Barbour County that also served as a boardinghouse for Black families new to the area.

Moore's mother found a school for her in Galloway, where she continued to the third grade. Moore said she had to go live with her mother and stepdad who ran a boardinghouse too.

"Well, finally, they gave in, and everybody started to work, doing scab work; and they stopped being so hostile with the shooting. But they kept the state police to guard Galloway since that was the most dangerous place."

UNITED STATES PATENT OFFICE.

HENRY THADEOUS FRANKLIN, OF DAWMONT, WEST VIRGINIA, ASSIGNOR OF ONE-HALF TO MATT EDWARD HOOD, OF DAWMONT, WEST VIRGINIA.

COAL-LOADING MACHINE.

1,304,869.

Specification of Letters Patent.

Patented May 27, 1919.

Application filed November 26, 1918. Serial No. 264,194.

To all whom it may concern:

Be it known that I, HENRY THADEOUS FRANKLIN, a citizen of the United States, resident of Dawmont, in the county of Harrison and State of West Virginia, have made a certain new and useful Invention in Coal-Loading Machines; and I declare the following to be a full, clear, and exact description of the same, such as will enable others skilled in the art to which it appertains to make and use the invention, reference being had to the accompanying drawings, and to letters or figures of reference marked thereon, which form a part of this specification.

Figure 1 is a side view of the invention with shovel retracted and lowered.

Fig. 2 is a similar view with shovel raised.

Fig. 3 is a similar view partly in section and broken away, showing the shovel thrust forward.

The invention has relation to coal loading machines, designed to load the mined coal upon the car in the mine, its object to relieve the miner of much laborious work in lifting the coal and throwing it upon the mine car, and to accomplish the loading of the coal more rapidly.

The invention consists in the novel construction and combinations of parts, as hereinafter set forth.

In the accompanying drawings illustrating the invention, the numeral 2 designates a post or standard, having at its upper and lower ends rotatable supporting engagement with the floor and roof of the mine, and fulcrumed to said post at 3 is an arm or beam 4, adapted for movement in a vertical plane, or upwardly and downwardly, through operation of a hand lever 5, the latter having a flexible rope or cable connection 6 with the free end of said arm, an intermediate lever 7 being fulcrumed to said post at 8, and being operated by said hand lever to assist in raising said arm. At the end portion of the upward movement of said arm, the hand lever acts through the medium of said intermediate lever alone, the cable being slack.

A shovel 9 is carried by the outer end portion of the arm 4 through the medium of links 10 and 11, respectively pivoted to the arm, said links being respectively pivotally connected to the shovel at the outer or

The shovel is designed to be worked forwardly and backwardly as a workman would operate it in throwing coal upon the car, and to this end a hand lever 12 pivoted to the post at 3, has a rod connection 14 with the upper end of the rear link 10, and upon operation thereof in one direction or forwardly will withdraw or retract the shovel and at the same time put a coiled spring 13 under tension, said spring connecting the rear end portion of the handle of the shovel with the forward end of the arm 4, and the tension of the spring being held or maintained by a pawl 15 carried by the hand lever 12 and engaging the teeth of a rack 16 upon said arm.

It being then desired to throw or thrust the shovel forwardly into the coal pile by a sudden movement, the pawl 15 is knocked down out of engagement with the rack 16 by a blow upon the handle end thereof, the spring 13 at once acting to accomplish the desired quick throw of the shovel.

The shovel being now located in the coal pile is lifted thereout by an upward movement of the arm 4 through operation of the hand lever 5, the shovel carrying therewith its load of coal, and the lifting movement of arm and shovel being stopped when the shovel has arrived at a proper degree of elevation to retain its load, the shovel being then substantially horizontal or slightly tilted rearwardly.

The shovel being in the raised position stated, elevated above the coal pile, is given a bodily movement of rotation through rotary movement of the post 2, in order that the shovel may be placed in position adapted for discharge upon the mine car, this discharge being accomplished by a second working of the hand lever and operation of the spring 13 as first described for these parts.

In the quick movement or thrust of the shovel last stated it is necessary to stop the shovel suddenly, in order that its load of coal may leave it properly or be properly discharged upon the mine car, and to this end the handle of the shovel where it is pivoted to the link 11 engages a slot 18 of said link, and contacts with the upper beveled wall 19 of said slot, the rear link 10 at the same time being brought into alined

While all of that was happening, Franklin was becoming quite successful in the mines, making good money. His wife was also doing well working for a white family in Philippi. That family bought a house for the Franklins with the understanding that Franklin would repay them. Moore had been out of school for about a year when her grandfather decided it was time to reestablish a school for the growing population of Black children.

He headed back to the school superintendent and was told that if he could find ten Black children to attend, a school would be opened. And the degree of darkness of the skin of the children wouldn't matter. The school board would pay the teacher and the rent and provide furniture, but Franklin would have to find the building. He was determined to have the school, but all the buildings were occupied in Barbour County.

"We'll give them our bedroom, and we'll move upstairs," Moore recalled her grandfather saying. Then he found a credentialed teacher, Dorothea Brown. For two years, she slept in the front bedroom with Moore and her grandmother. After two years, there were enough Blacks in and around Galloway to open a proper school. Classes met in the very same building from which Moore had been expelled. Conditions at the school soon grew crowded, so Franklin expanded. He built a new school himself, on his own property, next door to his house.

When the mine superintendent at Franklin's latest employ discovered he was building a school, he was demoted to a common laborer. He was given the worst place to work in the mines, described as "a day vein in a water hole," meaning he couldn't earn any money there. After he quit his job, the mine superintendent gave him a bill for the grazing that his mule had done on company property. He gave the mule to the company for payment and opened a restaurant in his home, the first Black-owned eatery in Barbour County.

But the Depression closed the restaurant and school. Five generations of Franklins were under one roof. The coal industry, a major source of employment for many African Americans, suffered a severe decline following World War I. And it received another with the Great Depression in the 1930s. Many Blacks lost their jobs and left the state. The Franklins remained, and Moore was back at the Galloway school.

"Rough times, really rough times." She leaned back in her broken recliner. "We ate soup and drank milk at school. We had so little food at home. Then, after the eighth grade, we didn't have a school. The school had closed. Blacks had to go to Fairmont or Institute (West Virginia State) or the Kelly Miller

The Franklins
A Barbour County Family Story
By Barbara Smith
Photographs by Ron Rittenhouse

The Franklins.

School in Clarksburg. But we didn't have transportation and would have to pay for room and board. I was just out of luck."

She said her grandfather was heartbroken. There were lots of white high schools. Franklin and others still pushed for a Black high school. Finally, the Barbour County Board of Education gave them a one-room experimental high school with transportation. It was about a twenty-mile school bus ride each way to Moore. Both Blacks and *mulattos* attended. "But the *mulattos* wouldn't sit next to us on the bus," Moore said as a matter of fact. "We didn't complain. Wouldn't have had a school if it hadn't been for them."

But once again, school doors shut for Moore and the other students. They were given the old options of faraway schools with no way to get to them. "We had to go to Fairmont or Institute to finish." She wiped her tears. "I never did, and I'll always regret it. But it was just too hard. My dream of being a teacher crushed me to the bone."

Henry Franklin died in 1956, two years after *Brown v. Board of Education.*
He lived long enough to see the public school integrated in the academic
year of 1955–56.

"I was chosen to represent the Mt. Vernon School District and was elected
vice president of the PTA that same year," Moore said with pride. "Granddad
would be so proud today. My granddaughter is a junior at Philip Barbour
High School. She'll graduate next year. My son, Frank, wanted to go to college
too. Now, wouldn't that be something?" She slapped her lap with both hands.

"There is a tradition of educational pioneering in the family. My granddaughter has her bedroom in the very room that housed the first school for
Blacks in Barbour County. Lord, have mercy."

Moore had made a good life for herself, despite some rough patches.
Like when she ran off with her first husband ignoring her family's pleas
not to do it.

"He was abusive and disrespectful," she said. "I came back home in about
three months. I was lucky to have a home and family to come back to." She
said feeling inferior because of her brown skin played a role in some of her
bad decisions.

For the first time in our interviews, Moore cried, recalling how horrible
she felt when she was sent home from school because of her brown skin.
She had never thought of her skin as a problem since it was a gift from God.

"Colorism," a term credited to Alice Walker in the 1970s, became a problem
for her beginning in third grade. "I am so sorry." Moore said she just thought
everybody was the way God made them. She couldn't imagine God being
color-struck. She felt ashamed and unloved.

She turned to me. "Did folks ever treat you different because of your skin
color?" She asked.

"Not at eight years old and never so outright hostile," I said, a bit surprised
by the question. I explained it was clear to me that light skin was considered
pretty and dark, ugly among our people. But I had received such positive
experiences from my teachers, who were different shades of brown. As long
as I had a book to read, I was okay and didn't pay a lot of attention to what
was going on around me. "And, of course, by the time I got to college, the civil
rights movement was in full swing, and for a short time, Black was beautiful."

"Well, that sentiment or the civil rights movement never made it to the
mountains of West Virginia. I guess when the first man told me I was pretty for
a dark-skinned girl, I thought that was love, and I ran away with him," she said.

"And from my own people, not from the whites. I found more hate and evil in my own people." She looked down at her swollen leg and closed her eyes.

But the civil rights movement did make it to the mountains of West Virginia, just not as obvious and quick as it did to other places. West Virginia could hide behind the mountains. Moore's grandfather Henry Franklin was a leader and a pioneer. Now her son, Frank, and her granddaughters and their children carry a torch handed down from the mighty legacy of her grandfather. The CRM is also about people we don't read about in history books, although many were history makers.

Moore said she better understood herself when she traveled outside of West Virginia with the Jewish family, the Cutlers, she worked for. They lived in Bethesda, Maryland, and traveled all over the Northeast. New York City scared her. She loved being at the beach house in Delaware.

"That was my favorite," she smiled. "I could swim and just enjoy nature like I did when I was a child. Even taught the Cutler children how to ride horses and a lot about nature and memories from my mountain childhood." She learned to observe people, just like she used to do with the trees and streams of water.

"I saw that folks of all races could be friendly and open-minded," she said. "I will always be thankful for the experience even though I didn't become a teacher." She looked to the heavens. "The Cutler children had even visited me in this nursing home; they never treated her like 'the help.'"

Moore had two children; one preceded her in death. Moore's only living son, Frank is named for great grandfather Henry Franklin and Moore's beloved grandfather. Moore adopted Cassidy when she was five years old. Her mother died of ovarian cancer. Cassidy described her grandmother as very sharp, like the stories she heard about her great-great-grandfather Henry Franklin. Cassidy has one son, Devone Moore is twenty-three years old.

"She wore long skirts with beautiful blouses and always wore a big sunhat," Cassidy said about her grandmother Blanche Moore. One of her favorite memories is jumping in the car with her grandmother and driving to Cool Springs on Route 50. "She was always teaching me something about maps and places she had traveled with the Cutler family. My grandmother was a great teacher, just like her grandfather."

She was always prepared with a picnic basket of delicious food since she was a great cook. And her bag of medicine was always nearby. "Two things my grandmother never got over the trauma of what happened to her when she was kicked out of school and her grandfather's patent being stolen from him," Cassidy said.

"Grandmother could've been like Katherine Johnson in *Hidden Figures* if she had had the opportunity to attend college at West Virginia State." She and Johnson were nearly the same age. "She didn't live long enough to see the movie. That makes me so sad," her granddaughter said.

Cassidy's sister, Amber Lamar West, said a favorite memory is that her grandmother used to come and pick her up to go sightseeing at Black Waterfalls and Seneca Rocks. They would have the best time while Moore would point out different sights to her and her sister Cassidy. And afterward, she would take them to the grocery store and allow them to get all the snacks and drinks they wanted.

"One of the most important lessons I learned from grandmother was, 'not to worry or stress about things you cannot control. Leave it in God's hands.'" Amber especially remembers the joy and happiness her grandmother expressed when her sons Jarrod and Jaidyn were born. They came with her to visit Moore at the nursing home too.

"My grandmother wore beautiful clothes and loved going through them and spreading them out on the bed. Sometimes she'd hang her clothes all around her room. I wanted to grow up to be just like her. Our time spent together while she was in the nursing home was about reminiscing about the past, especially her grandfather. She loved talking about him. Even though we never met him, but we always felt like we knew him and he was watching over us. I have tried to pass the same stories down to my children and hope they will do the same," Amber said.

The last time I visited Moore, she wanted to know more about my students at West Virginia University.

"In my creative nonfiction writing class, a white female wrote a piece about her grandfather."

"I would have loved that assignment. What was the student's grandfather like?" When Moore talked about her granddad, her face always lit up. She was so proud of him and his accomplishments, even though he faced unimaginable discrimination working in the coal mines.

"Maybe. The student said her grandfather had a Black man working for him, and they became friends. She said one day, her grandfather cooked up a plan to turn the Black man white. They were going to boil some oil, and when the Black man dipped in it, his black skin would turn white."

"What?" Moore roared back in her recliner.

"I know. Anyway, I told her that her story was very dramatic and needed to another voice." She started to cry and said she knew what she knew. "That's when I learned that her grandfather was still alive. I then suggested that she interview her grandfather to give her work more creditability."

"What happened then? Did they ever put him in oil?"

"No, they couldn't find enough oil. So her grandfather thought water might work. But when the Black man step in the scalding water, he received serious burns and ran away."

"Lord, have mercy."

"When I suggested that no one would believe that story, she reported me to the chairperson of my department; she told him I called her a lie in front of the class. He put a letter in my file, saying I shouldn't harass students about their work."

"I didn't expect that."

"Nor did I."

Coal Companies

The Century Coal Company built two mines and coal camps in southern Barbour County and named them Century 1 (a shaft mine) and Century 2 (a slope mine). An article in a 1918 issue of *The Black Diamond* stated that coal was first shipped from Century Mines in 1897, but state mining records don't show Century Coal Company mines before 1916. The article also was about how Redstone Seam Coal was mined in Century; Pittsburgh coal was also on the lease, with a daily capacity of three thousand tons of coal. Finally, there were six electric locomotives and electric underground mining equipment and more than thirty horses and mules used in the mines. Coal was shipped to market on a spur built by the B&O Railroad. From the 1950s–1970s, the Century Mines were owned and operated by Bethlehem Mines Corporation, a coal mining subsidiary of Bethlehem Steel. In the early 2000s, the mine complex at Century 1 was idle, but coal mining activity at Century 2 was observed at the time.

In February 2018, a Randolph County man was killed in the Sentinel Mine in Barbour County. Mr. Leonard Griffith, of Valley, was killed. He was an electrician at the mine and was struck by a coal rib roll while working on a continuous mining machine. This was the first fatality of the year. The mines have since been temporarily idled while an investigation into the fatality continues. The mines are still unsafe. In 2017, there were eight mining fatalities.

◆ ◆

The construction of the Chesapeake and Ohio Railroad in the late 1860s and early 1870s brought many African American laborers into southern West Virginia. An estimated one thousand African Americans helped dig the C&O tunnel at Talcott, now Summers County. One of these laborers was supposedly John Henry, remembered in the folk tradition. New steam-powered machines were considered by many to be more efficient than human labor. Legend has it John Henry defeated one of these machines in a digging competition at the Big Bend Tunnel at Talcott. The folklore often forgets to tell that he died afterward.

The C&O railroad accelerated the development of southern West Virginia's coal industry in the 1870s, creating more jobs and attracting more Blacks to the state. The Norfolk and Western Railroad did the same for the southwestern part of the state.

According to courthouse records, McDowell County experienced an influx of migrant laborers, increasing its Black population from 0.1 percent in 1880 to 30.7 percent in 1910. During the same time, the Black population of the entire state increased from 17,000 in 1870 to 64,100 in 1910 and reached a high of nearly 115,000 in 1930. Today the African American population in the state is about 2–3 percent, less than 60,000 citizens.

By 1900, voters had elected a state government controlled by Progressive Republicans, who wanted to reform the way the government took care of the people. They established a number of public institutions to serve the growing Black population.

During the first three decades of the twentieth century, the legislature created an orphanage, a home for the aged and infirmed, a tuberculosis sanitarium, industrial homes for boys and girls, a deaf and blind school, and an insane asylum, all for African Americans. Before 1900 African Americans had been forced to travel to other states to receive these services despite the fact that the same services were available in West Virginia for whites.

A few months after my last visit with Moore in 2016, I called her to say hello and tell her I had been awarded a fellowship at Ernest Gaines Research

Center at the University of Louisiana at Lafayette for the summer. She was very proud of me. "When I get back, I'll come for a long visit," and tell you about my experience. "You'll probably have a new chair by then."

"That will be lovely," she said cheerfully.

While I was in Louisiana, I received a phone call telling me she had joined the ancestors. She had promised me she was going to make it to one hundred. But she was able to tell her story. I will always carry her in my heart and the amazing story of her grandfather, Henry Franklin, son, pioneer, activist, inventor, educator, coalminer, leader, builder, husband, parent, neighbor, Christian, and friend to all.

METEOR

We agreed that there would be no "colored people's time." We needed to get to the mall when the doors opened. We had serious shopping to do, find our prom dresses. Little Mama woke me when she left for work at the white woman's house. I was out the door at 7:00 a.m. Eve Sharpe steered her father's new black Chevy across rural Alabama. "Black is the color of the dead," she joked. Her family's funeral home's name was on the side of the car.

We felt so grown up, even though we were only sophomores but had been invited to the prom by juniors or seniors. Our hopes were as wide as the pastures we passed. Our smiles were into the future, after high school graduation and then on to college. And somewhere along the line, we'd get married and have brilliant, beautiful Black children and strong Black families.

At the mall, we hit Baskin Robbins 31 Flavors first. I couldn't imagine so many flavors. I only knew chocolate, strawberry, and vanilla.

Ruth ordered vanilla. "Make sure I know what I'm gettin'."

"Me too. Chocolate, please," Eve said.

"Cherry." All of the flavors were pretty as rainbows. We sashayed around, giggling and window shopping.

Eve found her dress first at a store called 5.7.9. She was petite and hadn't locked herself into a color scheme. Her dress was lilac, size seven, and a perfect match for her sweet tea-colored skin. We cheered and told her she looked good enough to be on TV.

Next, we went to Steinberg's. Some of the church ladies shopped there because the Jewish owners treated them with respect. The fashions weren't flashy but were good quality. "Only de family work der. Dey ain't got no big business backin' dem," Miss Carrie Mae said like she was their best friend.

I never understood what they meant about them being Jews. Mr. Reed, our high school history teacher, would know. He knew everything. But he was fired because some people called him a "hippie," and he marched with Dr. King. He talked to us about how we could change the world if we were prepared, which started in our segregated classroom in Alabama's Black Belt. What was wrong with that? I wanted to ask out loud to the world.

I had saved twenty-five dollars from working at the white woman's house after school and with Little Mama on Saturdays. The only thing I liked about the work was I got to read *Newsweek Magazine* when the white woman threw her copies in the trash. I took them home after getting permission to do so. I had read a lot about the "race problem," Martin Luther King, and civil rights.

When I left for the mall, Big Mama slipped me a few dollars too. "Don't be actin' no fool now, and be careful 'round de white folks."

Finally, I found a rose-colored A-line taffeta dress with spaghetti straps and a below the-knee-hemline, and it was a perfect fit. Steinberg's was one of the few stores that allowed Black people to try on clothes. I looked glamorous. The church ladies would object to the straps and the hemline; a big grin spread across my face. I bought a pair of white satin shoes and a clutch purse.

The friendly clerk suggested I dye the shoes to match my dress. I opted not to. Two years ago, Miss Pearl, our bus driver, dyed her shoes green for her daughter's wedding. It rained, and the dye stayed on her feet for three weeks. Rain was not a friend to *us*: it could turn our pressed and curled hair into a nightmare if we weren't careful. I stocked up on coffee brown nylons. The only color available to us back home was Red Fox, which didn't match anybody's skin. It just made our legs look like they were burning. But the worst was not being allowed to try on clothes.

Ordering from catalogs was one way of not having contact with mean white folks. Big Mama and Little Mama didn't allow us to go into stores that didn't let us try on clothes. I didn't understand why whites hated us so much. We were hard-working Christians. Sometimes I felt ashamed that more folks in Barbour County didn't stand up about how we were treated. In *Newsweek*, I read about sit-ins and boycotts, and marches. Mr. Reed was the only white person I knew, and he didn't hate nobody. But a haircut and some dandruff shampoo might have helped him keep his job; he didn't notice such things. I wondered what white folks thought about since they had so much free time not having to think about being Black.

In Steinberg's, rich-colored scarves of gold, red, and green and pastel gloves beckoned from glass cases lined up like little soldiers. The soft sage-colored carpet felt like I was walking on cotton. The perky clerk offered us hints about mixing and matching our clothes. She even showed us how to wear a scarf in three different ways. "Fashion is all about illusion." She repeated and threw the pink and blue scarf around her shoulders. I didn't know what she was talking about. I just smiled.

Eve and Ruth giggled, pointing to the glass case that seal'd ladies' lingerie. "I hear a lot of girls lose their virginity on prom night," Ruth blurted out.

"I did." The clerk surprised us.

I had never heard anybody admit they'd had sex. The only thing I knew about sex was don't until you're married, then you had to; it was the husband's right. Something was wrong with that theory; too many unmarried girls turned up pregnant. At times like these, I wish my dead sister Daisy was alive. She would know the answers. Little Mama didn't bother about giving us any information. I used the book the Prell Sisters gave us, *Growing Up and Liking It*, to teach my sisters about the beginning of womanhood.

"Really?" I wanted to ask the clerk questions, like how do you learn to do it? And how do you know if you are doing it right?

"What was it like?" Eve asked.

She popped from behind the counter and peeped around the dressing room to make sure nobody was there. Her cream-colored sweater set matched a green plaid pleated skirt. She was older than us, maybe in her early twenties, with a round pale face. Her hair was big and curly like Eve's.

"Well, it hurts a lot, your cherry has a layer of skin, and it's broken. It can even be a little, well, wet." She talked like a teacher as she made a face like she had tasted a green plum. She used her large dark eyes and long fingers to help her explain.

"Gross." Ruth made a face like she ate the same green plum.

"You'll get used to how messy it is. Make sure you have a nice soft towel." She placed her hands over her heart.

"What does it smell like?" Eve asked.

"Natural. Like your bodies." She smiled.

"Does it hurt?" Ruth asked.

"A little. You'll bleed some, so don't be scared."

"Does it ever stop hurting?" I can't stand pain.

"I've been doing it for about a year, and it still hurts some," the clerk said with authority.

"Really?" I felt stupid not asking a real question. I was supposed to be the smart one. But words were stuck in my throat.

"But not nearly as much as it did in the beginning."

"Were you embarrassed the next time you saw him?" Eve asked.

"A little, but that's why you need to be in love with the person. Just having sex would be just pain." The clerk put her hand over her heart again.

"Somebody is coming," Ruth yelled.

"Remember, if you give him too much, it won't be special. Make him beg a little and give you chocolate often," was the last advice the nice clerk had time to offer.

Ruth was the only one who hadn't found a dress. I thought she was being too picky. When she finally called home, her mother gave her permission to treat us to dinner and charge it on her BankAmerica card. We proceeded to the Great Wall. They even knew Ruth's name. It was times like these that I didn't like her much. She always took over for everybody. But what I didn't understand was how she was so dumb. Her mother taught school with the Prell Sisters, and her father was the best carpenter in Barbour County. I always thought that smart people had smart children.

I learned a lot about etiquette from working at the white woman's house. And I knew how to order from a menu, even if I hadn't done it since I went to Shoney with Miss Pearl. I had read about it in books and seen it on television. How could that be?

While we waited for our orders of chicken with garlic sauce, spicy shrimp, and pepper steak, I blurted out. "Do you think we'll lose our virginity?"

"The only time I'm going to lose my virginity is on my wedding night. Charlie Frank knows I don't play." Eve shook her head.

"Me too. I might let John Earl get to first base, but kissing will be the only exchange of body fluids."

"What if things get hot and heavy?" I asked.

"Only guys get hot and heavy."

The waiter returned. "Thank you." We said at the same time but didn't speak again until he left.

"I don't believe that. What do you think the girls are doing?" I whispered.

"Only whores are supposed to like it," Ruth whispered back.

"It all seems pretty gross to me," Eve said.

"We oughta send off for some of those books," I suggested.

"What books?"

"The ones you get in the mail wrapped in brown paper." I knew this from reading the white woman's romance magazines.

"We don't have time. The prom is less than two weeks away."

"We can still order them. Sex will come up again." I was proud of my *True Romance* magazine knowledge. One time when I was sick, Big Mama let me watch the soap opera *The Guiding Light*; it was all about love and trouble.

The waiter brought fortune cookies. I opened mine first since I wasn't in the mood to hear a story from Ruth. "You're going to lose your virginity soon," I read out loud.

"Really?"

"You oughta stop it."

"Well, we could, you know."

"Just can't let it go, can you?"

"Why can't we have some fun?"

"What are you talkin' about now?"

"We could guess who . . ." I started, but Eve Sharpe cut me off. "That sounds too much like gamblin', and when you get right down to it, it's none of our business."

"You sound like the church ladies. This is our one and only prom night."

"Just remember, I took care of my sister last summer. I know where this can lead."

"Where?" I wanted to know. This was the second time Eve talked about taking care of her sister. I thought her sister had a baby, but Eve never mentioned a baby.

"We ain't ready to go there," Eve answered.

"I hear once you start doing it, you can't stop," Ruth said.

"Sure, I want to have a good time on prom night, but I don't think it's necessary to go against the Lord. And I'm sick of you talkin' about that silly white girl."

"She wasn't silly. No one has ever told us anything about what to expect the first time. We get the same the advice, 'keep your skirt down.'"

"Let's get going." Ruth picked up the check and headed out. We followed like a small procession. She said she told her mother what time they were leaving. "Don't worry," Eve said with confidence. "We don't have to be afraid.

White folks are scared of anythin' to do with the dead. We never get stopped. And if we do, they let us go real fast."

"It's good to know they're scared of something."

We laughed. Eve gunned the car toward the main highway.

Eve found the soul radio station and the sun set in coral streaks across the starless sky.

"I really like your dress," Eve said to me.

"Thank you. I like yours too."

The Supremes' "Someday We'll be Together" played on the radio, and we joined in. When the song ended, Eve was about to change stations when the programming was interrupted for a special report. *Reverend Martin Luther King Jr. has been killed in Memphis, Tennessee. Shots were fired at the Loraine Hotel, killing King. No one has been arrested for the killing of King. We repeat. Martin Luther King Jr. is dead.*

I covered my face with both hands. The sky seemed to shower us with a meteor. Fear took the steering wheel and guided us into an unknown place in history.

CHAPTER 6

Designing Dreams

Ann Cole Lowe (1898-1981)

I am an awful design snob. I love my clothes; and I am
particular about who wears them. I am not interested in
sewing for café society or social climbers . . . I sew for families
of the Social Register.
—ANN COLE LOWE

The wedding of Jacqueline Bouvier and Senator John F. Kennedy was the
social event of the season and a big break for fashion designer Ann Cole
Lowe, who already had a relationship with Bouvier's mother long before she
knew her daughters. Eleven years earlier, she had designed Janet Lee Bouvier's
wedding dress for her second husband, Hugh Dudley Auchincloss Jr.

In addition, she had also created and made the Bouvier's girls "coming out
dresses," according to Lowe's biographer Julia Faye Smith. It's not clear how
Janet Lee Bouvier and Lowe met and developed a relationship.

The year before, Lowe had been commissioned to design an earlier wedding gown for Jacqueline Bouvier when she was to marry stockbroker John
G. H. Husted Jr. But after meeting the young Senator Kennedy, she called
off the wedding. Bouvier had met with Lowe to discuss her ideas for a wedding dress for Husted. Lowe remembered her as being quiet. She promised
to deliver some sketches of the gown at a later date. Before the appointment
date, Bouvier had broken her engagement to Husted.

For her wedding to Senator Kenney, Bouvier declared she wanted a "tremendous dress . . . a typical Ann Cole Lowe dress." She wanted her bridesmaids to wear red, but Lowe talked her down to pink.

Lowe had so many challenges in her life, but she always battled them with grace and dignity. Ten days before the big event in 1953, a pipe burst in Lowe's Harlem studio, ruining the dresses, including Bouvier's wedding gown. The gowns had taken Lowe and her staff two months to make at a cost of $2,000.

Sizing up the disaster must have taken Lowe back to another critical moment in her life when she was sixteen and saved the family's reputation. Her mother and grandmother, accomplished seamstresses, owned a successful business in Montgomery. They were working on gowns for the first lady of Alabama, Lizzie Kirkland O'Neal, and her two daughters when Lowe's mother died suddenly. A grieving Lowe pulled herself together and finished the gowns with great approval. She must have called upon the same grit and determination some thirty years later because she recreated the gowns, bought more fabric, and hired additional seamstresses; they worked night and day.

The bride was stunning in Lowe's portrait-neckline dress and bouffant skirt that was crafted from fifty yards of ivory silk fabric. It became the most photographed wedding gown in American history. Ann Cole Lowe was fifty-five years old.

Lowe's grandmother and great-grandmother were enslaved seamstresses; she struggled to get recognition as a Negro fashion designer to honor them. In her early days, high-society women sought out her distinctive designs, but she was rarely given credit for her work. Later, as in the case of the Bouvier dress, she was dismissed as a "colored woman dressmaker, not a Negro haute couture."

But Lowe was a visionary, driven by her exceptional eye. She designed thousands of hand-sewn masterpieces for the rich and famous. Olivia de Havilland donned a pale-blue, floral hand-painted Lowe to accept an Academy Award in 1947 for *To Each His Own*. The actor had found the dress at a New York salon, but it was the salon owner who got the credit, not Lowe.

Family Thread

Cole was born in Clayton, Alabama, a small rural town in the Black Belt of Alabama, between Montgomery and Dothan, where about five hundred citizens lived when she was born. Today the population is closer to thee thousand citizens.

Jacqueline Bouvier Kennedy's
wedding dress.

I went to high school there, and one of my best friends, Olivia Cole Welch's father, was Lowe's first cousin. Welch reminded me that we knew Lowe's work when we were teenagers because she made dresses for a few family members. I remembered those beautiful dresses. "Annie could make a paper sack look good," the Cole women boasted. I always wanted to meet this mysterious woman who believed in dressing everybody in beautiful clothes and dreamed of being a top Negro International designer. "I feel so happy when I am making clothes that I could jump up and down with joy," family members said she was known to say.

Lowe's story began on a Tompkins' plantation in North Georgia. The mistress of the plantation owned a talented enslaved seamstress. She was skilled with her needle and had an eye for design. Her services were in demand; she sewed everything from family ball gowns to work garments for the enslaved. In 1844 an unnamed enslaved seamstress gave birth to a baby girl. The father of the baby was the owner of the plantation. That baby girl was listed as Georgia Tompkins and identified as "mulatto." The girl learned to sew with such skill that she joined her mother in the "big house," doing housekeeping and sewing for the family with expertise in embroidery. Georgia passed her skill down to her daughter Jane and eventually to her granddaughter Ann Cole Lowe, according to family members.

Lowe's grandfather, General Cole, was also instrumental in her success. In 1853 the twenty-three-year-old settled in Clayton and was known as a master carpenter and a free man of color. In Clayton, he joined the construction crew building the new Barbour County Courthouse, which had been a log cabin. He mail-ordered a wife from Louisiana and bought her freedom. They had seven children, one of which was Jane.

After the courthouse was finished, General Cole stayed; he liked living in Clayton. He worked as a carpenter on other projects, which included building a house for his family members in the Clayton area. In fact, all of the Coles built houses on Parish Avenue, a block or two from the courthouse that had brought them to Clayton.

When I was growing up, it was a beautiful block of painted houses with shutters and street addresses. Everyone I knew had a rural box number. Those cookouts were a place you probably kissed a boy for the first time and learned to "Jerk" or other new dance steps. Dancing to the music of the Supremes, the Temptations, Smokey Robinson, Clarence Carter, and the Commodores made us feel so special that a Black family had enough stature to close off the whole street.

For instance, General Cole was never in the military; it was a common practice for African Americans to honor noted Black people with titles. Whites in the Jim Crown South often referred to Black citizens in derogatory ways, nigger, mammy, boy, uncle, and the like. Of course, many still do today. Black folks showed each other respect by giving the notables deserving titles. This was Lowe's heritage.

Lowe's mother, Jane, married Jack Lowe in the early 1890s. None of the family I spoke with had any memories or knowledge of Jack Lowe. Their first child was a daughter named Sallie, and their second child, Ann, was born in 1898. Shortly after her birth, her parents moved to Montgomery by wagon. It probably took several days to make the seventy-five-mile trip. Montgomery, the state capital, was growing; in 1866, it became the first city in the country to install citywide electric streetcars. The modern transportation allowed Jane Lowe, a burgeoning designer, to reach her high-society clients.

Front of house General Cole and his brothers built in Clayton, Alabama.

Back of house General Cole and his brothers built in Clayton, Alabama.

After General Cole died, Lowe's grandmother joined them in Montgomery. Georgia and Jane were known for their designs and stitching, mostly evening-wear like debutante gowns for the city's society women, which, of course, included the governor's wife and daughters.

Young Lowe observed everything around her, especially the variety and beauty of flowers. Living in Montgomery allowed her to see manicured lawns filled full of camellias, roses, lilies, and magnolias, along with azaleas and dogwoods, and she was amazed that in Montgomery, there were such a huge variety of colors. She was also paying close attention to the artistry of her mother and grandmother. Soon she was combining the two in her own artistic manner while she played for hours with the scraps of fabric she found on the floor of the sewing room.

When Jane and Georgia sewed, Lowe designed and made dresses for her paper dolls and taught herself to make fabric flowers. Those early flowers led to a signature of her clothing design, exquisite handmade flowers. Lowe watched and learned as she grew up surrounded by creative women and beautiful fabrics.

After her mother's death, Lowe had to drop out of high school after just one year. With her grandmother and other family members, she continued the family business of dressing the society women of Montgomery. For many, that would've been the dream, but Lowe preferred to choose her own clients from the white upper class of society.

The only African American bride she designed for was Elizabeth Mance De Jonge; her father was Dr. Robert Mance Jr. There were twenty-one in the wedding party. Lowe made all the dresses and even attended the wedding. Family members said she was very proud. "This is the first wedding party I have made for my own race."

Through her clients, she not only had access to places that would've otherwise been out of her reach. She was able to control some of the circumstances of her life. She felt welcomed in her clients' homes as a valued employee, even if there were times when she was still told by servants to use the back door, which she did not. Lowe was her best advertisement, dressed in her own natty creations.

Society Ladies of Tampa

Lowe met a woman who would help her on the next leg of her journey of designing dreams. According to her biographer, one day in a major Montgomery department store, Lowe felt she was being watched. "This is not unusual, for we Negroes are always watched when in public, but I often visit smaller stores where I know the owners and have never felt threatened there." She looked around and eventually spotted a well-dressed white woman across the store. She went back to her browsing. Soon she felt the eyes on her again. She turned as far away from her as possible and put on a sweet smile.

Ann Cole Lowe gown.

Abruptly she turned to catch the woman off guard; instead, she caught Lowe off guard. Only four feet from her, she smiled.

The woman apologized and introduced herself. "I'm sorry, but I am Mrs. Lee from Tampa. Could you please tell me where you purchased your dress and hat?"

Lowe wore her own signature style. After her hair started to thin, she always wore a stylish navy or black hat with large-framed glasses.

"After I regained my senses, I told her that I not only made but also designed my own clothing." The woman was impressed.

Mrs. Josephine Lee and her daughters were members of Tampa's elite social set with a wedding in the near future. She asked Lowe to come to Tampa and design and make dresses for her daughter's wedding party.

Tampa's business elite also put on the Tampa Gasparilla Festival every year modeled after New Orleans' Mardi Gras. Lowe designed Gasparilla costumes for many of the wealthy women. "This was a chance to make all the lovely gowns I'd always dreamed about," she said.

The Lee family loved Lowe and her designs. After the wedding, she stayed on with the family, making Ann Cole Lowe dresses for the daughters. Friends were begging for dresses, and Lowe's business grew.

The Lee family recognized her talents but knew Lowe needed some formal design education. With the encouragement of the Lees and the $20,000 she had been able to save, Lowe left her privileged life as "Tampa's design darling" for school in New York City.

Even though she enjoyed the fame and fortune of Tampa, she knew a larger world of fashion was waiting for her. For the second time, with the support of the Lee family, Lowe left Tampa. When news spread to her clients, there was much dismay. The *Tampa Tribune* wrote: "There is much 'weeping and wailing and maybe gnashing of teeth,' to use the old expression, among Tampa society maids over the fact that Annie is going to New York . . . feminine society is wondering just how it will be able to survive the future events."

To further her dream, once again, Ann Cole Lowe took another giant step forward. "I just knew that if I could come to New York and make dresses for society people, my dreams would be fulfilled." She was eighteen when she moved to New York in 1917 to attend a segregated school.

In New York, Lowe found race discrimination too. The director of the school hadn't seen pictures of her. When he saw her for the first time, "he appeared not to be expecting a Negro," Lowe remembered. "I felt like he wanted to send me away, but he didn't."

Still, she was isolated; none of the students would work or study with her. "I was segregated and worked and studied alone in a separate classroom. I felt that most of the teachers and students didn't think a Negro girl from the South would succeed in the fashion design world."

In spite of the isolation and racism, she declared, "Now assuredly, I am pursuing my dreams." She told friends, "Maybe the next Negro who attended the S. T. Taylor Design School wouldn't have to sit outside and study in isolation because it was the wish of white folks." She learned later that her designs had been leaving her solitary classroom and being used as examples to other students. She completed her two-year program in one year. She and her son, Arthur, returned to Tampa.

Lowe celebrated her twenty-first birthday with happiness and confidence of a bright future. She was a Negro woman from the Black Belt of Alabama and owned her own Tampa dress design shop that employed eighteen dressmakers. In 1919 she was also married a second time to Caleb West. They were married for ten years before divorcing. Lowe was known to often explain, "My husband left me. He said he wanted a real wife, not one who was forever jumping out of bed to draw dresses." Family members remembered that Lowe wasn't to be disturbed when she was in the throes of creating. "Don't talk to me right now," they remembered her saying. "I have a gown."

I Prefer to Be Referred to as a "Noted Negro Designer"

After Cole designed Olivia de Havilland's gown, she met Christian Dior at the first Paris Fashion Week since WWII. Dior achieved great success with his "New Look." Lowe was there as a reporter. She described Dior's "New Look" as figure-shaping suits and billowing gowns, which were particularly appealing to Lowe. Many thought of Lowe as the most important designer at Fashion Week, but it soon became clear that it was Dior the world would come to know.

Years later, Dior and Lowe became friends and got to know each other's designs. But as their careers continued, Dior achieved great financial success and name recognition. Lowe received neither. Fashion journalists adored Dior but mostly ignored her. Ten years after that Paris show, Dior died, but the House of Dior lives on. When Lowe died, her labels died with her.

Even in her sixties, after Lowe had established herself as the master of the debutante gowns in Tampa and her clientele list included names like DuPont, Roosevelt, Rothschild, Post, Rockefeller, Whitney, Smith, and even some European families. She was often asked to maintain confidentiality. This was the case with the Bouvier-Kennedy wedding. Since Lowe liked Bouvier, she agreed. But she was still hurt when in April 1961, *Ladies Home Journal* characterized her as a "colored woman dressmaker." She wrote the new first lady:

Dear Mrs. Kennedy: The reason for writing this note is to tell you how hurt I feel as a result of an article, the last of a series, about you in the Ladies Home Journal in which the reporter stated your wedding gown was made by a "colored woman dressmaker, not the haute couture." I realize it was not intentional on your part but as you once asked me not to release any publicity without your approval, I assume that the article in question, and others, was passed by you.

You know I have never sought publicity, but I would prefer to be referred to as a "noted Negro designer," in every sense I am. My name does not need to be mentioned as many of my socially prominent customers know I did your wedding as I have your wedding portrait in my studio.

Five days later, Kennedy's secretary from the White House telephoned Lowe to assure her that the first lady did not see the final text of the article before publication. Lowe wanted a retraction or at least a correction. She was told that the White House tried, but one never came. Lowe did not hold any animosity toward the Kennedys. In fact, she designed a debutante gown for Nina Auchincloss, Jackie Kennedy's stepsister. She wore the Lowe original to her debut in 1955, which was featured in *Vogue*. Lowe was credited in the caption this time. "*Her [Nina Auchincloss] pale pink and green tulle dress was made by Ann Lowe.*"

Family, Financial, and Health Woes

Lowe first married shortly after her mother's death in 1914 and had a son named Arthur. Her husband, Lee Cohen, was ten years her senior, and she was sixteen. Some records state that she was fourteen. She was more involved with the family business, and Cohen was unhappy about it. He demanded she give up her involvement with the business because he wanted a stay-at-home wife and mother. In my research, I wasn't able to find anything about him or what he did for a living while he made such demands on his talented wife. Lowe tried to accommodate her husband for a while by limiting her dreams and designs for herself and her family. But she was never happy with her husband's demands and her submission to them.

She left him for work in Tampa. "I left my husband today. I packed my belongings, grabbed my young son, and sought my freedom," she declared.

Ann Cole Lowe.

"My great-grandmother was a slave, and my grandmother was a slave, and my mother pretty much a slave, but I will not be a slave." She was eighteen years old.

Her son, Arthur Lee Cohen, was educated at Wilberforce University, a private, co-ed, liberal arts HBCU in Wilberforce, Ohio, affiliated with the African Methodist Episcopal Church. It is also the first college to be owned and operated by African Americans. He grew up with his mother in and around her shops and clients. They were close. He escorted her to social events and was her business partner. He tried to keep her business affairs in order, but in 1958, he was killed in an automobile accident; he was only forty-two years old. She and her sister Sally visited his grave often in Hartsdale, New York. "I will never go to a party again. My escort is gone," Lowe cried. She was sixty years old. And there was more bad news to come.

In spite of working mostly for the wealthy, Lowe was known for selling her dresses at very low prices and often talked into even lower prices. Financial disasters were constant in her life. Noted department stores profited from their arrangements with her since she had to purchase materials and pay her employees. She barely covered the cost, most of the time, taking a loss.

Three years after her son died, the IRS wanted $12,000 from Lowe for back taxes. Her tax records were considered incomplete and in disarray. The IRS seized and closed her salon in Harlem. A year later, she had eye surgery because she was losing her sight. One eye was removed as it was ruined by glaucoma, and she developed cataracts in her remaining eye. Her days as an independent force in fashion were numbered.

When she left the hospital after having her eye removed, she learned that her back taxes had been paid in full. It is believed that Jacqueline Kennedy was the friend who paid off the IRS for her. But there were still private debts of more than $10,000 owed to merchants. By 1963, Lowe had filed for bankruptcy. She was unable to maintain a salon and again worked for another house, Madeleine Couture. Through this shop, she had her only fashion show. It was described as "a small Champagne affair with the models coming from her clientele." With decreasing eyesight, she continued to work at other stores—Saks Fifth Avenue's Adam Room, Neiman Marcus, I. Magnum, Henry Bendel, and Lillian Montalso.

Nearly a hundred years later, another seamstress from Montgomery, Alabama refused to sit in the back of the bus. Rosa Louise McCauley Parks started a movement that could not be stopped. Lowe was fifty-seven years old when Parks refused to give up her seat to a white person. Although Lowe was living in NYC by then, according to family members, she not only knew of the famous protest but supported it and Mrs. Parks. Race pride was very important to Lowe.

Parks worked at the Montgomery Fair Department store as an in-house seamstress, tailoring and fitting garments for the city's white folks. Her hours were long, and the work could be humbling for the educated Parks. Her mother, a schoolteacher, taught her to read and write at an early age, which allowed her to do well academically. She attended a laboratory school (a modern-day charter school) for secondary education led by the Alabama

State Teacher's College (now Alabama State University). Although she was forced to drop out of the program in her junior year to care for her sick grandmother, she never returned. Instead, she took a job as a seamstress in a shirt factory; sewing became her daily life. Parks learned to sew from her grandmother and secretarial skills at the Montgomery Industrial School for girls in 1932. With the support of her husband, she did receive her high school diploma at age twenty.

Because of her involvement with the bus boycott, she lost her job at the department store. Her husband was also harassed at his job as a barber. Later they moved to Detroit, where her mother and brother already lived. She continued to work as a seamstress and later worked as a secretary for Congressman John Conyers.

More than one hundred years before Lowe began sewing, another Black seamstress sewed and designed for the rich and famous in Washington, DC. Elizabeth Keckley was a former enslaved-turned-dressmaker for high society, including Mary Todd Lincoln. Keckley's work is in the Smithsonian. In most of Lincoln's portraits, she's wearing designs by Keckley, but little was known about the dressmaker. Like Lowe, Keckley's relationship with the powerful was a mixed bag.

Lincoln was demanding, and it took valuable time away from her thriving dress business, but it gave her access to the private world of the Lincolns. She found support for her own social and political work of feeding the poor and sheltering the newly freed. But Lincoln's erratic behavior also created many political and social enemies for Keckley.

After President Lincoln was assassinated, Keckley lost contact with the first lady. Much was written about Keckley's life as a result of the unusual friendship with Lincoln. In 1868, she published a detailed account of her life in the autobiography *Behind the Scenes: Or, Thirty Years a Slave and Four Years in the White House.*

Maybe on the winds of history but also by her own determination, in 1968, just as the civil rights movement was at one of its heights, Lowe was able to open a new store on Madison Avenue in New York. Ann Lowe's Originals was run with the help of her sister Sallie and other employees. They completed thirty-five debutante gowns and nine wedding dresses in six months. Lowe created the dresses by feel since she was continuing to lose her eyesight.

By 1972, with her eyesight nearly gone, she was forced to retire. She and Sallie had lived together for thirty years, but after losing her sight, Lowe moved in with her adopted daughter Ruth Alexander. Ann Cole Lowe died at Alexander's home in Queens on February 25, 1981. She was eighty-two years old.

An unknown reporter gave her the name "Dean of American Designers." Her gowns are displayed at the Metropolitan Museum of Art and the National Museum of African American History and Culture. Lois Alexander Lane, founder and director of the Harlem Institute of Fashion, remembered Lowe. "This woman was class; she was also a very proud lady, and she made the elegant little black dress and the string of pearls a status symbol," Lane said.

Lowe got lost in the shuffle of history among high society women who did not want the world to know who she was, not just because she was African American, but because they didn't want to share her unique and original designs. Her obituary in the *New York Times* called her "society's best-kept secret." She is not mentioned in the art of the Harlem Renaissance, nor is she a noted feminist who chose her design dreams over almost all else. I can only imagine how crushed and lost she was when her son was killed. "I will never go out again," she said after his death. She was sixty years old. I am sure it was her work that saved her.

We are indebted to Ann Cole Lowe; she created a path for other African American fashion designers to achieve success.

SAM

The Vietnam War touched all Americans since there was the draft. According to *Newsweek Magazine*, the rich could run to Canada, go to college, or even receive a medical deferment for a bone spur without serving their country. Many of my high school classmates went to war, and when and if they returned, many of them with maimed bodies and minds. Drugs were a huge problem too. Even my gentle and sensitive sweetheart, Sam, had enlisted in the Air Force; knowing that he was going to be drafted, he enlisted. That was his dream. He saw himself flying planes. It made sense for him to enlist since he was going to draft anyway.

"When he was a little boy, he loved putting airplane kits together." Miss Cora, his grandmother, said. "Always in the backyard watching planes. Since Ft. Rucker is right down the road, lots of planes flew by here."

"My husband and I used to drive over to Ft. Rucker. He could've stayed all day." She smiled with pride. "Then my sweet husband subscribed to magazines about the military and airplanes."

I liked Miss Cora. Everything in her house seemed to shine. The radio was turned down low to soft music. When the news came on, she'd turn up the volume. Her house was filled with peace and beauty. Both of Sam's grandfathers had died. Miss Cora used to teach home economics at the high school in Troy. She could take a Sears & Roebuck catalog and turn it into a make-believe tree.

"Who needs to be spending good money when you can create anything." She was dressed like she was getting ready to teach. Sam lived with her rather than his mother, stepfather, and brother in Clayton. That's how I met him; he was visiting his family in Clayton. His mother was helping me with a reading list for the summer. She wanted me to be prepared for college. She taught school just like her mother.

She introduced me to her Sam, who was home from Vietnam. He smiled at me. And he had dimples and sexy eyes. And he had on a casual version of his uniform. I thought I would faint or melt. This was it, being in love. I was beginning to understand why the women in romance magazines were so crazy for love.

He became my official boyfriend while he was home. I would be starting college by the time he was home again. Sam liked me for being smart. Other boys just wanted me to do their homework. One time Rufus Rogers copied off of my paper for a test. He was so dumb; he copied my name.

Sam and I didn't see each other that much, even when he wasn't in Vietnam. He only came to Clayton a few times a year. I went to Ozark one time with him to visit his other grandmother. That made being in love even more special. Sam and I wrote letters. He loved sending me postcards of airplanes. We were allowed to talk on the phone once a week.

When he returned to the Air Force, he said he would be in a less dangerous zone. "Don't worry. Do your job in college, and I'll do mine in the Air Force, even flying planes one day." I was only sixteen. It seemed so romantic to have a boyfriend far away, so far that I couldn't imagine where it was. All I knew was you couldn't drive there. Sometimes his mother would call me and talk about when Sam was little and how much he loved airplanes. And what a good student he had been. I loved Sam's family as much as I did him. They were educated and talked about college and how Black folks needed to stick together more, own land, and have the right to vote. They didn't order you around like Big Mama and Little Mama. Both of Sam's grandmothers liked engaging with me.

A week later, he was shipped to Nam. I wrote him letters and bad poetry and sent him Girl Scout cookies. When I received a letter from him written on thin military stationery, with only an APO box number address, I felt as though I was receiving a letter from God. Almost every day, I would storm off the school bus asking if I had any mail. I had no idea where Vietnam was, just some very faraway place "over there" that was always hot or windy. I knew that from Sam's letters. He called it a jungle. The only thing I knew about the jungle was *Tarzan* from the TV show. Sometimes folks would associate Africa with the jungle. Of course, none of them had ever been to Africa.

The maps shown on television during the news didn't help me. They only flashed. Despite having only studied a map of the state of Alabama, I learned a lot from Mr. Odell, our history teacher, about where exactly Vietnam was on the map; his younger brother was over there "fighting for a cause we didn't understand," Mr. Odell told our class.

When I got to college, Sam's letters were shorter and darker. Sometimes they scared me. He didn't belong there. Sam was kind and gentle. He, too, didn't understand this war, but he had no real choice. He was angry and felt like they had been tricked into fighting Communism. They only saw poor families trying to survive. It was the most evil he had ever seen or imagined. The killing of innocent people, especially women and children, destroyed too much of his humanity. I could feel hate taking over his heart. We weren't going to have that beautiful Black family we desperately wanted and needed.

His letters warned me to get on with my life because he could not make promises to me. Earlier, our letters had been about our future. I would go to college on his G.I. Bill, and we would build a house with a VA loan. We would raise smart and happy children, "like me," he used to say, since he would be a career military man. We would live all over the world in peaceful places. And our children would speak other languages. Who could have a better dream?

Being at college was exciting, and I was learning so much and making new friends. Sam was falling off my radar. I loved college. I worked in the library and earned good grades. This is where I belonged.

Then I received a letter from Sam that he was coming home. I was elated but nervous. Sam's mother was my teacher in elementary school and later became an important mentor. She gave me the love and attention that Little Mama couldn't and Big Mama didn't know how. Sometimes I wondered if that's why I loved him so much. We hardly knew each other. Three months after we met and declared our love, he was shipped off to Vietnam again. We knew each other through letters against the backdrop of war. That's why I felt like I knew him well, his family.

Since they lived in Clayton and I lived in Louisville, about ten miles away, it took me a while to get there since we didn't have a car. I had to wait until someone could give me a ride. He would drive me home; his mother would be home from work. I wore a yellow sleeveless A-line dress with matching sandals. I had a book of poems, *I Am an American*, by Langston Hughes, to give him as a gift. I bought it at the college bookstore.

When I finally saw him, I didn't recognize him at first; he was wearing a huge afro and had grown a full beard. He looked so grown up. If I had seen him on the streets, I don't think I would've recognized him smoking Winston cigarettes. His voice was deeper. He's still the only man I ever knew who had dimples, which always made me smile, and his dreamy eyes always made my knees weak. He hugged me so tight I thought he would break my bones.

He was happy I was in college. "That's where smart people oughta be," he said.

"What about you, your plans for the future?" I asked.

"Our plans for the future," he corrected me. "We signed up for this. We military folks. Our country is calling us."

"What? Why?" I wanted to scream.

"Remember, Little Girl, that was the plan. When I get out, you'll be finished with college, and we can start our lives."

I hated that he called me "Little Girl," which he did for the rest of his life. Everything was moving so fast. "Will we be able to spend time together?"

"We're spending time together now." He lit up a Winston.

"When do you leave again?"

"Three weeks, maybe a little longer. Whatever the orders say. It won't be the same. I promise. I won't be in danger. I'm a Sergeant now." He held me in his arms, smelling like English Leather cologne. "No more dark days. No more dark days." He buried his head in my chest. He was tall and was able to kiss the top of my head while he was holding me.

Sam was my first boyfriend, my first love. Even Big Mama and Little Mama liked him since he came from a good family and had the means of supporting one. And he brought them flowers when he visited, which was probably the real reason they liked him. "Ain't nobody give me flowers 'fore," Big Mama almost smiled.

"You'll see it will be different. I will even be able to call you sometimes."

His family prepared a big dinner. Everybody was thanking the Lord for his return and praying for the safety of our troops in "harm's way." I wondered about the ones that didn't make it back. What were those prayers like? My head was still spinning at the rate of speed as my life was about to change.

During the three weeks that Sam was home, we visited his other grandmother. I was nervous since it was my first time meeting her. Her house was clean and smelled like lavender. Books and newspapers were neatly stacked in every room. Pictures of Sam and other grandchildren graced her walls and mantels. She was a petite woman dressed in her good clothes but not church clothes. She wore a pleated shirt-waisted seersucker blue and white dress. She had gone to the hairdresser; her curls were still a little tight.

After I gave her the lemon pound cake that Big Mama baked, she took over, and showed me to the guest room, painted light blue with white ruffled curtains and matching bedspread. The blue walls were the same color as her dress. A quilt was spread on top of a cedar chest. Fresh flowers were in a glass vase on the dresser. I only recognized the daisies. Small cotton rugs were spread on the sides of the bed, and a bigger one took up most of the hardwood floor.

"I hear you're smart," she said without looking at me.

"Sam thinks so." I grinned.

"He's not the only one; my daughter-in-law thinks so too. And she oughta know."

"Yes, ma'am. Thank you."

"Don't thank me. Thank the Good Lord."

"Yes, ma'am."

Sam had disappeared into his room. It was clear why he was so gentle and had such good manners. He always opened the door for me or any other female he encountered. He was the man of my dreams, according to *True Romance* magazine.

He shipped out the following week. I was brokenhearted. That convinced me that I was truly in love. He kept saying: "I'm gonna fly planes. How good is that? And I'll always fly back to you."

⤙ ⤚

After I graduated from college, I moved to Atlanta and took a job with JCPenney in their management-training program. Soon after that, I was transferred to a store in downtown Paducah, Kentucky. I had not heard from Sam in nearly a year. I was happy to have a new and different focus. I did not contact his parents, nor did I try to find him. I was busy adjusting to my new world. My workdays were long. The only days I had off were Wednesdays and Sundays.

But one early spring Wednesday morning, I was cleaning my apartment and doing laundry, listening to Sam Cooke's "A Change is Gonna Come." It was my first spring in Kentucky. And I wanted a clean house for my birthday. A few folks from work are coming by. Dogwoods outside my window had started to bloom. I hadn't had time to explore my new world. Someone knocked at my door. There he was, tall, brown, and a shell of the person I used to know. He was dirty and disoriented. I was speechless at first.

"What are you doing here?"

"I drove all night to get here?"

"From where?"

"Columbus?"

"Columbus, Georgia?"

"Columbus, Minnesota. I needed to be with you for your birthday and explain things."

"Come in." I had so many emotions, surprised, shocked, and scared. He looked like somebody who could harm me.

"Would you like a shower?"

"No, I just need sleep."

"Sure," I showed him to my guest room. He was snoring before I turned the light out.

He stayed for a week. While I went to work, he puttered around my apartment, cleaning and fixing all things broken. We didn't talk much. He cooked dinners. We went for walks and held hands in the park. I didn't ask him any questions. I thought one day he would start to talk about his life; he didn't. Our talks were pleasant, mostly about the past. One day I came home, and he had gone. No note, no nothing, just gone.

That was the last time I saw Sam. Years later, my sister called and said Sam was in a nursing home. His oldest son had been killed by an eighteen-wheeler on his way from college. Sam had a nervous breakdown. By the time he turned fifty-five years old, he was dead. No one offered me an explanation, nor did I seek one. I couldn't believe my first love had crumbled just like ashes.

CHAPTER 7

Walking Is Like a Prayer

Louise Bruyn (1931–)

I felt that I must break my own routine in order to make my
protest heard . . . I am speaking as strongly as I know how. It is my
deep hope that others will be moved to take some action which to
them is right—as strongly as they know how to end the war.

—Louise Bruyn

The day before Louise Bruyn left to walk from Boston to Washington, DC, a
450-mile pilgrimage through the Northeast to protest the Vietnam War, a *Boston
Globe* journalist asked her, who was she doing this for? She was moved by the
question and, nearly in tears, said: "I am doing it for us—I am doing it for all
of us, but especially for the poor and Black young men who don't have a voice."

It was 1971, and the slight, suburban mom and former dancer was respond-
ing to what she described was a calling to her soul. She was forty-one years
old, and the country was exploding with protests of the unpopular war and
draft that fed unprecedented numbers of Black and poor young men to the
frontline, where they were four times more likely to be killed than whites. A
war with no end in sight. A war where news outlets regularly reported the
US military atrocities against the Vietnamese people. Forced relocations,
bombing, and torturing of prisoners. Why wasn't Congress doing anything
about this? Bruyn wondered, as did many other Americans.

127

I met Louise and Severyn Bruyn in 2001 when they opened their home to me in Newton, Massachusetts, outside of Boston. I had received a fellowship from the Women's Studies Research Center at Brandeis University. Sev was a retired sociology professor from Boston College. He was jolly, almost like Santa Claus. I remember him always trying different remedies, vitamin supplements, the latest cleanse, or detox to stay young and healthy. His wife always laughed.

"Easy for you to say," Sev said to his wife. "The woman who can eat cakes every day and not gain an ounce."

I was a victim of his wife's baking skills. Often when I walked in the house, the smell of something delicious like banana bread, apple pie, or blueberry muffins would greet me.

The Bruyns had a permanent renter. I never ran into him. He left for work at 4:00 a.m. He drove some kind of delivery truck.

"When did you know he was going to be permanent?" I asked Louise.

"He had a heart attack, and we were listed next of kin."

"Wow."

"Don't forget he had signed his Social Security check over to us earlier."

"As you see, he's almost never around. It's been like that for maybe fifteen years," Sev said, testing a sleeping gadget.

I ate breakfast with them every morning except Sunday. We would sit around the breakfast table, read the *Boston Globe* together, and talk about the news. Mitt Romney had been elected governor of Massachusetts. "How in God's name could this happen here?" They both asked out loud. Louise's favorite part of the newspaper was the funnies, Sev, the sports, and mine, the lifestyle section. We always ended up reading the entire newspaper.

On Sunday mornings, I would read the *New York Times* in bed. And afterward, go to the Newton library to work on my writing. Having breakfast with them and talking about the news reminded me of what my life might have been if my parents had been educated.

The Bruyns are Quakers, green and peace activists, and involved in any cause of human rights. I admired them and their commitment to justice for all. Some kind of meeting was always happening in their home. I loved the huge Victorian house. It was warm and inviting. And their home was the go-to neighbor; friends and strangers would come to them for help with any issue of human rights.

❧ ❧

The Vietnam War had been raging for six years before Bruyn decided on the walk-in protest in 1971. Although it started in 1959, she said she felt a growing numbness towards the daily horrors reported on television and the newspapers. She knew the war was wrong. She also knew she had to walk alone and hoped to encourage others to find their own ways to protest. Her walk took her through small villages, big cities, like New York and Baltimore, and college towns, New Haven and Storrs, Connecticut. She walked in snow and rain. Word spread of her mission, and she was greeted along the way by the press, celebrities, elected officials, and everyday folks. Her family and friends joined her for part of the way, but it was mostly a solo mission of protest.

When I interviewed Bruyn some twenty years ago, the spark was still in her eyes. I tried to encourage her to turn her journal into a book. It was already typed. This was right after 9/11/2001, and the country was talking about wars again. "Years ago, I tried once, but to no avail." "Now is a good time to try again," I tried to convince her. "You have a story to tell, and folks want to hear it, and they'll be encouraged to tell theirs."

She shot back at me. "I don't have time for some publisher to have power over me. I tried three publishers already." "But that was a long time ago. And with all due respect sending your work out to three publishers isn't much in the publishing world."

Finally, she allowed me to edit her manuscript. And by that time, she was also beginning to appreciate the internet. The stubborn midwestern dancer was softening.

Her journey started months before she walked her first mile. She was having coffee and reading the *Boston Globe* like she did every morning with her husband, Sev. She was convinced when she read an article about the US sanctioning the relocation of hundreds of thousands of Vietnamese from the five northernmost provinces of South Vietnam to the southern provinces. It reported the previous US military attacks on single villages, forced relocations, bombings, and torture of those who refused to leave their homes. Some reluctant villagers were burned out. "They would torture the whole providences,

Louise Bryun.

what they had done to one village at a time," she said. The writer went on to say that even though this project had been reported in the *New York Times*, the press and television had failed to comment on it. And the writer concluded that the nation was "sunk in anesthesia." Bruyn was determined to rouse people. She supported the civil rights movement, not just in spirit but financially too. Since she couldn't be part of those marches, she created her own.

While I was finishing high school in the Black Belt of Alabama, trying to figure out where Vietnam was on the map. Bruyn wanted to act. What could she do to stop the war? The protest walk slowly took shape and would begin in February 1971. I couldn't even imagine a place so far away, maybe heaven. Many folks couldn't understand why and how this forty-one-year-old petite woman could do such a thing. She was a nice upper-middle-class white woman from Newton, Massachusetts. Only Bruyn could understand what she had to do. Even if she didn't understand totally, she knew she had to do something.

What did she have to worry about? She had no perceived notions or strategic plan, nor did she have any illusion that her act would end the Vietnam War. But she had a moral compass and took her responsibility as a citizen seriously.

"Carnage" was a word often used by television newsman, Walter Cronkite, on the nightly news that brought the war into American living rooms.

At our home in the Black Belt of Alabama, Big Mama allowed us to watch the news more, since Sam was "over there," as they referred to Vietnam. It was all everybody was talking about. In our small community, everybody knew somebody who was drafted. "Dis a scary time, but we done seen worst." Reverend Hill preached, "Dat's why we gotta trust in de Lord to help our brave soldiers, who's a long, long ways from home. Pray for them and our country. Amen and glory to de Good Lord."

I wrote letters for some of the church members who couldn't read or write to friends and families who were "over there." Big Mama told me not to accept the quarters that they usually gave me if they had them. When I asked her why she looked at me like I was crazy. "Folks dyin', and you can't give up a quarter? Lord, have mercy."

Bruyn said she thought, "Walking was like a prayer." What was she praying for if not for the war to end? Not for self-redemption. "There comes a time when confronted with outrage, we must act to remain human," she said, recalling the moment of epiphany. "Not just any deed, but focused action floating the injustice to the level of public visibility."

As her mission became more defined over the objections of family and friends, she decided to do it alone with no signs. She thought that might discourage engagement with strangers. She craved forging a conversation, not preaching to the choir. Bruyn learned that walking alone on such a grueling journey was transformative. The visible self-sacrifice and loneliness of it evoked empathy, stirred her curiosity, and raised questions about what it meant not just to be an American but what it meant to be a peaceful human being. Many accused her of inflicting pain on herself. Why was she doing this? The curiosity of strangers led to discussion, which instilled doubt, and at times, she questioned her motives. But by walking alone, she was no longer alone. But she made the pilgrimage an argument. "I was speaking from the deepest part of me to the deepest part of everyone on the way."

When I moved in with them in 2001, I was treated like one of their daughters. My only responsibility was to drive to Brandies University every day if I wanted to and work on my writing. After surviving the grueling world of the tenure process, I felt free and was excited to emerge in my new world. I had earned this sabbatical. Plus, Boston is a major city, and I had other friends there.

Sev and Louise have two daughters and one son. All about my age, and maybe that's why it was so easy for them to be so parental toward me. Bruyn is a pretty petite woman with short gray hair that was dark brown when she walked 450 miles in 1971. She and Sev were very physical; they raked leaves, took care of their garden. I adored their commitment to social justice, which included caring for the environment. Recycling was a big part of their lives. Their phone rang all the time. Miss Pretty, her fluffy white cat, always ran to the phone when it ranged.

When I arrived, Louise and Sev were welcoming and caring. However, she was up in roar because all of her organizations wanted to use email for their meetings and gatherings. "Never," Louise said to me.

"When you get used to it, you'll see," I tried to talk her down.

"It's just a waste of my time."

"The idea is to save you time. Whenever you get ready, I'll teach you." It was clear she was stubborn.

"Ump," she said and walked out of my room.

I loved living with them in their home. They were great conversationalists and lots of fun. We talked a lot about 9/11. I had been driving to NYC the Tuesday when it happened. I was to stay with my son in Jersey City for a couple of days, visit friends in the city, and he was to drive with me to Boston and take the train back to the city.

I ended up driving to Boston alone and terrified. It was the gospel music of Aretha Franklin and Jessye Norman that helped me to make the journey. My son couldn't get a train back to the city; everything was booked since planes weren't flying. There was so much chaos everywhere and in all forms. I was thankful when I reached the Bruyns' house. I was greeted with warmth and love.

As a couple, the Bruyns never fought. They did more laughing than anything. Louise got annoyed when Sev invited a group over for a meeting and expected her to entertain them and clean up. And he generally waited until the last minute to tell her. Anytime that happened, she'd knock on my door. "Let's go to the movies."

Protests and marches against the war had been escalating, a fact that influenced Bruyn. College campuses, city streets exploded. People burned draft
cards and US Flags. Five years before she began her trek, Mohammad Ali
explained to Black folks and all of America why we shouldn't "fight those
poor Asian people who ain't never done a thing to us," as he refused his
draft notification. I started thinking about the Vietnam War in a different
way. Ali's stand against the Vietnam War transcended not only in the ring,
which he had dominated as the heavyweight champion of the world but also
in the realms of faith and politics. "His biggest win came not in the boxing
ring but in our courts in his fight for his beliefs," Eric Holder, the former US
Attorney General, stated.

In 1966, when I was almost fifteen years old and my sweet Sam was graduating from high school. Some Americans started to really listen to Ali. Sam's
mother was one of them who paid attention to Ali. Every time she got a
chance, she would talk about him.

Ali's draft status was revised to make him eligible to fight in the war.
He responded by telling the world, "that as a Black Muslim, he was a conscientious objector and would not enter the US military." He had changed
his name and faith. His old name was Cassius Marcellus Clay Jr., which he
referred to as a slave name, and he converted to Islam. He famously said, "My
conscience won't let me go and shoot my brother, or some darker people, or
some poor hungry people in the mud for big powerful America. And shoot
them for what? They never called me nigger, they never lynched me or my
people, they didn't put no dogs on me, they didn't rob me of my nationality,
rape and kill my mother and father. Shoot them for what? How can I shoot
them poor people? Just take me to jail now."

A year later, Ali was twenty-five years old and appeared in Houston for
his scheduled induction into the US military. He repeatedly refused to step
forward when his name was called despite being warned by an officer that he
was committing a felony offense that was punishable by five years in prison
and a $10,000 fine. He refused and was arrested and later convicted.

Ali was able to stay out of jail while his case was being appealed. But his
boxing license was suspended in New York that same day. Not only that,
his title was stripped, and other boxing commissions followed. For three

years, he was not allowed a boxing license, which meant he was not able to make a living.

But Ali remained firm. "I ain't got no quarrel with them Viet Congs," he said. "I am America. I am the part you won't recognize. But get used to it—Black, confident, and cocky. My name, not yours. My religion, not yours, my goals, my own. Get used to me."

I agreed with Ali. But Sam was ready to fight for his country and fly planes and be an American hero. Sam and so many others saw an opportunity to get out of poor southern small towns. Ali didn't have to worry about that, but he was still right.

Ali appealed his conviction to the US Supreme Court, and in a much-anticipated ruling, the court voted 8-0 in his favor. Thurgood Marshall recused himself since he had been previously involved in the case as a Fifth Circuit US Solicitor General. The Supreme Court found that the government had failed to properly specify why Ali's application had been denied, and the decision was overturned. In part, the decision read: "The Court stated that the record showed that Ali's beliefs were founded on tenets of the Muslim religion as he understands them."

In 1970, the National Guard gunned down four students at an anti-war protest. Nine were seriously wounded. We were really scared. If the National Guard was killing white students, we knew they would blow our brains out, and only our families and friends would care. A week later, two students were killed by the National Guard again, and many were wounded at Jackson State University in Mississippi. I prayed as I sent Sam positive quotes and newspaper clippings. My last line in those letters was always: God is walking with you.

One time I sent him a copy of Mark Twain's "The War Prayer." In the essay, Twain raises the question, when there is a war, whose side is God on? I thought He had to be on our side. Nobody believed in God more than Black folks. And hadn't we paid the price with slavery, Jim Crow, and all the other injustices we still suffered? Wasn't that enough for God to be on our side? I wanted to scream out to the world.

Sam told me in his next letter that there was no God. And if there were, why would He be on our side? He had, after all, allowed Black folks to be enslaved for centuries. And when it ended, all we got was sharecropping and Jim Crow. What about the poor people we had invaded? Who was their God? Didn't they believe as much as we did? The letter went on to say there were only greed and evil, and they who had the most money ruled. I didn't sleep for months after that letter. The sweet and sensitive boy I used to know and love didn't exist anymore. A lot would change for Louise Bruyn too. She was restless and needed to do something. She heard a calling, and she followed it in the most courageous and humble way she could.

A Suburban Mom Hears the Call

In 1966, the same year Sam graduated from high school, Bruyn and her husband, Severyn, moved from Jackson, Illinois, to Newton, Massachusetts. Her husband was offered a faculty position at Boston College in the sociology department.

Four years later, Bruyn was preparing for the walk of her life; she was a dancer and dance teacher, and raising teenage daughters. Both daughters were used to participating with their parents in peace demonstrations, vigils, leafleting, and working for peace since they had lived in Jackson. Their older son, George, was still living in Illinois, studying music.

There, they joined the Society of Friends Quakers; today, they are members of Friends Meeting at Cambridge. Their children have always been well aware of their parents' depth of caring for a better world and the importance of working toward that goal.

After consulting with her family, Bruyn sought the counsel of not just trusted Quakers and other friends but also serious hikers. They would know and understand the practical aspects of such a journey. Their friends were surprised and reserved when she first told them about her plans, mostly concerned about how she wanted to do it. "Do you want other people to go with you? Do you want to carry leaflets? Will you wear or carry a sign? Do you need a station wagon to go along with you carrying supplies, sleeping bags, food, etc.? When would you be starting?" they asked.

While the walk was still in formation, the Bruyns received a telephone call from the Legal-Aid Service Program. A returned African American soldier needed housing for the night. He had thought about going AWOL because he didn't want to go back to Vietnam, but then he decided to try to get out of Army legally. During his time in Vietnam, he said, he'd witnessed some of the worst atrocities committed by US troops. He even wore a "necklace of eighteen" of Viet Cong ears. He saw heads impaled on stakes. He heard a commander tell a soldier who had killed a Vietnamese not to return without the ears. Since the soldiers didn't have a regular knife, they had to cut the ears off with a small plastic knife.

When she told me that story, I wondered if the soldier's story was an example of what Sam had mentioned to me about the evil and horror of the war. Sam would never offer specific examples; he just used language like "evil that eats away at your soul, and after a while, you didn't own yourself anymore."

I wondered where Sam had been during the time Bruyn did her unimaginable 450-mile walk. And what he'd have thought about it. I never told the Bruyns about Sam. They could get crazy about injustice. For the same reason, I didn't tell them that at the gala event for the new fellows at Brandies, one of the guests handed me his empty wine glass and when I didn't take it, the wine glass fell to the floor and broke. He then screamed at me. I stood and watched him without saying a word.

When the person learned I was a fellow, he sort of apologized by telling me how much he loved his Black stepchildren. I walked away before he could finish.

Bruyn told the soldier about her upcoming walk. He seemed interested and expressed how powerful that would be with one person walking. But he had more to say about the weather since he and a friend had hitched rides across the country in January. It was so cold his friend got frostbite. After that, the friend took the bus; his feet hurt so badly. "For some reason, even though the zero-degree weather and storms frightened me, but it didn't seem relevant," Bruyn said. "I will face it one day at a time."

Her husband said he thought the walk was a good idea but was concerned about her leaving so soon since it was February. Winter in Boston. Winter all over the Northeast. He wanted her to wait until later in the spring; it would be safer too.

But she said she burned with urgency. "How can I justify waiting for nice weather?" she asked herself, her husband, her friends, and her neighbors. There were no answers. "The soldiers in Vietnam couldn't wait until spring," she told them.

After she made the decision to go, she would go alone, hoping others would be urged to take the strongest actions they felt they could take wherever they were. The walk would not try to accumulate more people and, therefore, divert people from other activities. She now had to work out the logistics. February 17, 1971, was the date they chose.

What route would she take? Where and how would she rest? Eat? What would she wear? What would she carry? How? She and her friends went to a mountain climbing supply store. They looked for boots, jackets, ponchos, mittens, socks, hats, and backpacks. She would dress in layers. The owner was also against the war and gave her a fifteen percent discount on her purchases, she recalled, the delight still in her voice decades later. And what would she do when she got to DC? She knew she would try to see President Nixon.

"Am I hearing myself right?" She laughed to friends gathered in their home. One friend had suggested she call Nixon and tell him she was coming, Bruyn did. She talked to an aide whom she told about her walk and her feelings towards the war. The aide asked for her name and thanked her. No one else from the White House called her back.

"This just can't be a walk against something," Sev said. They were members of the United World Federalist, known today as World Federalist, USA. They had discussed the need for more cooperation between nations. Americans cannot be the police of the world. It has never worked. They discussed how in the sixteenth century, Martin Luther had nailed his ninety-five theses on the door of a church in Germany when he was protesting church domination. The Bruyns put together their own anti-war theses, five imperatives for US foreign policy in relation to Vietnam and to the world. This is what they came up with.

Five Theses on United States Foreign Policy

In 1517 Martin Luther made public his protest again church domination by nailing ninety-five Theses to the door of All Saints Church in Wittenberg, Germany. Martin Luther so impressed Daddy King, the father of Martin Luther King Jr., that he changed his name from Michael to Martin Luther.

In the year 1971, I Louise Bruyn made this protest against state domination by nailing five theses to the door of the United States Congress. I carry this message written by my family and friends who support my mission.

We love our country for its ideals but we condemn it war policies. We oppose the fact that we must support the war through our taxes or be forced to go to prison.

We demand that the foreign policy of the United States be directed toward creating the foundations of world peace and goodwill. The following five theses convey our beliefs about the imperatives of US Foreign policy now.

1. The American troops and air forces must be withdrawn immediately and totally from Southeast Asia.
2. An international commission composed of major capitalist and communist nations should be established to aid Vietnamese people to develop their nation and protect the lives of all people in Southeast Asia.
3. A Study Commission must be created immediately within the United Nations to review its Charter, looking toward the establishment of enforceable international law and a democratically constituted world government.
4. International agencies must be created with the authority to allocate economic aid for national liberation and development, and to prohibit separate aid from stronger nations seeking control over weaker nations.
5. An international agency must be established to control the use of nuclear weapons and ultimately banish their national production for destructive purposes.

This document is what Bruyn carried with her during her 450-mile walk, collecting signatures.

I wondered what Sam would've thought about Bruyn's walk. He often wrote that sometimes he and the other soldiers felt alone and didn't think America was doing enough to end the war. Living with the Bruyns offered me an opportunity to understand some of what Sam had experienced and long ago suppressed. Sam and I were kids dreaming about a dream.

Once Bruyn had made up her mind, she thought she could walk twenty miles for twenty-three days. Her hiker friends suggested ten miles a day. "But that would take forty-five days," she remembered, and her stomach tightened. Her friends tried to convince her that there were other ways to work for peace. She decided on a test walk eighty-eight miles to Voluntown. The highway was slushy with rain, and the countryside was covered with snow. A friend had a map and an itinerary from a group who walked from Boston four years earlier protesting nuclear testing. That saved Bruyn a lot of time.

Her husband oversaw publicity. He wrote letters to local and national newspapers announcing her walk and why she was compelled to take such a journey. He and other friends called television and radio stations. The response from the media was immediate; they wanted more details and access to Bruyn. Reporters were sent out to cover the story. A loose network of hosts offered her food and shelter as she journeyed to the White House.

The last thing she did before she embarked was to contact a Newton police officer she knew to explain the traffic at their house the next morning. He was aware of what was happening. "I am amazed," he said. "Would you like a few of the men to keep the traffic clear for your walk as you go through Newton? Since you're one of our people, we could help you and those walking with you across the intersection at Beacon and Centre Streets, Four Corners, and Washington Street. Then you cross over to the Wellesley line, our men will radio to Wellesley police, and they can take care of you there." He further offered a letter of introduction she might carry with her to show other police officers. She thanked him again. When Bruyn told me, I could only think of the policemen in children's books. I couldn't imagine a police officer being so friendly and helpful to African Americans. I am sure there are some.

⌐━ ━⌐

As expected, there was a large turnout to see her off, including the media. Bruyn remembered one newsman shouting to her to stay at the head of the crowd for the best photo ops. "Whose walk is this?" Bruyn shouted back.

As she was taking a rest on a grassy patch of the road, she said someone shouted: "Louise, why don't you immolate yourself too?" This was a reference to the protest action of Norman Morrison, a Quaker, who burned himself to death in front of the Pentagon in 1965, and to the many Buddhist monks in Vietnam who poured gasoline on themselves and lit a match.

By the time they reached the intersection of Routes 16 and 9 near Wellesley, about three miles from Newton, almost everybody had disappeared, and only four brave soldiers were left. She knew she was going to be walking alone mostly. But she hadn't expected it to happen so soon. Their press friends were still following her, but soon they had stopped. Bruyn and her small army stopped at Mister Donut's for a coffee break. They encountered a young man who had been in the Marines. "Our forces belonged in Vietnam to protect the South Vietnamese from being overrun by the Communists." He was courteous, patriotic, and soft-spoken. But he did not have an answer about the killing of innocent people. He did raise the question: "How does an ex-Marine protest?"

Bruyn and her soldiers marched on. They passed a church in Wellesley with a sign: "Hope is the art of perseverance." They saw that as a sign of hope and endurance about what she was doing.

One of the things that kept her going was she saw and read signs throughout her walk. While she was unpacking that first night, she found written on an envelope:

Onward . . . !
Our orange hope
Our super lady-bug . . .
Travel well, feel full of love—we love you.

Inside the envelope was a poem:

The weight of the world is love.
Under the burden of solitude,
under the burden of dissatisfaction
the weight we carry in love.

"Song" by Allen Ginsberg-for your way . . . Carry on! Jerilyn, a friend, had written.

Bruyn hadn't realized how much these words meant to her until she got ready for bed that first night of her walk. "I showered and bedded down for the night. I felt small but stronger than I had ever felt before. Before I fell asleep, I thought of all the quotes and words that had helped me on that very important first day."

The next day, light snow covered the ground when Bruyn woke up in South Natick, hoping to walk to Holliston. She wondered how much snow she would have to walk through. But she looked up and saw a quote taped on her host family's cupboard: "To thine own self be true, Baby do thy thing," she smiled. "I read it as a confirmation of my action."

Later in a drugstore, she was applying moleskin to her heel when a woman came up to her and handed her a package of moleskin, which she just bought. "My contribution," the woman smiled. But as she walked, her blister continued; she needed more moleskin. She wasn't able to wear her new boots for more than a few blocks. She had to put her sneakers back on.

Two teenage girls ran out of their houses as she passed. They wanted to know if she was "that woman." Did she need a rest stop? A glass of water? But they didn't understand why she was doing this. She gave a similar answer as she had the last group and walked on. "It was then that I thought about the 'whys' more carefully. I was walking first of all because it demanded a commitment from me, physical and emotional, for forty-five days on the war; my energy was focused on the war." She believed during that time, she would grow, learn more facts, do more thinking, and face the challenge of speaking to people of all backgrounds. But most importantly, she would be affecting people around her by talking with them personally and through the news media. And finally, it was a visible protest; the government and the nation would see it.

She met her host. After a hot shower and applying more Band-Aids and moleskin, she went downstairs and ate an elegant dinner with her host family. And like every night, before she went to bed, nagged with the question: where would she spend the next night?

Back home in Newton, Bruyn's home base was in full force. The organizing of publicity had gained a new height. Her friends and family were answering calls from the media, answering letters from other interested parties. They were being interviewed on television and radio stations. The media was always following Bruyn and always present at their house. With the same question: "Why?"

On her way to Mendon, Massachusetts, it turned colder, and she was alone again. She walked to an ice cream parlor and had a cup of hot coffee.

She heard a young man at the counter say to another man something about "protesting the Indo-China War." When she turned around, he asked, "Are you 'that woman' walking to protest the war?"

They exchanged a few words. He was against the war too. He mentioned something about being drafted. "Do you know about drafting counseling?" Bruyn asked.

"I don't want to do anything that's against the law."

She explained that counseling was legal and often there were laws people weren't always aware of. He could find out what his options were if he saw a draft counselor. He didn't know of one in the area. She suggested he contact the American Friends Service Committee in Cambridge. She even wrote the address and phone number down for him.

By then, her host had arrived. She asked Bruyn if she were a purist. The host knew of some shortcuts. After Bruyn talked to her husband, he advised her to be firm on taking no shortcuts. He helped to clarify her thinking. She understood she was involved in an inner discipline. She knew she was involved in something deeper than just getting herself from one point to another. She would abide by the discipline of the task.

During her Thursday walk, day two, an image kept appearing in the back of her mind. She realized that the image wasn't leaving; she looked at it full square. It was that of a housewife using wooden clothespins to hang clothes on an electric high-tension wire. But when she faced it head-on, she could see what it was telling her. She became aware of the internal tension and the external danger. There she was, a Newton housewife, dancer, dance teacher, and mother of three teenagers having the gall to walk to the seat of her government and tell her representatives and everyone on the way of her deep distress about the country's foreign policy. "I knew the inherent danger and the inner tension I had to accept. But I couldn't let either get in the way of what I felt; I had to do it," she said as she walked on alone. "It got even worse when I learned from Sev that one of our daughters had received an obscene phone call."

But like a good soldier, she marched on toward East Douglas and Webster. She remembered her friend from East Douglas; her only son had joined the Army in 1966. He was immediately sent to Vietnam. Three weeks after he arrived, he was killed, two days before his nineteenth birthday. Her friends hadn't been able to find a way for their son to become a conscientious objector. He was shipped out ahead of schedule due to heavy American losses.

In East Douglas, she was met by a friend; another friend sent a poem to Bruyn:

Sometimes naked
Sometimes mad,
Now as a scholar,
Now as a fool,
Thus appear
on earth—The freemen!

Near Webster, they walked in the cold and drizzle. Different friends would meet her at different places and walk together. She was thankful. This kept her from being so lonely. It was damp, cold, and kept getting colder. They stopped in the woods, dusted the snow from rocks and pieces of wood, and sat down to eat lunch. This was the coldest that she had felt; she wasn't sure what the temperature actually was. She was afraid her fingers were going to become frostbitten. Just at that moment, a friend drove up with hot coffee. They warmed up in the car and trudged onward. They talked about the war and what they all could do. Many people expressed the sense that they were gaining a new perspective just through her process of walking. "We saw birds, branches, and brooks that we never would have seen had we been traveling any other way. The process of walking made us feel human."

In spite of the cold, it had been a wonderful day walking together. But a chilling message had gone over the new wires "Hatefulness/hatefulness." It was the coded alert to signify a nuclear attack on our country. The code shut down radio stations around the country; they waited for further instructions like all Americans. One man they ran into thought it was important to "support our leader, President Nixon." Bruyn disagreed with that, although she didn't tell him. She thought that way of thinking was the foothold for the beginning of fascism. I would've been in total agreement with Bruyn. Most of my high school classmates in my small town went to Vietnam. I didn't remember any of them coming back as themselves. They were alcoholics, drug addicts, violent, and abusive, with serious mental health problems. The totalitarian state is built on loyalty to a leader. It is built on the trust of a "father figure." Whereby democracy puts responsibility for making choices on the people. This is the strength of our nation; we believed.

At her next host's home, a youth meeting drew a good gathering. The boys were more interested than the girls because they could be drafted. Women weren't drafted in 1971. The short answer everyone gave about why the US was in Vietnam and should stay there was always the same, communism. Finally, the youth leader spoke. He felt communism had to be stopped. He continued by saying the war was a way to keep the Asian population down, that they thought differently than Americans and didn't value life the same way we do. Bruyn heard more of the same from the other young people.

Finally, a minister spoke: "We've got to stop communism before it comes to the shores of America."

"It seems to me that the way to stop Communism from taking over here is by taking care of the problems we have—eliminating hunger, illiteracy, and poverty," Bruyn shot at them.

"Why we don't have poverty in America. Doesn't everyone in America live like us? Aren't we typical Americans?" the minister asked.

"You're putting me on. You're just saying that," Bruyn said, stunned she remembered.

"No," he said, "doesn't everyone live like we do here in Webster?"

"When was the last time you visited a ghetto? What about Appalachia? The tenant farmers in the South?" she asked.

"Well," he said, "communism is going to start a lot of little brush fires around the world, and we have to put them out."

"How do you propose to do that?"

"Well, you know how a fireman puts out a fire . . ."

Bruyn said she had to interrupt him. "I don't agree or accept your analogy. We're talking about people. What would you do if people wanted communism? If they rioted because of poor conditions in their country, what would you do, shoot them?"

"Yes, I would," he nodded.

"My heart sank in the knowledge that there were thousands who believed as he did," she recalled. She held her right hand over her heart. "I felt that all over the country, there were ministers willing to kill other people if those people wanted a form of government or a kind of economy different from ours."

Another man in the group thought young men owed the country their service. Bruyn suggested that if the older men in the country felt the war was worth fighting, they should fight it.

"Don't be silly. You know we can't do it. It's the young men who are strong and healthy." He tried to make a muscle.

"And they come back home broken, maimed, blind, or they come back in a coffin," she countered.

Finally, there was a moment of connection. His arms dropped. "Yes, you're right."

Just as Bruyn thought the conversation had ended, a Russian woman in the group spoke with great energy. Bruyn wasn't clear where she stood on the Vietnam War, but the woman felt that a person in society was responsible to other members of that society. She said that if they did anything wrong, they had no right to live, and she made a slicing motion at her neck. She believed individuals had no rights. Bruyn was emotionally and mentally wiped out after the gathering.

"That encounter with all of the different comments and reactions made me aware of the depth of fear that can exist in so many rationalizations that got expressed in violence as the solution to problems," she wrote in her journal. "It was a challenge for all of us to examine our reaction to fear. How might we, personally and nationally, find our way out of reliance?"

By the end of Bruyn's second week of walking, she had covered most of the state of Connecticut. She found herself in Storrs, speaking at the University of Connecticut, her first formal meeting. About forty individuals attended, half students and half from AFSC. The sky was gray, and the temperature was dropping, pure rotten weather. Before she arrived, she wondered whether it would be one of those days that she would have to sit out somewhere. Reporters continued to follow her, asking questions about the weather. She responded by saying, "It's bad and beautiful at the same time." There was light sleet. Trees and bushes were shiny with ice, and the pavement was slippery. She told them how the trees sparkled. She wanted to tell them that it was winter in New England; what did they expect? But she remembered it was free publicity. Their next question was if she had any regrets. "No, I do not have any regrets. I will keep walking; I feel stronger physically and spiritually. I hope my walking would stir a few others to take action the strongest they can take." After the meeting, a reporter who tried to find her earlier handed her a note, the words of the song he had tried to remember the day before:

Step by step
the longest march
can be won, can be won . . .

Her third week was much of the same. Columbia, Connecticut, turned out to be the friendliest place she walked. Total strangers offered her dinner and a place to rest. About a mile from the University, a young man ran over to her. "I just had to come and tell you. Today I'm dropping out of school to go to New York and work fulltime with the Vietnam Veterans Against the War." He had been "over there," but had returned to school. It mattered that he told Bruyn of his plans. She believed he supported the sense of the urgency of their protest and her hope. She remembered the conversation being brief and beautiful.

Finally, a reporter asked an original question: "What would your response to having other people join you as you walk into Washington, DC? Would you want that?"

"That would be beautiful," she said, suddenly realizing she hadn't given much thought to how she wanted to end the walk. If others were to join her, she would prefer that no one carry signs or banners. At that point, she wanted to walk in silence on the last day. She hoped that anyone joining the walk would remain silent as well. She was aware there was a call for thousands to appear in Washington on April 2, the project end date of the walk. Bruyn wasn't sure how she felt about that.

February 26 was her daughter, Becky's, seventeenth birthday. Bruyn woke up to a rainy and damp morning. The rain fell gently or hung in the air as fog. She was also feeling depressed and weary, but she knew she was going to keep walking. Her family was going to join her, and that made her happy. When they finally arrived, they threw their arms around her. The weather changed, and the sun became bright, and so were their spirits.

Halfway, Bruyn arrived in NYC to a great celebration and affirmation of purpose. After thirteen days on her feet, she was in New York City. It was a big emotional boost that she made it that far, her halfway point. She was happy and hopeful and had the attention of major news media, NBC, ABC, CBS, and the *New York Times*.

"Reaching deep within me, I asked God, my higher power, the universe, to give me strength to speak clearly," she remembered praying. "Don't let the focus stay on me. Let me be a channel for the voice of peace. Let me speak to the problem of ending the war, the insanity of our national policy. Use me, Lord; don't let me get in the way. Keep me a channel."

Somewhere along Fifth Avenue, she met friends. She wasn't far from the Metropolitan Museum of Art when she heard the mayor's wife had waited to walk with her for a few minutes, but she had other appointments.

Both Mrs. John Lindsay and Sen. George McGovern sent glowing telegrams to the church welcoming her and offering their deepest support. That lifted her spirits, as did her talk at St. Clements Church. The vicar asked her about her faith.

"I have trouble with the traditional Christian words, the set phrases, so to speak, that seem to define the Spirit in such a rigid framework," she explained to him. "But I believe in the Holy Spirit, that power that is more than human, that nourishes us if we will listen to it. I believe in the love that is divine, the divinity that is in everyone, that Jesus is the purest example we know of, of a human filled with the God Spirit, filled with power of the Holy Spirit. Yet, I cannot say words like, 'Jesus is my Savior' or 'Christ died for our sins.'"

Finally, in the small chapel, Bruyn felt that in the past had she witnessed such a scene, she would have broken down in tears. But as moved as she was by the beauty of the music and the service, "I felt clear and strong. I was coming from a place of power that seemed beyond myself." Her time in New York City gave her the strength to walk on.

◆— —◆

On Bruyn's final day in Washington, the cherry trees were draped with the most beautiful blossoms. She had done it! Even she couldn't believe it. She had started on February 17, and now it was April 2nd. But there she was with her husband, daughters, friends, and strangers walking by her side. She had never been happier. One of the most beautiful moments was when they turned and saw the Capitol. "This is what I had been walking for, and now it was within reach." Her husband placed in her hands the stack of signed Five Theses signatures that she had collected on her walk.

But there was confusion over what would be the order of events. She was to arrive at the steps of the Capital at 12:10 p.m., climb to the top, have a silent witness of ten to fifteen minutes, then say a few words and hand the Five Theses to Senator Kennedy and the People Peace Treaty to Congressman Drinan-D Massachusetts, and then she would be finished. But she and her group were still trying to figure out the order of events.

Hundreds of people arrived by buses. Another hundred or had gathered, and the group grew bigger. "I had to pray extra hard to contain the butterflies in her stomach. I fought with that pledge of silence. I kept trying to figure out whether it was better to keep the discipline or to let the Spirit flow freely," she remembered. "I wished I had the courage to break my own discipline. Instead, I made a feeble effort to hold hands in a long thin circle along the sidewalk, but nobody knew what I was doing. It didn't work."

The group sat on the stairs near the empty pool in front of the Capitol waiting, silently praying, and loving one another with their eyes and arms. We were one asking our government to stop the brutality, the bombing, and the inhumanity. They never saw President Nixon; he was out of town. But she stood between Rep Drinan, strong and steadfast, and Senator Kennedy, supportive, quiet, gentle, and compassionate. Both had supported her.

Bruyn remembered her journey ended in faith. It was a beautiful, scary, and deepening experience, merging with humanity. "It was a public outcry against inhumanity of war; it was my prayer."

Today Bruyn is ninety-one years old. Sev joined the ancestors in 2019. I stayed with them a few years ago. I felt like I was coming home. They were so thrilled. We talked most of the night. I remembered coming home from Brandeis exhausted from writing and researching. All I wanted to do was get home. Bruyn had always baked a cake, pie, or something delicious. Her blood sugar is low; she never gained weight. I was jealous. I gained fifteen pounds in the year I spent with the Bruyns. It was well worth it. They fought the good fight for civil rights and social justice, not as energetic as they had, but they clearly understood the struggle continues.

A CONSPIRACY OF
GRANDMOTHERS

Nana was Big Mama's oldest sister; she knew everything and everybody, and no one held it against her. She was a sin eater and a joy giver, according to Big Mama. I never knew what that meant. Lying, however, was not a sin she was willing to eat. "One lie just make ways to break all de other rules of de Lord," she always said, according to my family. Because of Nana passing her beliefs to Big Mama, we grew up with a strict adherence to the truth; we grew up with no belief in childhood figures like Santa Claus or the Easter Bunny.

After being married to Grandpa Jack for fifty-three years, Nana left him to spend the rest of her days in peace. Then Grandpa Jack went on a drinking spree and was stuck by a car. She moved back home and took care of him until he died two years later.

The day after he was buried, the white man they sharecropped for came to the house and asked Nana who was gonna farm the land. She looked him in the eye without blinking and said, "My husband ain't cold in de grave, and you come here showin' no respect for him or de Lord. We farmed dat sorry land forty somethin' years, and I 'spect hit will keep bein' worked."

The white man left without saying a word. Later, we heard he spread the word around town: "Never cross dat crazy woman."

Nana birthed twelve living children. When she left Grandpa Jack, she planned to stay one month with each of the children. The story was repeated so many times I thought I was there, but I wasn't born until some twenty years later.

In my memory which is based on stories repeated to us, I did remember her staying with us. Before Nana arrived, Big Mama told us the story of Nana not knowing any of her folks. They were all sold to an evil slave owner. "Dat's why we lucky to have family and know where we come from." I think that's why Big Mama allowed her to take over our house when she stayed with them.

⟵— ┊ —➤

During the winter, steamed windowpanes were juicy, like fresh blackberries. The round table graced the middle of the worn plank floor. Buttery smells, sweet smells, and sometimes smoky smells draped the whole house and seemed to hold on to our small house like there would be no tomorrow. When the wind blew the wrong way, the smoke burned our eyes. If the smoke lingered long, we opened the windows and doors. Sometimes we went to our room, closed the door, and put a towel at the bottom of it after opening the windows.

I could imagine Nana arriving in a wagon pulled by a mule. We ran to get her belongings and welcome her. Nana took over the cooking. Big Mama spent more time working in her garden and doing laundry. And Little Mama was at the white woman's house more. My sisters and I tried to just stay out of the way.

Sometimes before a rain, the smell of red clay quietly slipped through the house. It eased all of our immediate pains. Then the rain came. The first sign would be the pitty-pat sound on our tin roof. Then we saw it on the windowpanes; it was like a member of the family. We never worked when thunder or lightning crackled through the house because Nana said, "When de Good Lord is carryin' on His work, we oughta show some respect."

Everybody in the community knew Nana. She was a giant of a woman with red-brown skin that was smooth as a summer peach. For Nana, visiting the sick was just as natural as wearing her everyday aprons. She often gave more respect to people when they were sick or dead than when they were alive and well. When Miss Cora Lee's left leg was amputated, Nana sat with her for three days. She bathed her and fanned the flies away. None of Miss Cora Lee's family would come near her; they said the smell made them sick. Even Dr. Faircloth wouldn't visit her without a mask.

Taking care of the sick was a major part of living in our community. Dr. Faircloth made house calls every other Thursday. In between times babies were born, accidents happened, children had measles, mumps, chicken pox, and colds, and old folks died. If a place was too far to walk, Nana hitched her mule and wagon. Nobody knew when she would return, but we never worried about her safety; a double-barreled shotgun and two boxes of shells were always at her side.

Folks always knew when she was planning a sick journey. She would put a kettle of water on the stove to boil for the scalding of the feathers on a chicken and wrung a chicken's neck without flinching. Afterward, she would throw the chicken in the backyard; my sisters and I clapped and danced to the rhythm of the dying chicken. When the chicken finally died, we put it in a tin tub and poured the boiling water on it. Another kettle was put on the stove; we plucked the chicken the first time, and Nana completed the task. She worked harder than anybody I knew and had the appetite to prove it. She could eat one-half a chicken in one sitting.

Her hazelnut brown eyes were mostly kind, but if you looked deep enough, you could see her pain too. She birthed fifteen children, but only twelve lived. She never spoke of her pain. We knew about all the dead babies from the Bible on the front room table.

When she returned from one of her sick trips, she was particularly demanding about our chores and schoolwork. I always wanted to know what happened to the sick person. She would look at me and say, "Dat's grown folks' business, Gal." Later at supper, she would say, "We saved one moe." She raised her hands to the heavens like she was going to shout. "We" meant that the Lord was the main caretaker, and she was only a helper.

Nana wasn't big on going to church. She only went to funerals. "De Good Lord can hear me anywhare," she said. "Just a bunch of showy hypocrites sittin' in de amen corner. Hit don't mean nothin' what other folks thank of you, hit's what you thank of you dat counts."

Big Mama told us that Nana always got her way. If she went to church and the pew she wanted to sit on was full, she would go anyway, looking straight at the pulpit. Folks always found room for her, even if they had to move to a different pew.

When my sisters and I did our homework, we sat around the big oak kitchen table covered with a scruffy oilcloth. Nana sat in the corner by the stove in a rocking chair that had been painted so many times, nobody remembered the original color. What I do recall was that it swayed a bit to the left.

Her hair was bushy. She didn't bother to do anything to it, only washed it in rainwater; she said it was a gift directly from the Lord. Her spit can was always nearby since she was never without a dip of Honey Bee snuff. While we studied, the only sound in the room was her cutting okra or shelling peas. Sometimes she hummed "Down by the River Side" or "Amazing Grace." Her voice was as strong as an Alabama pine tree.

I was the arithmetic whiz; my sister, Ruby, was the queen of English. Ida would color in her coloring book. Nana was always the boss. At the end of our two-hour study period, I was always first since I was the oldest. We stood in front of her with our right hand locked in the left one, with straight shoulders, so that we could stand tall like we were somebody.

She asked questions that seemed endless. They always began with, "What was 'pose to do? Did you know how to do hit?" If there were no schoolwork, we had to read a book. The questions then were, "Who write de book? Did hit teach you anythang 'bout bein' a better person?" One day she asked who we liked in the book and how come. Often she asked the same thing about our teachers. We always had to raise our hand to speak.

Ruby had big reddish curly braids, and it had taken two years for her front teeth to grow back. She thought she was smarter than anybody. Once and only once, she tried to vex Nana. The sugarberry switches in the corner helped her remember that it was easier to just do your schoolwork. When Nana wasn't around, she giggled a lot.

When Miss Lucille, our neighbor, had to work late cleaning the drugstore, her son, Rufus, waited at our house. He was always mad when he had to sit around the table and study, but those switches in the corner kept him from fretting too much. He would rather stay at Mr. Gus Eustey's; they had a new floor-model television, but Miss Agnes, Mr. Gus's wife, didn't want nothing to do with Roy because she thought his daddy was Mr. Peck, the white man who ran the store on Junction Road.

One night I heard Big Mama and Little Mama talking. I was supposed to be asleep. Big Mama said she was glad that Mr. Jake, Miss Lucille's husband, wasn't Rufus's daddy because his brother, Junior, was dumber than dirt and would probably grow up to be a drunk like his daddy. And he was the only child she had ever heard of who had to repeat the first grade three times. "Don't know what high horse Agnes ridin'. Dat TV done gone plum to her head. And if she's goin wit old man Peck, I just hope she gettin' a good cut of meat for her trouble."

We children weren't allowed to repeat such gossip. Little Mama said, "Hard to tell from lookin' at Roy. He was reddish brown, but dat didn't tell you much of nothin.'"

"Dat's just hit," Big Mama said. "None of dem look like much. But I know one thang, Lucille ain't never lied to me. But Agnes cheated me outta thirteen cents in 1941, and dat tell me all Auh need to know."

Often during supper, Big Mama and Little Mama would argue about who worked the hardest. Nobody ever won; it was always to be continued. Sometimes the insurance man interrupted our supper. Once when he did, Little Mama looked at Big Mama and said, "I know how to get rid of him." Big Mama nodded with approval.

Little Mama stepped into the front room to greet him. We continued to eat, but the kitchen was only a few feet from the front room, so we could easily hear them.

"Maudie, I want to tell you 'bout a new program we have," the white insurance man said.

"You ever been to New York City?" Little Mama asked.

"Can't say that I have."

"I took the Greyhound bus to NYC to visit Cousin Buford; he was in de horspital."

"That's nice, Maudie," the insurance man said before she could hardly finish.

"You know what's funny? Dat was ten years ago, but everybody up there called me Mrs. Baker."

"That's nice, Maudie, but I wanna explain our new program."

By the time Little Mama got to the part about coloreds and whites living side by side in NYC, the insurance man would be ready to leave.

When Little Mama got back to the supper table and looked in the direction of Big Mama, who nodded with approval, my sisters and I always giggled. But we stopped when Big Mama reminded us that having enough burial insurance was not a laughing matter. She said Mr. Pig Walker didn't have enough burial insurance. His family had to take up an offering at the funeral. Mr. Pig Walker was still turning over in his grave over the disgrace. We wanted to giggle when Big Mama got to that part.

Finally, Big Mama and Little Mama would pick up their argument about who worked harder. After supper, my sisters and I washed, dried, and put away the dishes, and then we went to bed. I never felt safer when my sisters and I washed dishes after supper, particularly when the insurance man disrupted us without saying, excuse me, or asking permission to come another time. Big Mama and Little Mama seemed so powerful. They didn't allow anybody to disrupt our lives, not even white folks.

CHAPTER 8

Drinking from the Cup of Equality

Dr. Mary Emma Bruce (1910–2010)

I never thought I'd see the day that this community would
have running water. We had been begging and praying for it as
long as I can remember.
—EMMA BRUCE

Hollins University thrived in the early days, founded in 1842 with a work-force of mainly enslaved people. This is a truth shared by many colleges and universities North and South in America. But what may distinguish Hollins is how slave quarters, "Oldfield" and later the Hollins community, grew up in the college's shadow. It is a difficult and complicated history, the relationship between a poor but dignified place called the Hollins community and the privileged women's college that never enrolled a Black student until the 1960s.

◄— —►

I was a graduate student at Hollins University in the late 1980s, and it was the voice of that past that spoke to me from the graveyard. The church and the rolling fields of the community will always be a snapshot in my memory. I would come to understand the ways of its people and grasp the poignancy of its history through a short but powerful force: Mary Emma Bruce.

155

Dr. Mary Emma Bruce.

When I first met Bruce, she was eighty-two years old and cleaning the house of three white families. Sundays and Tuesdays were her only days off. On Tuesdays, she visited the sick, shopped, and cleaned her own house. On Sundays, she sang in the choir at her church, served as Sunday school superintendent, was active in the women's missionary groups, and played the piano for the other choirs—the Hollins Community Baptist Church, which is just around the corner from her house.

"The church has no debt and a congregation of more than three hundred members," she told me proudly. That church is where I first approached her about talking to me about her historic community.

I was surprised and delighted when I walked up to her, introduced myself, and asked if she had any interest in meeting with me. She said, "yes" before I could complete the question. I had been trying to get some of the other African Americans working at the college to talk to me about the history of their community, but they hadn't been willing. They were friendly but guarded. Sometimes at the post office or in the dining hall, I could almost, but not quite, generate a conversation. They were quick to say, "I don't know nothin.'"

Their responses left me wondering what happens to the history of a people not accustomed to writing things down. Does this make oral history fiction? It's usually futile to search for letters, wills, and diaries of the poor and unlettered. Birth and death certificates, tax receipts, and other official records offer glimpses but do not show their everyday life. Because of that, Bruce was a most precious resource. Her stories are grounded in the ordinary occurrences of the world between Hollins University and the Hollins community that grew out of slavery and had been serving the college since 1842.

Our first visit was on a Tuesday at her house in the Hollins community on Old Mill Drive. She greeted me warmly, declaring I could have all the time I needed. We sat near each other in her airy living room.

"I looked in on the sick this morning, and I can clean this house anytime or not." She threw her head back with a laugh and clapped her lap with her hands, and glasses fell on her nose.

Outside her window, it's easy to see the road that divides the community that stands on thirteen and a half acres of land between the college and Tinker Mountain. The main road through the community is Reservoir Road. On both sides stand derelict houses and naked chimneys, a reminder of what the community once looked like. Other homes are like Bruce's, ranch-style brick with no front porches. The Hollins community stands on the border of Botetourt and Roanoke Counties, about equally divided between the two. Bruce and others believed that's why it took so long to get running water; the officials of both counties fought about who should pay for it.

In 1989, public improvements put in a two-hundred-thousand-gallon water storage tank, water and sewer, and five fire hydrants. A local reporter quoted a resident saying, "I never thought I'd live to see this day come. You look forward to it, pray and pray for years . . . it's a dream come true."

Bruce (she goes by Emma and doesn't use Mary, her first name) is a petite paper-sack brown woman with sparkling eyes, standing four feet ten inches and weighing less than one hundred pounds. But she could fill up a room with her tough but warm personality. She demanded and earned respect from everyone who knew her.

Other than talking about her faith, which was everything to her, she loved talking to me about the history of "Oldfield," the former name of her community. Black settlements like this were common to plantations and places outside of the South. There was a need to house a number of enslaved people and later servants to provide service to students and staff. Other names for such settlements were: the quarter, the bottom, the narrows, and others. When the enslaved people first came, they lived at the college in the rooms with the students. But later, they used to have little houses down where the horse stables are now, right down the hill from there, about four houses. Bruce continued in a soft, clear voice. "That's where they first lived. That's what I was told." Bruce pointed to the area.

All refer to the usually poor lands allotted for housing African Americans. Today, the residents of "Oldfield" call themselves the Hollins community to rid themselves of a name that grew out of slavery. But slavery casts a long shadow, defining relationships today.

More than one hundred and fifty years after the founding of Hollins, many from the community are still employees there, performing the same tasks as their ancestors did—cooking, cleaning, moving, planting, and weeding—serving the college rather than being served by it. Other employment was limited. Many of its young, educated people reject the old relationship with the college and, in a way, their own history.

The key to understanding many histories lay with their dead, in addition to attending church and spending time with some of the employees in the dining hall. At the church, I explored the cemetery, established in 1882, which is right across from the Hollins First Baptist Church. I was nervous when I first set foot in the cemetery. I had not yet interviewed Bruce, and most of the community refused to talk to me beyond polite greetings.

But once there, I lost myself in the moment. I felt like Alice Walker must have when she was searching for the grave of Zora Neale Hurston—except I didn't know what I was looking for. But the cemetery told me volumes. The names Boldens, Bruces, Hunts, Johnsons, Langhornes, Meades, Mortons, Phillpots, and Scotts spoke to me. These last names carved on the headstones are the same as many of the early students who were enrolled at the college. Some had no headstones; rocks were placed on those graves. Of all the places in the world, I knew that the Hollins community was where I was meant to be. And when I stopped and listened very carefully, I could hear them urging me on. I received that experience as a "calling" to move forward with my research. I stopped being so concerned with what I could not find and discovered satisfaction in knowing that whatever I found would be valuable.

Families had lived, worked, and died in this community. They were young, old, war veterans, mothers, fathers, and children. Thinking about the name and dates, I came to appreciate that communities, no less than individuals, need to know their origins—their heritage in order to gain self-respect. We are as much a product of our communities as we are of our parents.

When I got home after my graveyard foray, my telephone was ringing. Reverend Calloway was on the line. He said he heard I had been in the cemetery. And he knew who I was; then he told me I needed permission to go into the cemetery. With an apology, I told him I meant no disrespect to the church or community. I asked him how to go about getting permission. And I saw that what I was trying to do was urgent and important—shedding light on the shadows of slavery. He said the members of the church would probably not be interested in talking to me. In all of my life, I'd never heard of anybody having to get permission to enter a cemetery.

Hurt and surprised that Reverend Calloway felt this way, I began to realize what a difficult task I had ahead of me. But I remembered the voices in the cemetery, and I knew they wanted me—counted on me—to push forward.

Bruce had warned me that it might be hard to get folks to talk to me. Her spoken words and the spirit of her voice created one of the strongest bonds I had ever experienced. I knew that I would forever be transformed because of her. She lit a spiritual light for me that I hope will never stop burning. Her voice was tied up with the creation of an authentic public and political voice that she didn't even realize. But what she did understand so well were her duties and responsibilities as a Christian and a citizen.

"Child, these folks pretend they're scared of losing their jobs. You see, a long time ago, before we had cars, malls, and such, this was a special place to work. Nobody in the community ever went hungry, no beating or any of those horrors." Bruce shifted on her sofa. She had grown comfortable with my visits. "We had our own church, even had a little school for a while. But now folks can go to other places to work or wherever they want."

I didn't see what that has to do with their history.

"Let me tell you something, Child; they get suspicious when folks start asking them questions." She sat back in her recliner and pushed her glasses up. "They're used to being told what to do, not what they think."

"I thought they'd see me as a benefactor rather than a troublemaker," I admitted. "How naïve I was?"

"But don't you worry; some will talk. Our history is all that we have."

Talking to Bruce always offered me courage. She was the community historian, an explainer, and the spiritually conscious. But I found myself lost in thought about the direction of my project. What would I do with the information I had gathered? Would anyone else from the community ever talk to me? I believed the college reflected the city of Roanoke. Even though the city had a long-termed African American mayor, there never seemed to have been a civil right movement in the city. Middle-class Blacks had their churches and schools and the neighborhood of Gainesboro until the government robbed them of it when Interstate 81 cut through the neighborhood and left many African Americans with only enough resources to move to the projects. Most of the homes had been in families for generations.

I thought I would remember the spring of 1992 because it marked my fortieth birthday. But instead, I, along with most of the world, remember Rodney King's crying voice raising the question, "Can't we all just get along?" We watched the videotaped recording of him being beaten inhumanely by members of the Los Angeles police department. The incident, fueled by other racial unrest, was the beginning of rioting in cities all over America. Black folks were scared, especially if they had Black boys like me.

By now, I had known Bruce for more than a year. I knew her schedule and was generally able to track her down. She also knew which days I taught at Virginia Tech and my tennis schedule. We both liked it that I didn't call for appointments anymore; I just dropped in like folks do in the country. If she was home, she was; and if she wasn't, she wasn't. I didn't feel like I was interviewing her, but we were having conversations and getting to know each other.

One time we met at my house in the Old Southwest section of Roanoke. I had just planted pansies in the huge urns on the steps and hung Boston ferns from the ceiling of the front porch. I thought she would enjoy the change since she had never seen where I lived. From my front porch, the steel star on top of the Mill Mountain, representing Roanoke as a progressive "star city," could be seen easily. We sipped lemon tea with mint from my yard, and we talked while watching the star on the mountain.

Bruce referred to Roanoke as another place separate from the college. She was born in Hollins and went to the little school in the community. She remembered her elementary school teacher, Mr. Samuel Carrington, who taught all grades up to seventh. "Believe me, you, we worked hard," she recalled. "When he gave us a recess, he said, 'get your playing done outside; no playing in this classroom.' And he meant it."

Going to high school meant she had to leave the community and travel to Roanoke because there was no high school in the community. Bruce and a friend took a bus to Lucy Addison High School, which today is a middle school, but still has the name Lucy Addison, a teacher and principal, born enslaved in 1861 in Upperville, Virginia. After Emancipation, her people bought land and sent her to school at the Philadelphia Institute for Colored Youths. She spent her life educating African Americans. She's known as the Patron Saint of Education by Blacks in Virginia. Bruce and her friend eventually had to board in Roanoke for two years with a woman named Ruth Hughes in order to finish school. The school had opened in 1928; Bruce was a graduate of the class of 1931. She felt thankful for the opportunity.

After she graduated, Hollins asked her to come to work. She joined her Black community members and worked with one of the elder maids, Aunt Bill Hunt. Then she went to Roanoke and worked for Dr. A. Willis Robinson. Later, the head of the chemistry department at the college, Dr. Harriet Fillinger asked for her; she knew of her work with Aunt Bill. She started to work in the chemistry department in 1934.

"Dr. Fillinger and I talked about school for me. I wanted to major in chemistry, but Papa had an accident at the quarry, and there was no money for me to go to college," she said without regret. "Soon after that, I started to study freshman chemistry on my own with Dr. Fillinger. I learned which chemicals caused which reaction."

After about two years, Bruce was in charge of all the chemicals in the department. She gave out all of the chemicals and prepared all of the experiments for the freshman class. She made up all of the solutions and tested them before they were put back in the lab for the students to use. She worked there until four in the afternoon. "I never had one accident," she smiled.

Then Dr. Sitler asked her to come and work in the biology department after she finished working in the chemistry department. She took care of the little animals when they mounted birds and killed snakes by drowning them. "I was there to assist. I worked there until 1976, when I retired. After that, I started to work for different faculty and staff members in their homes."

"Sounds like the chemistry lab was your favorite." I judged from the bright look on her face.

"Sure was. It was a different world. I was in charge rather than being told what to do for a change. I even took the exams along with the regular students," she nodded.

"Did the professor know?"

"Dr. Fillinger knew; it was her idea. But the students didn't know." She covered her mouth with a lace handkerchief and laughed. "Dr. Fillinger probably could've gotten in trouble by teaching me."

"Well, how did you do?"

"Child, I made 100 all the time. Except that time I had to stay up all night with a drunk student. I got 98."

When she left the chemistry department, she was sixty-five years old. They asked her to consider staying on for another year. She chose not to. Dr. Fillinger and others she'd worked for had passed.

"Young people came in every year, somebody new and something different, just didn't sit right with me, so I said, 'Emma's getting old, and she better get on out from here while the going is good.' So I retired." She often referred to herself in the third person.

"Of course, they said they were lost without Emma; and asked again if I would consider coming back, but I didn't go," she said, waving her hand at the pansies. "I was established with other friends, and I was enjoying what I was doing. I still enjoy my work because every day I see somebody new. Don't have to be bothered with the same person." She frowned like she had tasted something bitter.

She remembered one of the best parts of working in the chemistry lab; she and the students had a secret flower garden on the landing onto the attic, and they used to grow tomatoes up there too. That's when she first started growing African Violets. She's known around Roanoke for growing prize-winning African Violets; they graced every room in her house. "We sure had some fun. That professor left early on Fridays and came late on Mondays.

That would be our chance. We ran up to the top of the roof. Good-tasting tomatoes. Wish I had one now."

"Why did the professor leave so much?"

"I'm not in the habit of asking white folks about their business. Since he was a man, I didn't have a relationship with him like I had with the women professors."

"How much money did you earn?"

"Let's see; what did I get in 1934? I know I had some extra work since Miss Moore paid me fifteen cents per hour. Back then, they paid me six dollars a week when I first started. Each year they would give me a little raise, but basically, I was getting six dollars a week, five days a week. I worked on Saturday mornings too. With the six dollars, I was also getting three meals a day if I wanted. I worked about fifteen years before they put me on regular payroll; my salary went up some too."

"Do you receive any retirement benefits?"

"Not from the college. Faculty children can go to the college for free. That offer was recently extended to us, so I've been told. I tried to get my granddaughter to look into it. But she just wanted to get away from Hollins." Bruce has one son, Sonny, who is the father of her grandchildren, George and Cynthia. Later she was the great-grandmother of Taylor, Cynthia's daughter.

"Does the community have a relationship with the college today?"

"Not like we used to. They don't come to our church. There was a time when we could always depend on those students in our church, but not now. Since they all have cars and everybody seem to be so busy. And they're just not aware of us, the connection the community had with the college. No community, no college. Faculty used to come around too, especially if someone died or got married. Students used to tutor children in the community. We knew we could count on the college to be there."

"Can you remember when the relationship started to change?"

"Well, let me see: I haven't worked over there since 1976, but it seems to me when the civil rights movement started, the college dropped us like hot potatoes." She laughed. "So hot they would burn our hands. I saw it as an opportunity for them to take some leadership or at least do better than they used to do. I meant the running water situation should've been a college issue too. It shouldn't have taken over a hundred years to get a water system. Lord, have mercy." She poured herself another cup of tea.

"Let me know if you're getting tired."

"Child, I'm enjoying myself too much." She pushed back in the rocking chair. "I'd like to just sit here a while. It's so peaceful, rocking and hearing the world."

"But you're busy doing for everybody. Just think, if more folks were like you, the world would be so much better off."

"Well, I do what I can."

Bruce and I sat on my front porch and sipped lemon tea, witnessing the late afternoon fading into the early evening. There was no need to talk as we listened to the end of the day at the top of the hill, folks coming home from work, and early spring critters humming; even the red cardinals were singing.

On a bright Sunday morning in November 1992, I attended church services at Hollins First Baptist to honor the life and work of fifty-eight-year-old Audre Lorde. Her death had been announced on NPR. She had finally lost her fourteen-year battle with breast cancer. I knew her poetry well; it exhibits a strong sense of responsibility to the truth with the collective history and experiences of women all over the world.

The Black church has always been at the helm of African American communities, especially in the South, whether the occasion is political, economic, social, or, of course, religious. The Hollins community is no different. I often raised the question to myself: How can Black folks be such dedicated Christians after being enslaved and the continuation of inhuman treatment of Black folks throughout history? Bruce taught me that in God, there is strength and the source for patience to wait for freedom. But she also believed that one had to work while waiting. That was a compromise I could live with.

I wanted to talk to Bruce about her role in the church over the years. I knew that she had served as church secretary for, as she put it, "more years than I can remember." She said she wasn't officially an officer of the church, but for a long time, she was the only one who could read and write in the church, so she performed the duties of church secretary.

"Well, I was secretary for a long time . . . but since I am a woman, I was officially not allowed to be a member of the board of directors."

"How did that make you feel?" I asked.

She threw her head back, took off her glasses, and looked toward the iron star. "I see it like this: I was working for the Lord, not silly people. Don't care about some title that folks made up to make themselves feel good," she said. She did whatever the church needed, cleaning, cooking, or working with the young people. "And since I was doing the work, and everyone knew I was doing the work, I was the church secretary."

"Child, the Lord keeps me." She clapped her lap and laughed.

She reminded me of Mrs. Willie Mae Ford, the mother of gospel music, who traveled the country singing and preaching in a vibrant and intense style, often in opposition to established church practices. "When I would go to their meetings, the preacher would say, 'you can sit down there; you don't need to come up here. Don't get in my program. You're a woman; don't you realize that.' No respect at all. Well, it didn't make no difference to me. I turn around in my pew and sang to that audience. Next thing I know, 'Come on up here, get up and let all of them see you.' See, God don't wants no filter on His work. To be a gospel singer, you got to be a gospel person," she said.

I also thought of the irrepressible Dorothy Height, the president of the National Council of Negro Women since 1957. Mary McLeod Bethune founded the organization in 1935. Height said, "Black women are the backbone of every institution, but oftentimes they are not recognized, even in the civil rights movement." There was a myth across the South that only two free people were the white male and Black woman; and that Black women had better chances at jobs. "Well, that was because they scrubbed floors," Dorothy Height pointed out.

For our next meeting, I decided to ask Bruce out to lunch. We dined at the French Asian Café, a cozy restaurant in downtown Roanoke. "I am just tickled pink to be eating out." She spread her cloth napkin across her lap.

Nelson Mandela had just been released from prison after twenty-seven years. A feeling of hope energized the air. It was indeed an exciting time in America and, of course, South Africa and probably other parts of the world. The world had changed. Friends had telephoned me from everywhere to talk about Mandela. We wanted to remember the moment forever. The sun shined brighter on that February day.

"I never thought I'd live to see the day that Nelson Mandela would be a free man," I said.

"What do you mean, Child? I'm the one who should be saying that."

I smiled and nodded my head in agreement. After the waiter took our orders, I turned to Bruce. "I want to know more about your jobs in the labs."

"Primarily, I was in charge of maintaining and setting up equipment and chemicals for science labs. All of us Blacks were assigned to other work as needed. I was expected to work in the dormitories and other departments during school vacation and while other workers were doing other jobs."

"Would you have liked to been a scientist?"

"I don't know what scientists do exactly, but I sure loved being in that lab figuring out stuff in those glass containers. I loved how the containers sparkled after I cleaned them."

The waiter appeared with our food. She said a short grace before we ate. "I'm starved." I tore into my salad. This is the best tomato. After we finished our meal, Bruce suggested that we have a glass of sherry and toast to Nelson Mandela and may freedom ring all over the world.

My research into the life of Black people and Hollins took me to the Fishburn Library at the college. Deep in the basement was a box marked "Servants." I wasn't allowed to check out the yellow loose-leaf pages (financial ledgers, for the most part), but I was able to read them uninterrupted, which I did over and over. And I took notes. The librarian apologized for the state of the box, explaining that many important documents had been destroyed or misplaced due to the 1985 flood. Because of that, she allowed me to photocopy them.

But the highlight of that day was when I examined back issues of the *Spinster*, the college's yearbook. In the 1903 issues, I found photographs of some of the earliest members of the community. But the most stirring photographs were of the women walking with baskets of laundry on their heads. They marched toward the spring, south of the college, to wash the clothes of the students, faculty, and staff members too. Chills ran all over me. Those women could've been from anywhere in the world—Africa, Brazil, The Caribbean, India, or Turkey—but they were from the foothills of the Blue Ridge Mountains, carrying on a tradition that was so old they probably didn't recognize its origin. I felt claustrophobic as I choked in that hot musty basement of the library. "Breathe. Breathe," I told myself as I ran out and left the books on the table.

The DuPont Chapel, three buildings over, embraced me with quietness and serenity. I didn't know why I ran into the chapel since I had never set foot in there before. As the atmosphere of the chapel soothed me, I realized for the first time I had seen members of the community as enslaved people. Of course, I knew that intellectually, but now it was emotional, coming to grips with the fact that slavery had existed right upon the grounds I walked, studied, and played tennis, was quite a challenge.

From Bruce, I learned that after washing the clothes in the spring that surrounds the college, they hung them on a wire fence at their homes. When the clothes dried, they were carried to their homes, ironed with heavy starch, and then returned to their owners.

I returned to the library an hour later and photocopied what information I could. The image of the women carrying clothes on their heads made me wonder if they were aware of the timelessness of the custom and its antiquity. Another photograph showed a picture of a little girl with happy and proud eyes. I tried to calculate her age; I wondered what she would think today if she knew I was trying to piece together her life and write about her world. Would it matter to her? I wanted to know more about her than what she did. That part of her life was clear. I wanted to know her unvoiced thoughts and dreams. What did she like to eat? Where did she get her dress-up clothes for the "Thursday Afternoon" event to collect dirty clothes? How did the white women treat her? Who were her people? Was she told stories of life before the college? Did she piece quilts like my Little Mama and Big Mama and all the women in my family before them? Did she can fruits and vegetables in the summer? Did she love flowers like me?

Later at home, I couldn't stop thinking about the people of the community; and I knew I never would. The women in the photographs were real to me. I thought of my own mother, Little Mama, who for fifty years labored for a white family seven days a week, with the exception of the fourth Sunday of every month, when she attended church. I never understood why my sisters and I couldn't have our mother with us on Christmases and Thanksgivings. I often prayed for Little Mama to be home with us, even for the weekends. That never happened. I allowed myself to be angry—angry for all of the Black women who had and still toil in houses and institutions of white folks for very little money and oftentimes less respect.

But I also remembered Bruce's response when I first asked her how it made her feel that she had worked at the college for forty-six years and still had to work three jobs at age eighty-two. "Child, I thank the Good Lord every day that I have my health and strength," she had answered. "How else can I be but thankful?"

⊷ ⊶

A year later, my graduate program was nearing an end, and I needed employment, which possibly meant moving from Roanoke. I wasn't ready to leave Bruce or the Hollins community, or my project.

I didn't know where to look for more information. After Reverend Calloway's warning about the cemetery, I felt awkward about attending church. But every time I said out loud, "early students came to college with enslaved people." I found it unbelievable and probably always will.

On the afternoon of July 20, 1990, Supreme Court Justice William Brennan retired. On that same day, the niece of Mr. Zachariah Hunt Jr. telephoned to tell me that Mr. Hunt had died; they knew about my work. Before he died, he had granted me permission to look through a box of old photographs and other materials that might be helpful to my research. I could keep all I wanted. I offered the family my deepest sympathy. We agreed to meet the following Saturday. I called Bruce; she was willing and delighted to join us.

Mr. Zach Hunt was the grandson of Mr. Lewis Hunt, who worked at the college for fifty years. Mr. Lewis Hunt gave himself the title "dean of servants." For a family to continue in a line of service work is not progress. In fact, in this case, I believe its regression. When Mr. Lewis Hunt was the headwaiter for the colored kitchen employees, he held a very formal position with respect and dignity. He wore a suit and tie to work every day, and he supervised. The college took pride in telling the story when an African dignitary was a guest at the college in the 1940s. Hunt refused to serve him since he was "black as tar." He told the African dignitary that he was the head Negro in Virginia. I was always shocked that white folks took such pride in telling that story.

The elimination of waiters and waitresses at meals is of particular interest in its correlation to the retirement and death of Mr. Lewis Hunt, Mr. Clem Bolden, Mr. Caesar Morton, and others who waited tables for the college. During the 1955–56 school year, shortly after he retired and right before he died in 1954, waiters were no longer hired for breakfasts and on weekends. So by the time Mr. Hunt's children and grandchildren began their tenure of employment at the college, the world and even Hollins had changed. Most colleges and universities had long switched to cafeteria-style dining. None were serving students with waiters dressed in formal style anymore. So Hunt's heirs had no opportunity besides being food-service employees and earning minimum wage salaries. Many of them had to take on additional jobs in Roanoke to keep from being destitute. The college offered members of the community none of the educational opportunities or benefits that it offered the white employees.

⸺ ⸺

We arrived at 9:00 a.m. on a rainy spring morning. Redbuds bloomed all over of mountains of Virginia. Hunt's house didn't look like other houses in the community. Most of the other houses looked like Bruce's ranch-style brick. In fact, Little Mama's house in Alabama looks almost the same. The front porch of Hunt's Victorian-style house was sagging and in need of some basic repairs. But it was clear that it had once been an elegant house. We almost thought no one was home.

But soon, Ms. Hunt came to the door. After a quiet greeting, she invited us in. The inside of the house looked like Bruce's house, with the exception of no flowers gracing the mantels or tables or photographs hanging on the walls. The furniture was covered with sheets. A glass-door bureau took up most of the space in the dining room, and a covered table filled the rest of the room. We sat around the dining room table. Ms. Hunt was maybe forty, soft-spoken, and looked at the floor when she spoke.

"Zack will be missed; that's for sure," Bruce said.

"Here's the box." Ms. Hunt offered me an old brown taped-up cardboard box that looked something like a homemade hatbox that Big Mama may have had.

"Thank you. Thank you very much," I said nervously. "I will take good care of them and will be happy to return it if you like."

"You can keep it," she said. "He wanted you to have it."

"Did he say anything else?" Bruce asked.

"Not that I know of," Ms. Hunt answered.

I raised the lid of the box; the swirling dust made us cough. It was the first and only time the young woman smiled.

"It sure was good for old Zach to leave something of his history," Bruce said. We had no idea what was in the box.

In spite of Bruce being small and fragile looking, she put on her large eyeglasses. But to me, that day, she was big as a mountain. I don't know if I would have been able to get through the meeting without her. It wasn't anything she did in particular; her presence alone offered me courage. Everyone in the community trusted and respected her. She could be counted on as the person who would always help. She can "never sit home for too long on the days that don't belong to the Lord." For herself, she grew African Violet and played the piano.

Back at Bruce's house, I was finally able to relax. We opened the box. Dust circulated in the air, making us cough again. The box contained old photographs of Hunt and his family, a newsletter from the college, showing a surprise birthday party honoring his fiftieth birthday. One picture showed him blowing out the calendars. He was dressed in a suit in every picture. We kept saying "wow" as we fanned dust.

I finally flopped down on a big sofa chair by the window full of pink and purple African Violets in her living room. On the table to the right of me sat her good wig that was set in curlers so it would be ready for church on Sunday. Photographs of her great grand and grandchildren and others graced the top of the brown piano. On another wall was her certificate for winning Hollins College's Algernon Sydney Award. She was the first African American to have received the award and probably the first staff person. She received the award in 1976, the year she retired after forty-six years of working at the college. The award states, "He reached out both hands in constant helpfulness to this fellow man." The award usually goes to a professor or benevolent alumna. After we had gone through the box from Ms. Hunt, Bruce fussed around in her kitchen for coffee and a "little something to nibble on." Like my grandmother, Big Mama, I wasn't allowed anywhere near the kitchen. She appeared with coffee and sweet potato pie. The pie melted in my mouth.

"It's sad, isn't it? Our young people have no interest in our history," she said, picking at her pie. "They just don't understand how hard we've all worked and what we had to put up with."

"I guess I see it in my students. All they want to do is shop and socialize, especially the females," I agreed. "Not all of them, but too many of them."

"That's sho 'nuff the truth. Child, I remember when we were coming up, we used to go down to the college to shop. We didn't know what it was to go to Roanoke to buy clothes. The students sold their clothes to us to get extra money. Someone would say, 'I want a dress for Emma or a coat for Sister.' The next thing you know, you'll have it. My first pair of I. Miller shoes was from one of the students. And when I got a pair of blue suede shoes, you couldn't tell Emma nothing." Bruce slapped her hands and laughed.

"I bet they were so pretty."

"Pretty? They were beautiful! To think those girls used to sell some of the most expensive clothes. We used to love to see the girls come after summer. We bought coats, hats, just like at the store, but better. Good quality and didn't have to even think about if we could try on the clothes. Whatever we wanted." Bruce laughed.

"We would go through their trash and take out all of their paper, pencils, and ink. That would get us through the winter because Mama would take charge of it when we got home and gave it to us as she thought we needed it. We all missed that when we had to go to Roanoke and shop at Cato's, Phelps, and all of those kind of stores. No quality."

The records did not tell me much about the African Americans who were associated with the college. For example, in neglecting to mention the servants of the college, they did not record the fact that generations of Black folks had been a major force in the history of the college. Nor did they record the full names of the women who served the college despite the fact that it's a women's college.

It was the financial ledgers that taught me the most. Black women who worked at the college as enslaved and later servants were defined by the tasks they performed, unfairly sentencing them to anonymity in terms of written history. But why were only three women listed as paid employees in the 1861–67 ledgers and twenty-three in the next ledger? After the Civil War, women tended not to leave the workplaces of the enslaved as rapidly as men did, making it probable that some enslaved women, after Emancipation, gradually assimilated into college employment as servants after 1865. Chances were the twenty-three women listed as employees after the war had already performed those same tasks—as the enslaved had before.

"Other than a retirement plan and better employment benefits for everyone, what do you think the college owes you?" I asked. This was our last interview.

"Education! Education! That's what Hollins College is, an educational institution. It's what it's all about. If it was a grocery store, then it would be food owed to us. We have earned that right, not just for ourselves but all of the generations that will ever be from the Hollins community. To this day, only one child from our community has graduated from the college, one child every one hundred years. Well, that ain't gonna cut it." She shook her head. "No. No."

After I moved to West Virginia in 1993 to teach at West Virginian University, I talked to Bruce as much as I did my own mother. Sometimes I had to track her down.

"Child, Emma has places to go," she'd say. She always made me feel like my phone call was the best thing that had happened to her. I am sure all who called her felt the same. In later years, she didn't always recognize me; but she would say, "Sweetie, I am just not so steady today." I was never disappointed, I would ask her about her African Violets, and her voice would change, and she would begin to talk.

Whatever Bruce did, she believed in doing it well, whether it was working in the church, visiting sick, cleaning a house, or drowning a snake. I remember calling her and telling her I was coming to Roanoke and wanted to see her. "Some of us have to work, you know." I offered to go to work with her. I just wanted to be with her.

We arrived at the to-be-cleaned condo. I was ready to work, rolled up my sleeves, and asked where to start. "Relax, I have to see if Janie fixed my favorite chicken salad with grapes." She had; we ate.

"What's next?" I asked.

"We have to watch *The Young and the Restless*. Janie doesn't know how to work the VCR." She picked up the remote for the television. "I will call her tonight and give her the updates. I get $5 extra." She smiled.

This was unlike any cleaning I knew about; I decided not to ask any more questions. But I decided to dust in the high places since Bruce was so petite. She just looked at me and pointed to the high places. "I can't even reach up there."

When we finished, she looked around. "Janie is not going to know what hit this place; it's so clean. If she had any sense, she'd hire a cleaning service and take me to lunch."

THE PROBLEM WITH EVOLVING

"I have some news I need to share with you." I hate it when friends start a sentence with I need . . . My oldest friend Sarah says over the phone. We met more than forty years ago when our sons were the new kids in the third or fourth grade at the Fernbank School in Atlanta. Sarah says third grade; I say fourth. We volunteered to help with the Halloween party that year.

"Is everybody okay?" I try to prepare myself for bad news.

"Oh yeah."

"In that case, I can take anything," I say with confidence.

"We sold the Park Avenue place."

"You did what?" I gasp.

"We knew this was going to be hard on you."

"You damn right, this is hard on me. This is worse than somebody dying. I've had a Park Avenue address since forever. You just can't take it away."

Both of us had left Atlanta more than thirty-five years ago. I was awarded a fellowship to graduate school, and Sarah moved to Rye, New York; her husband, Charles, had accepted a new position at Pace University. In Atlanta, he had been the dean of the business school at Emory University. A few years after they moved to Rye, he died from a massive heart attack at age fifty-six while he and Charley, their son, were scuba diving in the Caribbean.

By then, our children were college-aged; our friendship not only continued but grew stronger. Sarah visited me in Roanoke, and I visited her in Rye and later at *our* 94th and Park Avenue place. Of course, it wasn't *our* place, but I knew I was welcome whether Sarah was there or not. She was the big sister I never had, and I was the little sister she needed.

"I need that address. If you've forgotten, I live in West Virginia, meaning I need as much cache and glamour I can get. Some of my best pickups have been because of that Park Avenue address." We laugh.

"We didn't want to tell you until it actually sold."

"Thanks for being so thoughtful."

"And you know, life hasn't been the same since the Towers . . . Well, you know."

"I know; I feel the difference too. Even when I try to forget, but when I look up and don't see them, it's like the sun or the moon not being there."

"It'll never be the same. And Saul is getting older. Life will be easier in Atlanta. Even though we'll be living in our cars."

"I have no idea when I'll visit the city again with Adam in Boston and you in Atlanta. I will miss you NYC, especially *our* Park Avenue."

"I know, me too, but Maggie asked me to come. You know with the baby and all. I never thought I'd be moving back, but we're pretty excited. And Saul has never lived in a house." Saul is a Holocaust survivor from Romania, but came to the US via Australia.

"You should be excited. I am, too, and a big congratulation to Maggie and John. They're going to be great parents. Well, here we are, entering a new era."

"And, of course, you and Adam will come and visit." Sarah paused in between tears.

"Of course. What neighborhood are you moving to in Atlanta?"

"Northwest. You're such a snob."

"Tell Maggie she owes me her second child." Maggie was the only girl born between her brother, Charley, and her stand-in brother, my son Adam. With her athletic abilities and bubbling personality, she hardly needed two brothers to look after her. She probably could've protected them. But we all enjoyed the gesture.

One year after Charles's massive heart attack in the Caribbean, Allen, my partner of five years, was struck with stomach cancer; he died two months after his diagnosis at age fifty-three. He had been promoted to top-level management at his company's headquarters in Minneapolis. My son and I were to join him as soon as the school year ended to look for a house. Allen had completed his Executive MBA, and we would finally get married and settle in as a family. But instead, the universe insisted that I needed a new battle. At least I didn't have to fight it alone.

The next spring Sarah and I went on a well-needed holiday, Club Med, to Guadeloupe. I played tennis and rode horses on the beach. Sarah tanned and smoked cigarettes on the beach. We ate lunch and dinner together. Sometimes we slept, but mostly we wept and tried not to talk about anything that wasn't alive.

Two years later, Sarah met Saul. I was thrilled, but, of course, like any good girlfriend, I had to check him out for myself. He passed all of my checks for Sarah: smart (Sarah's men always had to be smart), charming, and funny. But mostly, he was attentive to my best friend. They seemed to have art, culture, and politics in common.

But most surprisingly, Sarah had not only claimed, but she had embraced her Judaism. When we first met in Atlanta, she told me she was German. I didn't care what she called herself. But I did find it odd that we never conversed about her conversion. I felt like I was seeing my oldest friend for the first time in two years. And she had remarried and had another baby without telling me? How could this be? But she had never mentioned it to me during the times we talked over the phone, which was often. I thought we were talking about everything. Nothing about Sarah was the same. Her hair was dyed very blonde, she wore tight designer clothes. We used to shop for clothes at vintages places. She loved talking about her newly found political party. We had served on the boards like Planned Parenthood, Violence Against Women, and feminist organizations. She didn't even sound the same. How could this have happened?

Our lives had changed. We had grown up, reared children, and buried men, but we were still evolving, evolving to be the best of ourselves, be that a newly found culture or becoming a writer. I was not upset about the conversion but stunned and shocked that I didn't know anything about it.

—◆ ◆—

I was driving to Sarah's on September 11, 2001. My son was going to drive with me to Boston over the weekend and take the train back to the city. I was so excited; at Brandeis University, I'll be working on a book about my experience as an African American Fulbright scholar in Germany. I felt very Jewish, at least "honorary."

I had never driven from Pittsburgh to NYC. The night before, I had lectured at Carnegie Mellon University. The next morning, I left for the city. My sleepy friends gave me the best sendoff they could. They had offered to fly me back for the lecture. I said no. I wanted to tie up all loose ends. "Be sure to call us when you arrive," they all said.

"I have my first cellphone, and I think I know how to use it." We laughed. It was a glorious Tuesday morning; the sky was clear as glass and blue as the Atlantic. I felt like the luckiest person alive. I was listening to Sam Cooke singing "A Change is Gonna Come."

After about two hours on the highway, my phone rang. Everybody was calling me, wanting to know where I was. The first call came from Melbourne. "Where are you?" Australian friend asked.

"What do you mean?" I am on open highway driving toward freedom and listening to Aretha Franklin sing "Driving on the Freeway." I laughed. "Freedom."

"You need to turn on the radio." She faded. I felt connected to the world, zipping along the expressway, watching the soft colors of early fall embrace the trees. I would be in New England for the autumn season. What could be better? I turned on the radio and found a sketchy NPR station. It seemed as though a small plane had landed on one of the towers in the city. "What a bad pilot," I said out loud. The radio station died into static. The phone rang again. "Hi, Ethel, it's Ken (one of my son's friends). Adam wanted me to call to let you know he's fine." Thank you, Ken. Before I could ask him about his parents, he said he was in a hurry and had to go. What a nice young man, I thought.

Australian friend called again. "Do you understand what is happening?"

"I heard about the small plane landing on one of the Towers."

"Ethel, listen to me, the United States is under attack; two planes have flown into the Towers. Thousands of folks are dead. Both Towers are gone."

"What?" My hands shook while searching for a radio station. My heartbeat fast. *Stay focused on the highway.* "Hello." We were lost again.

The next phone call was from my Morgantown friend. "God, Ethel, it's horrible. Everybody has been calling about you. They knew you were headed to NYC."

"I am so scared, Jane."

"Of course, you are. Have you thought about turning around?" I lost her before I could answer.

NPR finally came in clear over the electric skies of the Pennsylvania Turnpike. Another plane had gone down near Pittsburgh. *Where was I to turn around to? Planes were down in front of me and behind me. Am I going to die alone on this damn highway? Was the world coming to an end?*

Australian friend called again. "Finally, you've caught up with the news. Folks here have been up all night following this story. Everybody is walking around like zombies. Ethel, the world is with the United States."

"What am I supposed to do?"

"Don't turn around; if you do, you won't go back. All we can do is pray."

"I don't know what to do!" I cried.

"Get off of the expressway and get yourself together. You can do this. Recharge your phone and buy some ginger ale to help with the throwing up. Eat some saltines. And whatever you do, keep driving until you can't drive any farther. And oh, don't forget to gas up." We laughed for the first time. Australian friend and met when our sons were roommates in boarding school.

"You are so close. And remember, Adam is okay."

My son took the Path from Jersey City to work and changed trains every day near the Towers. Sometimes he had coffee with a friend who worked at American Express. Now I understood why Ken had called me. I felt thankful and terrified. I didn't think I could drive another mile when I heard the radio announcer, "All planes in the United States are grounded. No planes will go out, and none will come in."

I exited off of the highway at a Burger King. I charged my phone and talked to other teary-eyed weary travelers. Most were on their way to Pittsburgh. One woman volunteered to watch my phone while I went next door, filled my car with gas, and bought ginger ale, saltines, ice, and paper bags.

At Burger King, strangers were hugging and crying. We wished each other well on our journeys. I gassed up and cleaned out my smelly car, and then I pulled onto the main highway. All I wanted to do was to get to Sarah's and embrace my son.

I pushed on toward the Pulaski Skyway, although I didn't remember how. Since the traffic was so backed up, it was easy for me to throw up. Balls of black smoke towered high in the sky in front of me. I rolled my car window down; I smelled what seemed like a combination of human flesh and electricity. I threw up again. My stomach was twisted in extreme pain since I hadn't eaten all day. I drank more ginger ale.

While I was vomiting, two painters in a truck noticed me and my license plates.

"How long have you been driving?" one asked.

"Twelve hours," I tried to get out.

"You drove all the way from West Virginia? Where are you going?"

"Tonnele Ave.," I cried.

"We'll get you there. We know exactly where it is. Stay with us. Everything is going to be okay," I thought I heard. "You done the hard work already."

"Okay." I shook my head since I wasn't able to talk. Tonnele Avenue was the last exit before the Holland Tunnel, which was closed.

I was thankful for the two house painters and was even more thankful that I had keys to my son's apartment. His phone was working. I couldn't reach Sarah. Adam had left a message on my cellphone saying he was staying in the city since there was no public transportation. The only way of getting around was by bike or foot.

I took a shower and called my family in Alabama. Then I turned on the television. I felt as though I was watching a movie that friends told me I had to see. I stood frozen, seeing the replay of the falling towers over and over in disbelief and horror.

The next day I was able to get into the city, to Sarah's. Adam and I spoke; he was fine but had been worried about me. At Sarah's, folks gathered outside of her building at our 94th and Park Avenue trying to sing gospels. They were surprised and disappointed when they learned I couldn't sing.

Later, at dinner, the political ramifications of the bombing hit me; George W. Bush was president. "Oh my God, I wish Al Gore was president," I blurted out.

"Why?" Sarah asked.

"Because he's less hawkish than W. and a lot smarter."

"Not really; Gore dropped out of divinity school. Bush didn't."

"Sarah, Bush's mother wouldn't call him smart." I laughed. Then it hit me that my oldest friend had changed politics too. How did all of this change happen without me knowing? Was this what happens when you don't see each for two years? Friends must be informed about major changes in each other's life.

In Atlanta, we had volunteered for the League of Women Voters, Planned Parenthood, and United Way and had been on boards of many progressive organizations, especially those having to do with the right of women to make decisions about their bodies. I was confused, scared, and a bit angry. Why didn't I know about all of this?

Had I changed too? Maybe we all had. My politics were the same. How could they be anything else? My Harvard-educated son can't get a taxi in New York City. Black and brown males are frisked at a rate of eighty percent higher than white males just because they are breathing the same air. Police are supposed to protect and serve, but instead, they are shooting down our children in the streets. All of the hard-fought battles of the civil rights movement were disappearing by way of stripping those laws down to their last gem clip. *How can my politics be anything else?*

After 9/11, Sarah and I agreed to not talk about politics. I found our new reality strange and difficult. My oldest friend was a new person, and now we have rules about what we can and cannot speak of. I knew that Saul was a German Jew and had escaped the Holocaust. I had never heard Sarah mention the Holocaust in the more than forty years we've been friends.

Then it happened; I was so excited that I slipped and forgot our agreement. Sarah called me a few months later; we hadn't talked in a while. I was always careful not to express my excitement about Obama being president since she and Saul sounded more like FOX News when talking about the president; I wasn't willing to listen. I had other friends with similar political views to mine. After all, we can't get everything we need from one friend.

"What's going on?" Sarah asked.

"I am so excited. Angela Davis is coming to my university, and she requested that I sit at the dinner table with her." Sarah was quiet; then she had to go soon. I thought nothing of it since we're all busy. When she didn't call me back, I replayed the telephone conversation in my head; and kept reminding myself that I didn't think of Angela Davis as politics. By that time, Obama was serving his second term as president.

About six weeks later, Sarah emailed me, telling me that she was sorry to just be getting back to me, but she was so put off by my love for Angela Davis that she couldn't talk to me. Angela Davis had been negotiating for peace between the Israelis and Palestinians, and for that, Sarah hated her. This is what the woman does, travel around the world, including South Africa, trying to negotiate peace. I was shocked and angry. I rewatched the documentary *Free Angela* and felt even more proud of her. She was hunted down like a criminal, but she never broke. I wanted to be on her side of history.

Finally, I wrote Sarah back; the first thing I said was: *In the words of Nelson Mandela, your enemies are not my enemies.* Then I went on to ask her what did she want from me. Was I supposed to contact her to see if I could admire, care about, etc., folks she hated? I was damn angry by then.

We wrote each a few emails to each other. I was puzzled, hurt, and didn't know what to do with my emotions. Sarah told me that her mother had been a Holocaust survivor. I wrote back and told her she didn't own all of the pain in history. My mother worked as a maid for fifty years earning $15 per week, and when my father was killed when the gas truck he drove exploded, we received not one dollar.

With the killing of Trayvon Martin, Michael Brown, Tamir Rice, Eric Gardener, and too many other Black bodies, along with the incarnation of Black bodies, my political radar was overflowing.

Sarah and I haven't seen or spoken to each other since. I still don't understand.

CHAPTER 9

Another Other: White Negroes

Andrea Lee (1953–)

What I like to investigate when I write is what people dream
about. What fascinates me is fantasy, the dream of being away,
the state of being foreign, of being apart.

—ANDREA LEE

I first met Andrea Lee through her writing in the *New Yorker* more than a
decade ago. I was a university professor teaching African American literature. My white students and many of my Black students thought all African
Americans had always been poor, even if they are wealthy today. I searched for
books about middle-class African Americans. *Sarah Phillips*, Lee's first novel,
became a mainstay in my teaching portfolio. The novel is autobiographical
and would probably be called a memoir today. The main character is born to
educated parents and grew up in an affluent Philadelphia family, sheltered from
much of the violence and racism of the 1960s. After the death of her father, a
well-known minister, who graduated from Harvard University, Sarah goes to
Europe; and finds a world much larger than that of her childhood and stays.

Lee's own life is even more interesting than the characters she writes about;
she wears many hats as an expatriate. She has lived outside of the US all of
her adult life, first in Russia and now in a castle in Turin, Italy, where she's
a Baroness. She's a novelist, short story writer, journalist, and memoirist.
Whether celebrating her birthday in Stockholm, writing in Switzerland or

Andrea Lee's Home, Turin, Italy.

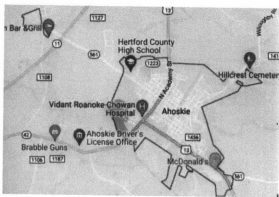

Map of the area where White Negroes lived.

hanging out in Amsterdam, she's always someplace else. Not because she's running away, she says, but because she's running toward the new, learning, and embracing worlds that appear in her writing.

"I was born to be a foreigner," Lee says. "I write often about the experience of outsiders like me. I grew up in an African American family deeply involved in the civil rights movement and one with a long history of being both privileged and mixed raced."

An interesting part of that history resides in a small county in North Carolina, near the Virginia line, in a place where people referred to themselves as "White Negroes." One of Lee's memorable visits was in 1962 when she was nine.

White Negroes

Lee's mother's side of the family is from a small county in North Carolina near the Virginia line. In the essay, she recalls her visit to spend a week with her Aunt Lucy in Ahoskie, Hertford County, North Carolina. It's where her "White Negro" relatives lived. About five thousand people lived in the area not far from the Great Dismal Swamp. Her Aunt Lucy was childless and related to Lee through marriage and was an old friend. Lee had never cared about patchwork or quilts until she spent that week with her Aunt Lucy. She fell in love with the names of some of the patterns: Rising Sun, Brown Goose, Children of Israel, Churn Dash, Chips, and Whetstones.

Map of Ahoskie, Hertford, North Carolina.

As early as 1719, Ahoskie, North Carolina, was known by the Native American name Ahotskey, which was used by white settlers when they arrived. There, of course, were many different spellings. The town of Ahoskie was established in the mid-1880s as a railroad and lumber town. Ahoskie, Hertford, North Carolina, is located in North Carolina's Inner Banks region. Since no other town is known by this name, its nickname is "The Only One."

Lee had taken the overnight train from Philadelphia to the Carolinas. When she woke up, she wanted a patchwork quilt. It was all that she could think about. She was curious how obsessed she had become with longing for a quilt. Aunt Lucy showed her two old quilts she had made some fifty years ago, stitched in a stylized pattern of red and green, called Baskets. The other one was a fan quilt that her aunt had also made, probably about the same time.

The next day, Lee's aunt asked a friend, Miss Dessie, to take her to a nearby town to look for a quilt. During her journey, Lee learned that English, Irish, Native American, and, of course, African American blood run through her veins. And that was just on her mother's side of the family. She would see gray-eyed, white-skinned people who described themselves as African Americans.

On the way to Cofield to find quilts, Miss Dessie stopped at the Pleasant Plains Baptist Church to show Lee the grave of her husband and the plot beside it where she'll be buried. The brick church was established in 1851 as the Free Colored Baptist Church. Miss Dessie pointed out to Lee that the land stretching to the skyline along the nine-mile stretch of highway that joined Ahoskie and the small town of Winton is entirely owned by Blacks, specifically "the White Negroes." It has been in their families for generations.

When Lee asked about a shack or a dilapidated house, Miss Dessie would respond, "Honey, I don't know, probably tenants." Lee understood that this small place seemed to have a rigidly divided caste system. She didn't understand until years later when she was researching her family history. Her Aunt Lucy and Miss Dessie "were aware of the identity of tenants but spoke about them with innocent professions of ignorance as if the tenants belonged to a different planet. Similarly, they addressed white acquaintances in tones that were not quite deferential but suggested that the whites breathed a different air," Lee said.

By the time they arrived at Miss Julia's small turquoise-painted cement-block house, Lee had found herself getting excited about finding a perfect quilt. Miss Julia led them into her bedroom and opened boxes from her closet. Lee was immediately disappointed by the big pieced squares she pulled out, a pattern of Double Wedding Ring top, pieced patches made of stretched polyester. The woman must have sensed disappointment on her face.

"Most everything I do now is polyester. It's a lot easier to get remnants, and it holds the color," Miss Julia smiled.

Lee picked out two cotton quilts, a Log Cabin with narrow strips of fabric joined to form a complex system of rectangles.

"I see you like cotton," Miss Julia said. "We don't get much of it these days; folks just don't wear it much anymore."

On the way back to her Aunt Lucy's, Miss Dessie asked Lee if she was happy with her quilts.

"I like them, but not what I had wanted or expected," Lee said.

"You should have taken the polyester. It's bright and washable and makes a right nice quilt." Miss Dessie smiled.

Lee described this place of "White Negroes" as a "strange island." The Blacks were freed but lived together in isolation believing life was better there than on the outside. After slavery ended, freeing more than four million Blacks in the South, the younger "White Negroes" left and probably passed as white. The older ones died off. They had been prosperous and happy and lived in their own utopia.

"It's still a very old world," Lee said. "No one goes there anymore. Their attitudes are condescending. All of their lives, they were somewhere in between races and weren't going to divide themselves. That was the Old Deep South that we don't hear or know anything about. Everybody knew everybody else, and they got along and had been getting along for hundreds of years."

The old world of farm work and eating from the earth evidently made for exceptional health. Lee said her Aunt Mable, also called Aunt Mama, who died a few years ago, lived to be 105. "She was one of the 'White Negroes.' They all lived long, long lives . . . Aunt Mama's body was studied at the University of Pennsylvania hospital. They couldn't figure out why her body was so young, and she was so old." Lee said a professor even bet students they couldn't guess the body's age. "'I will give a bottle of whiskey if anyone can guess how old this lady is,'" Lee mimicked the professor. "They were guessing sixty-something, and at that point, she was ninety-seven. It was unbelievable."

Nine-year-old Lee found the women to be more practical than she had imagined. They were excited about McDonald's new sandwich, the McRib, although they hadn't eaten one.

Early Years

I first interviewed Lee by Skype in 2015; she was open and engaging. Since we hadn't met before, we dressed up for our introduction. Lee was feeling a bit chilly; she sat in her study surrounded by books and art with a pot of tea wrapped in a glamorous rose-colored Indian shawl. Once in a while, her 10-karat wedding diamond sparkled. I sat at my desk in my newly painted purple guest room, wearing a brown beaded barrette. Lee remarked that my lipstick and nail polish matched the color of my room. Later, we found ourselves giggling like we had known each other all of our lives. We only stopped talking when Skype broke, and we couldn't get it to work again. We still laugh about breaking Skype.

After Skyping, we talked on the phone often via Messenger and WhatsApp. And we've been doing that ever since.

Andrea Lee. Photo courtesy of Andrea Lee.

Her father's side of the family is from the same world as her mother, Lumberton County, Virginia. In the 1800s, some free Negroes moved to Washington, DC. Faith and education were always important and often intertwined values in Lee's life. She was able to trace her lineage back to her great-grandfather, who was a freeman employed as a servant in The White House. Muse, as he was called, was the illegitimate son of somebody in her family; he left small-town Ahoskie for DC in the 1820s. He had an enslaved sister, whose freedom he bought, and they set up a house together in Washington. That sister became a teacher, and the family opened a school for Black children.

"I am just thinking about how interesting that is," Lee said. "And he became a leader in the church."

But DC was a segregated city, and those color restrictions intensified during the Woodrow Wilson administration, especially after Wilson showed the film *Birth of a Nation* in the White House. Lee's family, like many other African American families of the Great Migration, continued to move north and ended up in Philadelphia.

Lee's parents, Edith Taylor Lee and Charles Sumner Lee, were descendants of the same "White Negro" world in North Carolina. They met in Philadelphia, and both went to the city's elite public high school and Lincoln University. Her father later graduated from Eastern Baptist Theological Seminary, near Philadelphia, and was the first Black man to do so. His brother, Lee's uncle Oscar, also went to Central High, Lincoln, and Yale Divinity School. Of course, he was one of the first Blacks to graduate.

"He was like a big star," Lee said. "He and my father were very active in civil rights and were political activists all the time."

Lee's father, a longtime pastor at First African Baptist Church in South Philadelphia, not only worked with Martin Luther King Jr., they were close friends. From Birmingham to Selma and in Philadelphia, her father was by Dr. King's side. Reverend Lee became a member of the National Council of Christians and Jews. Later he was elected secretary of the World Council of Churches.

Her mother taught at the Lansdowne Friends School, just outside Philadelphia, where Lee was a student. The two spoke French together at home. Lee was being readied for her life abroad and didn't even know it. The school allowed her to use her imagination, which gave her confidence. She recalled her mother had dreams of going to the University of Pennsylvania and becoming a French teacher, but her father, who ran a successful insurance company, died during the Depression. "I don't know why she wanted to be a French teacher, but that was her dream. She ended up going to Temple University, and then she taught elementary school and was unhappy that she was the minister's wife. Despite her very nice life, she was still bitter about that."

Lee described her growing up as urban and progressive. She was headstrong then but now realizes how progressive her parents and community were. The church was very diverse, even though most of the members were Black. When she was growing up, she thought the folks were so boring, and she couldn't wait to get away from them. Looking back on it, she thinks their church was full of wonderful people who were changing the world. They would do anything in the world to help their community and their people.

During the civil rights era, life was limited for African Americans, even well-educated ones. People in Lee's community were determined to improve their lives and that of their children. They moved to city suburbs that became Black middle-class enclaves. Lee's father and his friends started the Nile Swim Club in 1959 (named after the great Nile River) because Blacks weren't allowed to join the white swim club. And the Nile Swim Club is still around.

"They did all kinds of things for us, got us into those schools. We were the first generation of Blacks who got shoved into those elite white schools," Lee said. "Our parents thought that was the direction to go. I think they regret it now."

The Baldwin School on the Philadelphia Main Line is still one of the country's leading single-sex prep schools. When Lee went there for high school, she was one of a handful of Black students and on the frontline of racial and class harassment. The school has a famous English department in poetry and prose; Lee called it a wonderful school. Other than Andrea

African Americans weren't allowed to swim in the city's (Philadelphia) public swimming pool. Lee's father and community members established the Nile Swim Club, a swim club for African Americans. Photo courtesy of Andrea Lee.

Lee, many noted alumnae hail from the halls of the Baldwin: Shawn Michele Lacy, Jamila Kamara, Farah Jasmine Griffin, Jody Gerson, Maria Wing, and Julie Wollman.

In 2000 Lee was named alumna of the year at the Baldwin School. She was invited to give a graduation speech. "I told them how difficult it was for me feeling excluded, but I spent more time talking about the fine education it offered me and so many other students."

"When I mentioned exclusion in my speech, one of my brothers said everybody on the graduation platform begin to look terrified." She laughed and pulled her shawl around her shoulders during our Skype talk. "But now they're really turned that school around. The head of the school is an African American woman. There are so many diverse girls there from all over the place. When I was there, it was like *Upstairs Downstairs*. They would sneer at me, not believing that I was allowed in the front door. Today it's a whole different world."

She said sometimes it's hard for her to process the changes. Like when a white woman she attended Baldwin High School with suddenly wanted to visit her in Italy. As it turns out, the woman's mixed-race daughter was doing

research in Italy. "I was shocked since she had been mean to me in school . . .
I didn't want her in my house."

Lee's memory was that she and the only other African American students
at the Baldwin School took a lot of their hostility because they were the first
Blacks to integrate into the school. Although she received a wonderful education at Baldwin, she still felt a sense of being set apart because she was Black,
which made her feel like a foreigner. So why not be one? As a teen, she wrote
poems and stories about living abroad. It was fun; she said, "always reading
and writing, and dreaming of living in Europe."

Russian Journal

Lee pulled her shawl around her tighter as we began talking about Black
beauty. "Once in a novel, I can't even remember the title or author, but it
changed my life. I was quite small, the author wrote about Black women
being so beautiful. One of his characters opened the door for him, and when
she opened the door, she was so beautiful he fainted. I remember being so
shocked and imagined what it felt like in that little room. I used to go back
and read that description. It was the first time in print that I had ever seen
anything about Black women being beautiful. It blew me away and totally
surprised me. I became obsessed with that book."

She believes that the idea of female beauty in the US is corrupted by race.
African American women would fare better in Europe. "When I come back,
I'm shocked about the racism that I've forgotten about," she poured more
tea. "That's why I wrote *Russian Journal*. Living in Russia overwhelmed me
like nothing ever has. It was tough."

Lee associates *Russian Journal* with her first husband, Tom Fallows. The
book was published in 1981, nominated for a National Book Award, and
received the Jean Stein Award from the American Academy and Institute of
Arts & Letters. Lee was twenty-six years old.

When she and Fallows met, he was a graduate student working on a doctorate at Harvard. She was finishing up her undergraduate degree there. He
was a Russian scholar and was offered a fellowship to go to Russia with a
spouse. That's why they got married so quickly. She thought it was going to be
an adventure, and it was. They took lessons and learned to speak Russian. Lee
never learned to write or read Russian well, but she spoke it well by forcing

herself. "I didn't want to be left out," she laughed. She and her husband were young and in love and living at a very intense time. It was exciting; they were swept up in all kinds of experiences. "We were both very creative; it was a marvelous time." Lee threw her hands up, and her rose-colored shawl fell to the floor. Her diamond ring glinted when she picked up her shawl.

Lee and her husband came back to the States after a year in Russia. She got her master's from Harvard and kept writing, starting her next book, *Sarah Phillips*, published in 1984.

"And that's when I got to know Jamaica Kincaid. We used to hang out sometimes. And we read together at Harvard. During that time, my ambition was to dress like Princess Diana. Jamaica was really cool and downtown. We were a great combination: she was free-spirited, and I was so bougie."

When Lee's husband finished his doctorate, they moved to New York City and stayed there for a couple of years; she worked at the *New Yorker*. From there, he got a new post, and they moved to Rome.

"Tell me more about your writing."

"I started writing early. I honestly don't remember a time when I wasn't writing. I think it comes natural, really natural. I find it easy to see things that I am around all the time and turn it into writing. I don't think I could write science fiction, for example, but no problem with the other genres. My experience in the world has allowed me to see so much. I am good at spotting things and then figuring out how to put it together as a story or novel. But with some checking, it could also be nonfiction."

"I would agree with that. Don't you think *Sarah Phillips* would be called a memoir today? Just like *Invisible Man*, *Go Tell It on the Mountain*, and so many other books that are called novels."

"Yes, I agree; basically, I just write and see what shape it forms."

"What are the cultural differences between the States and Rome? How does it show in your writing?"

"The cultural difference that emerge in my writing are those that I've noticed repeatedly over the years since I married into an Italian family. There's a palpable sense of the past, the weight of tradition. The atmosphere is quite natural. I drive past over land that was successively occupied by Roman legions, by Napoleon's troops, and Italian partisans fighting the Nazis. Italians are more attached to family (like most Europeans) and birthplace more than Americans."

"So now you're in Rome?"

"Yes. My husband gave up his Russian scholar career. No jobs for a Russian historian that year in academe. So, he went into the trading program in Manhattan and became a banker. After Rome, we moved to Milan; my daughter was born there. At that point, I felt in love with an Italian."

"Your present husband?" She laughed and threw up her hands. We both laughed. "Of course not. My marriage seemed to be over. You know, he was a sweet guy; but I was young and impetuous. The Italians seemed so exciting and exotic. Now that I know Italians, they're not so exciting and exotic. After I ran off with him, I asked myself what I had done. I lived and worked in Milan for a couple of years. I had my three-year-old daughter. And there I met my present husband from Turin, at a party. We're married, and I am here."

⎯⎯ ⎯⎯

This was Lee's real introduction to Italian life. She considers her children to be American in spite of both being born in Italy and growing up there, but they went to boarding school and university in the US. They're very international.

"Charley came along years later. The American schools here in Italy aren't that good. First, Charley was with Mr. Italy; now, he's down with the 'brothers.' He wants to be a schoolteacher. Everybody in my family is a teacher. I want to say NO."

"What an honor to your legacy. And it's an honorable profession. When did you know this was home?"

"I think it's when I had kids, and life revolved around them. I always know where I am since I do a lot of coming and going in my strange bubble of a life. I can't really say I've settled into Italian life. I know how it works. I don't care anymore about settling in."

"Do you consider the States home too?"

"Yes, when I arrive in the States, I feel like I'm home, but I have to deal with all the race stuff, which includes how Blacks treat each other. I don't understand. We should have been helping each other out."

"I think how we treat each has to do with so much self-hatred that has been inflicted on us. They see racism everywhere; it gets internalized."

"I think you're right. Even in my family, with my uncle and my father, there was so much bitterness inside of them. Here they were helping the community, saving the world. Occasionally something comes out of them that remind me (and them) that they didn't like themselves that much. We have this poison in ourselves. It's so tragic."

Lee's mother died nearly twenty years ago. And her father died from a stroke while she was in college in the 1970s.

Living Away from "Home"

After that first interview, Facebook and Messenger made it possible for Lee and me to get to know each other better. She was gracious enough to write a blur for my second book, *Reflections of the Other: Being Black in Germany*. When I was looking for a model for that book, I turned to Lee again with *Russian Journal*, which impressed and intrigued me. I thought Lee was so brave in her exploration of living elsewhere. When I lived in Germany, I had nightmares about getting on the wrong train and would end up in Siberia, where no one spoke English. *Russian Journal* was a constant and well-needed companion during my Fulbright tenure.

Lee is the youngest of three children and a classic daughter and sister of educators. Her oldest brother, Lloyd Lee, is an attorney at the University of California–Berkeley and her other brother is a longtime educator in Philadelphia Public Schools. "He was about to retire, but they asked him to stay on, and he did, trying to raise money for ill-fated schools." Lee believes every child should have a good education. It doesn't matter if she knows the child or not. I don't mean just reading and writing, but cultural experiences as well.

An example of this is the mixed-race son of her manicurist, "a lovely pale blonde woman from northern Italy . . . The child's father is a Nigerian man who ran off and dumped her." Lee spread out her hands like a fan. "She has an adorable little boy whom she's raising very well. She has structure, and her parents, who are very conservative people who probably never saw a Black person in their lives." We laughed. "I got concerned about the little boy and started bringing him books from the States. He needs to know something about blackness. The manicurist told me that she introduced her son to the new priest. The mother was thrilled in that the new priest is also Nigerian. And the first thing the son said was, 'Hi, I am Derrick, and I am brown.'"

"Wow. The children give us back what we give them," I said.

"The child goes to the only person who looks like him," Lee continued. "He is clearly thinking of his own identity. Unfortunately, the priest didn't say anything specifically about his comments about being brown."

Lee's third book is *Interesting Women,* a collection of short stories published in 2002. Her writing is often referred to as the *International Sex and the City.* One critic noted she wrote "in vivid prose shot through with mordant irony. Lee takes us into the hearts and minds of a number of extraordinary women, intelligent, seductive, self-possessed, who, with wit and style, must grapple with questions of identity in a shrinking world where everyone is, in a way, a foreigner."

Phillip Roth said of *Interesting Women,* "Andrea Lee is the real deal. And there is nothing else to say."

Lee is one of those interesting women in her books. Her second husband is an Italian Baron Ruggero Aprile Di Cimia, and they've been married for nearly twenty-five years.

Golden Chariot Memories

But Lee, of course, is quite attached to her own history, as she wonderfully displayed in a short story, "The Golden Chariot." It's about a middle-class Black family traveling across the country in America in the early 1960s. She said her father always drove black cars because, as a prominent pastor, he thought it proper. But finally, she said, "He got this gold Rambler. We were shocked that it was gold. We called it the 'Golden Chariot.'"

And the family took off on a road trip to end all road trips: Philadelphia to the Seattle World's Fair. "It was an incredible odyssey. My parents had planned it all out. Underneath it all, they were worried about segregation and encountering racism. They clung to *The Green Book,* a Negro Motorist guide for Black folks by Victor Hugo Green, published in 1936. The book noted where it was safe for African Americans to stop for gas, food, and lodging. So, they were always asking and checking out information before we stopped."

The trip changed their lives because they really saw America and experienced how in the West, racial hate was more directed at Native Americans than African Americans.

"My uncle Oscar looked very much like Native Americans," she said. "I'm sure there's some blood there." Her uncle had to tell a white man he was an "American Negro."

And the guy said, "Well then, glad you're not one of them dirty Indians."

In the summer of 2018, fifty-six years after the first rip, Lee and her brothers drove the trip again. I'm anxious to read what happened.

Her latest novel, *Lost Hearts in Italy*, is unlike most of your work. It expands a number of years with a multitude of characters and a wide scope.

"*Lost Hearts* is the most challenging book I've written, mainly because of its complex structure, and it's divided into two time periods, the 1980s when the love triangle happens and the present time, and there are three points of view. It is, above all, a novel about the different ways people have been foreign to one another. It's about the basic curiosity we have throughout our lives that attracts us to new places and new experiences."

The Red Island House, her latest book, is about sexual tourism in the beautiful country of Madagascar, where she spends part of every year. Her husband is a deep-sea diver who traveled the world. But when he found Madagascar, he needed no other places. "It's only a six-hour flight with the same time zone. African and Asia, black, brown, and yellow people, who look like members of my family," Lee said. Her second project is a collection of linked stories about the complicated, sometimes scandalous life of a large Italian family from the point of view of an adopted South African daughter. Andrea Lee continues to explore race and culture and the many ways of being foreign.

DEFERRED DREAMS

In my late thirties, I received a fellowship at a prestigious graduate school in creative writing. Before that, I had reared my son as a single parent. He entered college as I entered graduate school.

My graduate program didn't offer teaching assistant jobs like nowadays since its main goal was to have students intensively focused on their writing. Not good if you needed income. Sometimes I substitute taught in the public school system for $40 a day. When I wasn't able to support myself from substitute teaching, I borrowed $7,000 in the form of a student loan program. I felt thankful to have access. To date, I have paid more than $21,000 toward the loan, and I still owe $3,000, which was paid off in 2013.

In 1990 after graduate school, I was fortunate enough to find a full-time position as an instructor in the Department of English at a state university forty miles from where I lived. I would teach four courses or 150 students a semester for $20,000 a year. The benefits package included health insurance and a retirement plan. Two weeks after accepting the position and before I set foot in one classroom, the state declared a freeze on hiring, and everyone who had been recently hired was to receive a two percent pay cut. So my $20,000 salary was figuring closer to $18,000 per year.

I bought a demo model 1990 Subaru sedan, which registered at 18,000 miles. I contacted the Virginia Department of Education to make arrangements to begin paying my student loan. We agreed on terms; I would begin making payments that September, when I would receive my first paycheck. I thought I was ready to start my new life.

By that June, the Virginia Department of Education started harassing me by calling more than three times a day, along with sending letters at least two times a week. It didn't help to try and call them unless I had hours to spend on the phone waiting. The first week of July, I received a certified letter stating that the wages I didn't have were about to be garnished. After spending an afternoon on the phone, I learned that the first person I had made an agreement with was no longer working at the agency, and he hadn't made any records of any of our conversations. I was able to get a deferment for six weeks since I was technically unemployed.

My main financial goal was to keep my son enrolled at an Ivyish college, where tuition, room, and board cost more than my annual income. I wrote a letter to the Department of Education and tried to explain my situation. And I raised questions about the aggressive policy of harassment that some of their agents had imposed on me. It made no sense. I needed just a bit of time to get organized. Since my roommate from graduate school had moved out, I had to pay the full rent and buy a new car, along with all of the expenses of driving. I hadn't had my teeth cleaned or a medical checkup in more than two years. Not to mention I needed clothes for work.

This is how the loan nightmare started: For three years, 1990–93, I paid the Virginia Department of Education $120 monthly, which totaled $4,320. That agency went out of business and sold its loans to private companies.

In 1993 I moved to West Virginia for a tenure track position at West Virginia University. By that time, the loan had been sold at least twice. Each time the loan was sold, the new owner would start my balance at the original $7,000, plus the amount they had paid for the loan, which raised the monthly amount greatly.

I tirelessly wrote letters and tried to call these new owners of the loan. If I could talk to the right someone, I knew the situation could be worked out. Loans are sold every day, but owners of the loans are given credit for the money they've paid. Between 1994 and 1996, these new companies ruined my credit with false reporting to the credit bureaus and garnished my wages. I had trouble buying a house and even had to have a cosigner for a loan from the university's credit union, a most degrading experience. There was never a time I did not make payments on the loan. This was a hardship since my son was in graduate school by this time, and I was living in a place where university professors earned an average of twenty-five percent less than in most parts of the country.

When I finally talked to someone, I was told they knew nothing about the history of the loan and didn't care what I had already paid. The facts were that they owned the loan, and I didn't have a choice. I was outraged. I knew this couldn't be legal, but it seemed so. This financial nightmare tumbled down and choked the life out of me.

I am an African American woman and associate professor of English at a state university with more than twenty some-thousand students. I was awarded tenure with a promotion in 2000. I earn right at $58,000 a year. From 2001–04 we (faculty members) received no raises. I teach graduate and undergraduate students three courses in the fall semester and two during the spring. That's not a problem. I love teaching. At its best, there's no greater passion.

One of the reasons I've always wanted to teach is because I had great teachers who changed my life by introducing me to the world of books, a gift that I've passed on to my son and all of the students I encounter. My teachers cared about me and were invested in every aspect of my life. I, like so many others, have dreamed of extending that same kind of gift, but with the system that governs student loans, more and more of these dreams will have to be deferred. I have paid almost $30,000 for a $7,000 loan. This is not just wrong but inhumane.

CHAPTER 10

Two Ways of Seeing the World

Gloria Naylor (1950–2016)

A writer will write, a singer will sing, a dancer will dance. You
have no choice. It's either you create, or you explode.
—GLORIA NAYLOR

In 1991, Nikki Giovanni and Virginia Fowler, my new colleagues and friends
from Virginia Tech, invited me to my first Wintergreen gathering. "They will
love you, and you will love them," Giovanni and Fowler assured me.

Wintergreen is a mountainside resort named for the abundance of wintergreen boxwoods. I felt adventurous driving to the resort that Memorial Day
weekend. Up the mountain, I imagined I could be in Vermont, Oregon, or the
state of Washington. But there I was, driving on the eastern slopes of the Blue
Ridge Mountains, a little nervous. All I had was the name of Joanne Gabbin.

When I walked up to the desk, I knew it was her. "Are you Joanne?"

"Yes, and you must be Ethel. We're so glad you could join us." Her smile
was as sweet as peach cobbler. My nervousness disappeared like the light
of day.

"Wintergreen is where we unburden our minds and renew our spirits in
the intimacy of conversations around the dining table or walk in woods,"
Gabbin told me.

The beauty and peace of the place took my breath away. And after more
than thirty years of gathering, it still takes my breath away. The Women of

Gloria Naylor.

Wintergreen are mainly scholars and artists who support and cheer each other on, give advice and make suggestions for our work, and our lives.

On my first night in the large rented house, Opal Moore and I roomed together. And we've been rooming ever since. Both of us suffered from insomnia long before the days of Ambien. Around 2:00 a.m., we decided to go outside and relax in the hot tub. Finally, we went back to bed and fell into peaceful sleeps. But to our surprise, we were awoken too early the next morning when some of the other women who had been awakened during our dip into the hot tub pulled us out of bed, just like sisters.

I remember our tenth anniversary being chaotic and joyful; we rented two houses, one for smokers and one for nonsmokers. None of us smoke anymore. It was a special year for me; I was headed to Germany, where I had been awarded a Fulbright fellowship. And my son had been accepted into graduate school at Harvard.

And to top that, Fowler asked me to interview writer Gloria Naylor. It was the first time the Yale-educated National Book Award winner had joined the Women of Wintergreen. Fowler was editing a collection of interviews/essays about Naylor for *Callaloo*. I was thrilled, nervous, and unbelievably grateful. "I can do this," I kept repeating to myself.

I had never met Naylor, but I felt prepared to conduct the interview. Not only had I read every book she had written at least twice, but I had taught them too. She was awarded The American Book Award for her first novel, *The Women of Brewster Place* (1982), adapted for a film starring Oprah Winfrey (1989). Her next novel was *Linden Hills* (1985), followed by *Mama Day* (1988) and *Bailey's Café* (1992). *The Men of Brewster Place* was published in 1998 after our visit.

Naylor roomed with Val Gray Ward, our great performance artist. Other than meals, we didn't see much of them. Their room was next to Opal and mine; the door was always closed, but we heard talk and laughter. Sometimes we'd hear Val singing an old spiritual.

Naylor and I met on the side porch, away from the laughter and sun. She wore an African loose-printed dress. Her glasses looked like Gwendolyn Brook's. She brought a tall glass of water and cigarettes with her. When she settled into the interview, she explained she was born in Brooklyn but was conceived in Mississippi. "I've always had two ways of looking at the world," she said. She was influenced by southern culture until she entered elementary school. Southern speech was all she knew. She came of age in a northern city and saw life through that lens as well. Naylor understood this duality. Her affinity for language, behavior, and food of her roots imbues each page of her novels. It shapes characters' frustrations and drives her plots.

"When did you decide you were going to be a writer?"

"When I was twenty-seven or twenty-eight years old. As an older student at Brooklyn College, I had discovered writers like Nikki Giovanni, Paule Marshall, Toni Morrison, and Alice Walker. Discovering all of their work led me to believe that I could add my own voice."

"Did you have any other mentors?"

"Only Rick Pearce, a white male teacher at Yale. In fact, I dedicated *The Women of Brewster Place* to him for nurturing and helping me to shape my dream."

"Do your southern roots have any impact on your writing? I don't think of you as a Southern writer."

"No. I write what I remember or stories I've heard since childhood."

"Did you ever go back to the South?"

"My father's mother stayed in the South. We went back for family visits. My mother's mother had moved to New York by then. But I knocked around the South about two years when I was in my twenties. I went back as a missionary for the Jehovah's Witnesses."

"Do you come from a large family?"

"Yes. I am the oldest of three daughters. My mother and father come from families of eight and nine children. I have some thirty cousins on both sides. My mother's sisters were her best friends. She's shy and has never done much socializing. It's heartbreaking to watch her lose them because they're getting older and dying out."

"I am sorry. Where were you in the South when you went back?"

"Durham, North Carolina and Jacksonville, Florida."

"When did you go back North?"

"After two years, I drove back home [New York City] and began to go back to school. The realization came to me that I was twenty-five years old with no marketable skills. If I wasn't going to make my life in the religion as a full-time missionary, I had to get a job. I always had jobs to support myself in the ministry."

"What were some of those jobs?"

"I worked for several hotels, including the Sheraton City Square in New York City, as a telephone operator."

"What did you think about those jobs?"

"That they were just that—jobs. There was no hope of any professional progression. The most I could hope for was to be head operator."

"You weren't interested in staying with the Jehovah's Witnesses?"

"No, I left that faith in 1975."

"How long were you a Jehovah's Witness?"

"Seven years. My mother was part of the faith all of her life. When I was thirteen years old, she was baptized. At age eighteen, I was baptized. I had been around the faith for a long time."

"How do your characters come to you?"

"Imagination and images. I'll see a person or a flash of two people doing something that might seem strange to me. I often go in search of that scene. Like Mama Day, very early on, I saw a woman carrying a baby through the woods to another house. I had no idea what that meant at the time, but of course, it turned out to be Bernice carrying her dead baby, who was killed during the hurricane. Because that image stayed with me for a long time, I knew it was important."

"Tell us how you write. What's a good writing day?"

"If I am working on raw creation, I like to start early in the morning; I am naturally an early riser. I get up, drink coffee, and smoke cigarettes. I know that's horrible, but I do it anyway. After an hour, I am ready to go to work. After about four hours, I take a break by going through the mail, doing the laundry, or just taking a walk. If I am editing a piece, it's nothing for me to sit in front of the computer for twelve hours."

"I find the style of writing in each of your novels different. Is that planned?"

"No, not at all. It's simple; I have a story to tell, and I write it in that voice."

"I've noticed a new wave of African American women authors writing in the genre of more contemporary romance with a generic-looking book jacket. What do you think?"

"I think it's wonderful. We [writers] have come before and built bases for these children to jump and excel. They're also bringing with them a different type of experience. For example, I, myself bring the experience of a tenant farmer or sharecropper's daughter. Alice Walker writes from the same experience. Toni Morrison writes from experience of segregated Lorain, Ohio, and working in the steel mills."

Naylor takes a draw from her cigarette and continues, "A lot of these children don't have that experience. They are third and fourth-generation middle class. Their mothers graduated from Yale, Harvard, and Howard universities, as their fathers did. Their perspective will be from those experiences. They shouldn't be expected to be their parents."

Naylor sounds more like a preacher than a prize-winning author. "And, yes, I've heard people say, 'oh, that's not real Black writing because it's not about the South or oppression.' I think that's nonsense because the middle class has changed, and they're bringing their own experiences. They have a valid voice from those experiences. And that's Black literature too. And this new middle class can graduate from these prestigious colleges and universities without being loaded down in student debt, like our generation. People gain comfort in pigeonholing you. They can pull out that one box and not have to think any more about individuality. That's why I am fascinated with Tiger Woods. He doesn't fit into any of the molds. America is slowly going to have to accept that about Black folks."

"What was your experience at Yale University like?"

"The graduate programs are different from the undergraduate school; it has more diversity. There is no assumption that everyone is rich, but I didn't like New Haven that much. I found it depressing and often had to get out of

town. My initial plan was to get a PhD in American Studies and get a position with a high-class union card. That was my idea of what tenure was. I
didn't have any idea how long and hard it was to accomplish. I realized that
after my years of graduate school. I figured that it could take me as long as
ten years to get a tenured position and be loaded down with so much debt.
And I didn't want to put my writing on hold that long."

"And we thank you. You're associated with *The Women of Brewster Place*
more than any of your other novels. How do you feel about the film version
of *The Women of Brewster Place*?"

"I think it's a decent enough job. It's television, and we know how stereo-
typical it could've been, but it wasn't."

"I want to say, as an African American literature professor, that book has
never let me down. Students respond well to it, especially the beauty and
elegance of the language, in both literature and writing classes. Did you have
any idea how important it would be to us?"

"No, not to folks on the outside, but I knew it was very important to me
because it was the first thing I had started and finished. I had a life of false
starts in ways. A religion that I didn't finish, a marriage that ended, and there
I was putting myself through college and wondering if I was going to finish
that since my track record wasn't good."

"A lot of folks don't have good track records with marriages, especially
those starters marriages."

"Well, Miss Ethel, where were you in the 1980s when I needed to hear
that?" She clapped her hands and laughed.

"We're better off for not being in toxic relationships."

She takes a drag of her cigarette. "I know you're right in my case. The
book was the first thing I completed. And I graduated from college the
same month."

"You must have been elated."

"Oh yes. Done it! Got it! Mine!" She beats her fist on the table.

"How long did it take you to write it?"

"One, two years."

"Then what happened with the publishing of the novel?"

"I finished it under contract. Yeah, I had four short stories; we took them
to a publisher at Viking Press. Nobody told me that I wasn't supposed to take
my work to a publisher. Wasn't that what they were supposed to do, publish
folks' work? So I took them to the secretary. She read them, loved them, and

passed them on to an editor. They called me in and said, 'finish the book.' It was like a fairy tale in a way."

"About the National Book Award, were you surprised?"

"Yes."

"How did you find out? Wow! Your first book wins such a prestigious award."

"I received a phone call from my editor."

"You knew it had been nominated?"

"Yes. I received that call from my editor about a month earlier. In those days, they'd let you know ahead of time before everyone else knew."

"How did it affect your writing?"

"I still had a blank page in front of me. I was working on *Linden Hills*, and I was stuck as to how to get my family from upper to lower Linden Hills. It was very humbling to receive the award, but I still had a blank page. At one point, I thought here I was with a National Book Award. You'd think that writing would come easier. But there I was, stuck. You're no better than your next work."

"Would you tell your readers what is *Linden Hills* about?"

"*Linden Hills* is about the Black upper class and their morals. However, there is no simple answer. Black folks were so eager to integrate into the white world so they could make believe that their good work would make them colorless."

Naylor sips her water and lights another cigarette. "After all, that's what America is all about. And then there's the government. After the civil rights movement, so much destabilization occurred because they couldn't let things get outta hand. They had to control. Systematic breaking down of organizations that said the same things as Black Muslims are saying today was common practice in the government.

"The Black Panthers and the Students for a Democratic Society said, 'if you want some results, you're going to have to get way deep down in this mother.' Meaning, tear it down and build it back up. I don't believe you have to do that, but I do believe you have to understand where the roots are. Because that's how deep racism is. Even if they are running around burning their own buildings, stores or neighborhoods, even if you burn a tree and don't kill the root, it'll spring back up."

"And when it springs back, we may not recognize it."

"Exactly. That's what the Panthers meant by 'getting way deep down.' That's what Louis Farrakhan meant at the Million Man March when he said,

'America is evil and rotten to its core.' And no one is willing to address that. And God knows I don't see a Black leader addressing it. But there is a bit of hope. The Million Man March demonstrated what we can do when we work together all by ourselves and treat each other right."

"What are some of your other projects?"

"I own a production company and have been trying to get *Mama Day* in film for more than six years."

"That would be so fabulous. How is that going?"

"There's some fresh action now. I am reluctant to talk about that project."

"How did you decide to build a production company?"

"I wanted to do something that no one else has been able to do for me, and that was to find an infrastructure for my work and other work that I believe in. That slowly evolved into us doing programs for children. I was asked by Nickelodeon to write a children's piece, which I did. Lincoln Center commissioned me to write a play for grades K–6. Since children are so media-minded, we're going to have to figure out a way to get their minds through that medium."

"Wow! Anything else?"

"Another theater project called *Candy*. It's based on a little girl, Candy, and her brother, who run away from their abusive foster home. They end up in the basement of a paper factory and meet a six-foot rat name Speed. He's a 'homeboy rat.' The brother and sister realize that they are not victims and have the power to do something about their fate. After the piece was commissioned, they changed the artistic director. You know how that goes. But the rights will revert back to me in August 1997, which will give me some freedom to work with the piece."

"What a great idea! Anything else?"

"Nothing much. I'll write a novel about a religious cult. It'll be called *Keepers of the Kingdom*."

"What is it that you want folks to know about you?"

"That I try to do decent and honest work."

"I want to know about your new novel."

"*The Men of Brewster Place*?"

"What would you like to know?"

"What is it about?"

"Well, there's the title" [*laughter*].

"Will it take place during the same time and place as *The Women of Brewster Place*?"

"You're going to hear from Ben, the janitor and Mattie son's Basil and grandson Michael. You're going to hear from Eugene Turner, whose baby was killed, and he didn't show up for the funeral. C. C. Baker will be heard from as well. The book is the voices of the seven men. All of them don't live in Brewster Place, but they're somehow connected to it."

"Did you conceive of this idea when you were writing *The Women of Brewster Place*? If not, when?"

"For two years, the idea ran in the back of my mind. I didn't think I'd be writing this novel now because I had been working on my historical novel."

"What's your historical novel about?"

"It will be called *Sapphire Wade*, the foremother of *Mama Day*. We will go back. Bascombe Wade and a Native American sail to Willow Spring, and that becomes a microcosm for building a nation. I've already done so much work on the book, including reading three to four bookshelves of books for research."

"That's fascinating. And it sounds very Faulknerian."

"A lot of people have said that."

"And, of course, it sounds like Ernest Gaines, with your use of place and time."

"That's a good point."

"This morning, I heard some of your conversation with Nikki [Giovanni] about the civil rights movement, will you talk a little bit about this discussion?"

"I ascribe to what Malcolm X said: 'no one has a true revolution by integrating a lunch counter. A revolution is about land and power.' Now, if the civil rights movement had brought Black folks big land ownership, then I'd say fine; it worked. But the older I get, the more I believe in the spirit of Booker T. Washington and Marcus Garvey. Don't be running after white folks for a few crumbs; build your bakery. Build your own house. Get yourself some land and a basic profession so that people will have to come to you. If Black folks had taken that advice, the texture of the Black community would be very different today. It would be stronger."

"Every nation marches on the spine of its merchant class; that's the solid middle class for any nation. But what I see is a huge gap for Black Americans. There's the middle and upper-middle classes, doing quite well, thank you. There's the poor who's not doing quite well or well at all. I see few in the merchant class, like mom-and-pop stores. I've seen that transfer of power from Jewish Americans to Pakistanis, Indians, and Koreans, who now make up the merchant class. Black Americans have resorted to selling their labor to the government, which is the largest employer of the Black middle class. Black

Americans also sell their skills to corporate America, who only uses them as drones. That's how I feel about integration. I think it's time to reexamine it."

"What do you think about Black folks regarding the civil rights movement?"

"The progress that has been made because of the civil rights movement has been for the middle and upper middle classes. Working class and poor people are probably worse off. At least during segregation, Black children grew up with Black doctors, Black teachers, and Black police officers. White women are often teachers of Black students, and most don't have our children's best interest. They need to learn some Black history rather than fall back on the usual stereotypes. Oftentimes white teachers assume Black students are stupid. Therefore, they are then misplaced in special education classes, and it becomes a self-fulfilling prophecy."

Naylor continued like she was preaching a sermon. "The power structure in Harlem was Black as it was in many cities like Atlanta and Charlotte. What integration did was push Black teachers out of the classrooms leaving no one to teach Black children about their history and culture."

"What's the most important thing you've learned about yourself through your writing?"

"I've learned that I am a decent kind of a person. And I have the ability to hang on when all seems dark and miserable. My work is part of me, even though there may be issues of balance."

Gloria Naylor also received the American Book Award and a Guggenheim Fellowship for her work. She joined the ancestors on September 28, 2016, while living in Christiansted, US Virgin Islands.

We've had other Wintergreen Women who have joined the ancestors: Maya Angelou, Ruby Dee, Mari Evans, Carmen Gillespie, Gary Giovanni, Yolonda Giovanni, Pink Gordon Lane, Mary Harper, Lovalerie King, Paule Marshall, Toni Morrison, Novella Nelson, and Sherley Anne Williams.

Every year I look forward to our Wintergreen gathering; it is a place where dreams are shaped, and memories from long ago are recalled. Wintergreen women gave me the support I needed to turn my project into a book. They wrote reviews, letters of recommendation, and blurbs, but mostly they applauded my courage. And I continue to count on them.

When we gather on the mountain of Wintergreen every year, I am reminded of the spiritual "Shall We Gather at the River." Some of our Wintergreen sisters have reached the silver river. Soon our pilgrimage will cease too. Soon our happy hearts will quiver with the melody of peace. Oh, how I love my Wintergreen sisters.

MOTHER

I am my mother's oldest daughter. And I look like her, except she was prettier with long curly hair, pecan-colored skin, high cheekbones, and a figure like the number eight. We were never close. I was the one who grew up and moved away.

My mother's life was difficult and painful. She ruined many holidays for my sisters and me by weeping about her dead child not being there. Her firstborn child was perfect. She could read at age three and recite scriptures from the Bible when she was four. This daughter died from hookworms at age seven, before my sisters and I were born.

When I was in elementary school and brought home report cards with straight As, my mother's response was always the same, "Your sister would've made A pluses." I was fortunate in that I had teachers and a community to support me. I never held my mother's pain against her as I grew into adulthood.

None of us could live up to the perfect dead sister, who would always be perfect. My sisters had no interest in trying. I tried all the time, maybe because I was the oldest and felt some connection to her. A sad photo of her hung on our living room wall. When the doctor told Mother that there was nothing he could do for her only child, she and my grandmother scraped together $10 in 1946 and hired a white man from Eufaula to come and take a photograph of her dying child so she would never forget what she looked like.

Little Mama worked as a maid for the same family for nearly fifty years; she earned $15 a week, plus food from the store, which couldn't be sold to white customers because it was slightly ruined. The white woman promised

Little Mama her house since all of her relatives were dead or lived up North and showed no interest in her or the store she owned. She even said we were more like family to her than her Yankee relatives.

Little Mama repeated this story to us all the time, especially on holidays. My sisters and I dreamed of living in the house with the big screened-in back porch, shady oak trees, and a yard full of flowers.

After the white woman died, the relatives showed up and stripped the house, even the red and white curtains on the windows that Little Mama had sewed and kept starched and ironed. The house sat and fell into ruins. Big Mama ordered us never to go by the house again, even if we had to walk an extra half-mile. She told us that one heart could only be broken so many times.

When my sisters and I had children, we saw a different Little Mama; she joked, played checkers, and cooked for them, but mostly she hugged and kissed them. The first time I witnessed this behavior, I wept with gratitude; she still owned some love, even though it had been buried deep in the folds of her pain.

My sisters and I were able to buy her a house on a special Federal Housing Administration program. She and our grandmother became companions. Other houses soon popped up in the area. Friends and neighbors planted gardens and flowers together. They watched Oprah and the soaps together. They went to church and doctor appointments together.

After Big Mama died, I felt my mother slipping away. Six months later, her best friend and neighbor of sixty years passed too. Little Mama tried to cling on, but she lost her bearing, but not her wit. She was known not to "bite her tongue." One day I received a phone call from my sister telling me a neighbor had found her wandering around the neighborhood in her nightclothes, saying she was going to be late for work.

Soon afterward, my sister took her to her home, but that didn't last long; Little Mama needed special care. We finally put her in a nursing home. She stopped eating. My sister told me that when a nurse tried to talk her into eating, Little Mama told her, "You eat it." Just a few days later, she was gone. I tried to get home but wasn't able to. I was in the middle of finals at my university. I wanted to say thank you to my mother and reassure her that the ancestors would be waiting for her with both hands. But most importantly, she would be with her little girl again.

One of my classmates from high school delivered the eulogy at Little Mama's funeral. He talked about how she had babysat for him and his wife;

half of the time, they couldn't afford to pay her the $2 a day she charged for caring for their two children. She never asked them for a penny, he continued. My son and I laughed a little and held hands. The classmate went on to say that when he was a little boy, my mother would tell all the little Black children in the community to come to the back of the store between two and four every afternoon. She would give them Ike Mikes and potted meat, saltine crackers, moon pies, Vienna sausages, spam, and RC Colas. And any other food that wasn't up to standards. He went on to say that most of the time, this would be the only meal they would have had that day.

Later my son and I asked the minister why they had to be there between 2:00 and 4:00 p.m. He told us that was when the white woman was taking a nap. My son and I toasted with a glass of champagne to Mother.

CHAPTER 11

We Reached out to the Arts, and the Arts Said Yes

Nikki Giovanni (1943–)

> We write because the human spirit cannot be tamed
> and should not be trained.
> —NIKKI GIOVANNI

Standing in the classroom coteaching with Nikki Giovanni at Virginia Tech, I often thought about the glorious chain of events that landed me an instructor position in the early 1990s. I felt like the most fortunate graduate student alive when Giovanni, a world-famous poet and social justice activist, and professors Roberta Green and Virginia Fowler invited me to apply for the position. It seemed like a dream that we were breathing the same air, but it was real. Her diminutive stature belied her immense hunger for discourse and debate. Her colossal love for people, especially Black people, is always apparent.

One day, students were hotly debating Margaret Walker's *Jubilee*, a historical novel about the life of a biracial enslaved woman. Some students disagreed about the novel being considered the first truly historical novel.

"I have an idea," she said over the clamor. "Why don't we just call Margaret and ask her what she meant?" Giovanni walked to the phone and dialed, mouths dropped open.

Walker said she was delighted to hear from "such a lively group of young people." However, Walker had no idea what the argument was about since she had written the book nearly thirty years earlier, and her research had been conducted even earlier.

Occurrences like this often happened in our classes. At the start of the semester, I felt more like a student than a teacher. Giovanni wasn't territorial, though; it was always *our* class. Those Tuesdays and Thursdays glided into weeks into semesters. I never felt the forty-mile commute to Blacksburg from Roanoke. Not only was the landscape stunning, but I was always driving against the traffic. As the semester progressed, I felt more comfortable and gained more confidence. Giovanni was generous and funny, with knowledge that spanned around the world. Students loved her and clung to her every word. She was not afraid to talk about difficult and complicated issues like racism and sexism with honesty and wit. It took us three years to build the Africana Studies Program at Virginia Tech. We worked with interdisciplinary texts—art, music, oral history, and books, of course. Guests were well-known scholars, artists, activists, and musicians.

While packing up my house in Atlanta to move to Roanoke, Virginia, I heard a familiar voice on NPR but couldn't place it. The familiar voice spoke of the beauty of the Blue Ridge Mountains and how happy she was living in such a place. I was so memorized I stopped packing and sat on my bare floor and listened.

"We are a restless nation whether driven by explores seeking gold or oil, the fountain of youth; whether by the slave trade giving birth to the Industrial Age; no matter that rotting potatoes started the Irish immigration or that World War I stopped it. We are a nation in movement—the Great Migration seeking relief from the terrorism of the KKK bring their help, their hope, their promises of a new land, or the soldiers bringing their blues and jazz to Europe. We move from cakewalk to break dancing seeking something new, something safe, and something warm." I heard from the radio voice.

"We'd like to thank poet and professor, Nikki Giovanni, who teaches at Virginia Tech," the commentator said.

"Wow," was all I could think and say out loud. Virginia Tech is less than an hour from Roanoke. I had to meet her! The voice was so familiar because Nikki Giovanni was my introduction to Black women poets. At Alabama A&M University in the 1970s, we students were demanding to study the literature of African Americans, our people. A few dog-eared copies of books by Nikki Giovanni, Maya Angelou, Alice Walker, and Gwendolyn Brooks were passed around in my dorm. I still don't understand why this was an issue. We should've been the creator of that ideology.

⊷ ⊷

By that time, Giovanni had published *Black Feeling, Black Talk* (1967) and *Black Judgment* (1969). Both were reissued as a joint volume, *Recreation* (1970). Poems from these early volumes gained wider recognition when she recorded them against a background of gospel music for the album "Truth Is on Its Way" (1971). Giovanni had also published the early militant volume of poetry *My House* (1972), *The Women and the Men* (1975), and *Cotton Candy on a Rainy Day* (1978). She had emerged as one of the most prominent poets of the Black Arts Movement. Her early work is distinguished by its alliance with the themes and forms of the movement, radical black power, and black pride. She also gained herself the attention of James Baldwin, who requested that she be the one to interview him for a PBS special on race. Later her poetry moved to more introspective and mellow in style and content. Throughout her career, her poetry has kept its focus on social consciousness and love.

If You Don't Understand Yourself, You Don't Understand Anybody Else

In 1971, twenty-six-year-old Giovanni snagged a major interview and discussion with James Baldwin. The event was hosted by the PBS television series SOUL! The interview took place in London since Baldwin was too busy to come to NYC. It was considered a dialogue between Baldwin and Giovanni as an effort to "begin to draw upon each other's strengths rather than wallow in each other's weaknesses"—an effort all the more urgent today. For hours of absolute presence, intellectual communion, and occasional respectful rebuttal, they explored justice, freedom, morality, and what it means to be an empowered human being. The transcript was eventually published as *A Dialogue*.

Baldwin dived in; he wasn't one for small talk. "You somehow have to begin to break out of all that and try to become yourself. It's hard for anybody, but it's very hard if you're born Black in a white society, and hard because you've got to divorce yourself from the standards of that society. The danger of your generation, if I may say so . . . is to substitute one romanticism for another. Because categories—to put it simply but with a certain brutal truth—these categories are commercial categories." I can imagine him smoking cigarettes and smiling that glorious grin of his and those wondrous eyes looking everywhere. His words are thoughtful but with a knife.

"My generation came with a level of burdens. We had to overthrow a lot. It's what Langston Hughes said: 'We will express our own dark-skinned selves.'" Hughes was a poet, whom Giovanni admired and wanted to meet, but he died in May 1967, a few months before she moved to New York to attend graduate school at Columbia University. The other artist that Giovanni wanted to meet was Lorraine Hansberry, who died in January 1965. Malcolm X was assassinated a month later.

I can imagine Hansberry and Giovanni being friends. Both were intelligent, angry, and owned so much fire. Both are passionate and a fighter for social justice and discrimination. And both beautiful Black women. Hansberry brought theatre for black folks into its own. There was so much excitement. Everyone involved with *A Raisin in the Sun* was nervous. So many things could've gone wrong. But with Lloyd Richards at the helm as director, it was splendid. White folks couldn't keep saying that, "black folks don't go to the theatre." I can imagine Giovanni and Hansberry smoking cigarettes, drinking black coffee, and having an intellectual exchange. I can hear them laughing too.

—◆ ◆—

"We were aware of representing a group," was Giovanni's response to Baldwin's comments. "But how do you always take yourself with you?"

"Wherever you go, take yourself with you." Baldwin continues, "You know, I'd be a fool to think that there was someplace I could go where I wouldn't carry myself with me or that there was some way I could live if I pretended I didn't have the responsibilities which I do have. So I am a cat trying to make it in the world because I'm condemned to live in the world."

"Condemned," Giovanni answered loudly. I imagine her throwing up a fisted hand, sporting an afro bigger than her bright and charming face, maybe smoking cigarettes too. They're drinking black coffee.

"Condemned. Condemned in the sense that when you're young, and also when you're old, you would rather have around you the expected things to know where everything is. And it's a little difficult, but it's very valuable to be forced to move from one place to another and deal with another set of situations and to accept that it is going to be, in fact, it is your life. And to use it means you, in a sense, become neither white nor Black. And you learn a great deal; you're forced to learn a great deal about the history out of which all these words and conceptions and flags and morals come: Something has moved—things move in a very strange inexpressible way."

Baldwin continued in yet another gleam of extraordinary prescience, peers at the crux of this shift: "I think that without quite realizing it and no matter what our hang-ups of our generation, and the terrible situation in which all of us find ourselves—one thing has changed and that is the attitude that black people have toward themselves. Now within that change, I don't want to be romantic about it, but a great deal of confusion and incoherence will go on for a very long time. But that was inevitable. That moment had to come."

Baldwin continued to speak about the most heartbreaking and pernicious way in which all bigotry infiltrates the psyche and shrinks it from the inside. "It's not the world that was my oppressor because if the world does it to you long enough and effectively enough, you begin to do to yourself. You become a collaborator, an accomplice of your murderers because you believe the same things they do. They think it's important to be white, and you think it's important to be white; they think it's a shame to be Black, and you think it's a shame to be Black. And you have no corroboration around you of any other sense of life."

Giovanni is great with the exploration of the complexities of race. She reflects on her experience with the civil rights movement, which the Black Arts Movement grew out of.

"I came up in the sixties, which is way after everything else. But we always assumed that we knew white people, that we really sort of understood them. And I found out that if you don't understand yourself, you don't understand anybody else."

Baldwin harmonized that insight into an admonition of piercing presence. "Power without some sense of oneself is, to me, another kind of inability, and Black people would then become exactly what white people have become."

"This act of understanding, ourselves as well as one another, is invariably messy. I think one of the nicest things that we created, as a generation was just the fact that we could say, 'Hey, I don't like white people.' It was the beginning, of course, of being able to like them too," Giovanni said.

"We got this far by means which no one understands, including you and me. We're only beginning to apprehend it, and you're a poet precisely because you are beginning to apprehend it and put it into a form, which will be useful for you, your children, and for the world. Because we're not obliged to accept the world's definitions . . . We have to make our own definition and begin to rule the world that way because kids, white and black, cannot use what they have been given," Baldwin said.

"It's very hard to recognize that the standards which have almost killed you are really mercantile standards. They're based on cotton; they're based on oil; they're based on peanuts; they're based on profits. When you begin to realize all of that, which is not easy, that you begin to break out of the culture, which has produced you, and discover which is really produced you . . . what really brought you to where you are," Baldwin continued.

With an eye toward Giovanni's generation and future generations of writers, he observes a spark of optimism, which is rare for him. He seems to be passing his literary torch to her.

"Something has moved—things move in a very strange and in inexpressible ways. I think that without quite realizing it and no matter what our hang-ups are as of this very moment—the hang-ups of my generation or the hang-ups of your generation, and the attitude that black people have toward themselves. Now within that change—I don't want to be romantic about it—a great deal of confusion and incoherence will go on for a very long time. But that was inevitable. That moment had to come."

Giovanni is probably dressed in a dashiki and jeans with a big colorful wrap around her. Baldwin is wearing all black. Maybe they smoke a few more cigarettes; she continues to drink black coffee. I see him sipping Scotch as they move into the evening. He offers her a few maps to her literary future, but before telling her the price of the ticket.

When I asked Giovanni about the interview with Baldwin, she shucked her shoulders and said, "I was shocked that he wanted *little old me* for the interview. I was surprised but, of course, delighted. They even paid for my son to come to London with me; he was just a baby."

Baldwin knew exactly what he was doing, just as Beauford Delaney, a great painter and impressionist, had done for him. Delaney taught him how to see beauty in everything, even the most disgusting. Like Giovanni, Delaney was

Nikki Giovanni and James Baldwin.

born in Knoxville, Tennessee, more than forty years before her. And like James Baldwin, he died in Paris. Delaney trusted Baldwin, and Baldwin trusted Giovanni with the commodification of lives—lives that matter goes back a long time in history. Black Lives Matter grew from some of these early seeds.

Everything Will Change. The Only Question Is Growing Up or Decaying

When my son and I finally arrived in Roanoke, Virginia, in the late summer of 1989, there was a telephone strike. Everybody apologized to us for the hottest summer they could remember.

We thought it was nice, no television, no telephone. During the day, we unpacked and set up house in our new world. We listened to the radio, mostly NPR. In the evenings, we'd take breaks by sitting on the front porch in Old Southwest Roanoke, and facing the Roanoke Star, also called the Mill Mountain Star. Constructed in 1949, and known as the world's largest freestanding illuminated man-made star at the top of Mill Mountain. Thus, giving Roanoke the nickname of the "Star City of the South."

My son and I spoke of the slave history in Virginia and Thomas Jefferson. And how our lives were about to change; he was about to enter college at

Wesleyan University in Middletown, Connecticut. And, of course, I was about to enter graduate school and study creative writing, bringing an old dream back to life. Every other day we'd walk to the corner store through a small alley, and make a couple of necessary phone calls and buy cheap wine. We appreciated our peaceful life compared to Atlanta.

One day while unpacking, I found my stationery. I sat down and wrote notes to friends giving them my new address and soon-to-be telephone number. I also wrote Nikki Giovanni at Virginia Tech about hearing her on NPR. Less than a week later, she wrote me back and welcomed me to Virginia. And invited me to her class at Virginia Tech. I couldn't believe it!

What Is the Duty of a Teacher If Not to Inspire?

Most professors dread having football players in their classes. Giovanni embraced them since she's such a big sports fan. They loved her, which also meant they were willing to work hard in her classroom. Her approach was friendly and thoughtful, but she wasn't a pushover.

One golden September morning in 1990, we walked into the classroom; most of the students were reading the newspapers, especially the football players.

"You can put those newspapers down. I can give you a briefing." Giovanni spread her hands out like she was beginning to preach a sermon. "A female sports reporter, Lisa Olson, was interviewing the Patriots in their locker room. Players complained that they thought she was 'a looker,' standing around looking at their goods."

The classroom burst into such a long laughter that some students were coughing. Giovanni shook her head and laughed. "Hey, I'm just an old lady."

According to an article in the *Boston Globe*, some of the players taunted Olson by walking around naked in her presence, making vulgar comments and gestures. One player even "fondled his genitals" in front of her. She complained by describing the experience as a "mind rape." Even the team owner called her a "classic bitch." He even told the attendees a crude joke about the incident. Referring to the United States military's use of "Patriot Missiles" during the ongoing Gulf War. "What do the Iraqis have in common with Lisa Olson? They've both seen Patriot missiles up close."

An investigation concluded that Olson was "degraded and humiliated." When the public learned of this, Olson was subjected to harassment by fans of the Patriots. Her tires were slashed, she received hate mail and death threats, and her apartment was burglarized.

"Well, here's what I think," Giovanni told the class. "Ms. Olson just want to pay her mortgage and her bills, like all of us. And who knows, she probably has a big hard *one* at home waiting for her every night."

I thought the class would never stop laughing and coughing. When they calmed down, the tone changed. Giovanni wanted the class to understand that sexism, like racism, is real, and it affects all of us even when we're trying to do the right thing, like doing your job. "Literature wouldn't make any sense if we couldn't relate it to our own lives. It may not answer all of our questions, but it will expand your knowledge and raise more questions." She proceeds to begin the discussion of *The Autobiography of Miss Jane Pittman* by Ernest Gaines. Later Gaines was a guest at Virginia Tech.

The class syllabus moved from Africa to slavery. Since Giovanni knew so many people from all walks of life, on any given day, a famous guest would grace us with their presence. For example, Alex Haley, the author of *Roots*, came to Tech for Black History Month. The night of the program, we couldn't find Haley. "I know where he is," Giovanni said. We found him hanging out with the janitorial staff. He was laughing and having a grand old time. Giovanni invited the janitorial staff to come to the program and sit with her.

I Wouldn't Take Nothing for My Journey

We taught African American history through the creation of Negro Spirituals. Students learned the Negro National Anthem, "Lift Every Voice and Sing," by James Weldon Johnson. Sometimes I think of those students now in their adult life teaching their children that most important song.

Later in 2007, Giovanni wrote a book, *On My Journey NOW*. Our main goal was to teach the class, mostly Black students, not just their history but hoped that they would see the pride they should carry with them for being Black people, beautiful black people.

Giovanni heard spirituals growing up in the church, as I did. We probably grew up singing the same songs—"Just a Walk with Jesus," "Go down Moses," "Down by the Riverside," and so many others. She has always loved them, regarding them as sacred songs created and first sung by our ancestors. Traveling from the slave ports of Africa and back to congregations in the US, she has listened to the roots of those marvelous songs. She told stories that helped students to understand why the spirituals are so important. This allowed her to rid some ignorance and misunderstanding surrounding the legacy of the spirituals. Once she told them about being in Cape Coast Castle dungeons, where they were holding Africans to take them to America to make them enslaved people, you could hear them moan.

"I was talking to Roberta Flack, and she said, 'Did you, girl? Did you? Did you hear it?' 'Ro, I did. I mean, you feel it. It's there. It's sort like a moan.'"

Giovanni tells us in *On My Journey NOW*, "We know from the diaries of slave captains that if they brought the African up the first or second day, they would jump overboard because the people could just look back and see home."

"I laugh at the myth that Africans don't swim, which is crazy. They lived near the Atlantic Ocean, and, of course, they would swim. When swimming pools were segregated, that made it harder for black folks to swim. Just more white folks lies." She strutted to the other side of the classroom.

In 2014, I remembered being in that same space with Giovanni. Leap for Ghana is an international educational organization founded and led by Kwame Alexander, a former student of Giovanni's. The John Newberry prize-winner invited us via the US Embassy.

The Queen Mother of Kinko, a village in Ghana where we worked with small children and raised money to send high school girls to school, said she had been in the dungeons more than twenty times and felt the same horror each time. The dungeons are cobbled, stoned floors, walls, and ceilings, no windows, and some five hundred years of stench. You've never smelled anything like it. There are two dungeons for the women; the smallest one is for the women who fought back.

"I would've jumped in the ocean." I closed my eyes. "I wouldn't. I would've fought until the last breath in my body," Giovanni said.

We learned that soldiers who captured the African women regularly raped them. And if their pregnancy showed before the next ship sailed, they were thrown into the ocean. Our hotel was on the ocean near Cape Coast. I never slept. I couldn't wash the five hundred years of stench from my body. Instead of hearing the roar of the ocean, I heard the moaning of the ancestors.

Giovanni wanted students to correct their misunderstanding by demanding that they understand by offering a new and fresh voice by expanding her intimate listening circle into an infinitely larger but still intimate community of intergenerational readers. From the time Africans were taken on board the slave ships, they had to choose to face an unknown and clearly harsh future or give up. Their choice was to fight and find ways to survive and pray for a better future.

She has such a keen poetic vision to guide us through the inner world of the brave Africans in bondage who created the spirituals. She helped students to discover for themselves some of the reasons why we needed the wisdom of the ancestors. Spirituals are the best way to make such a claim. Her discovery is profound and sometimes unsettling. "Read at your own risk and be aware that the changes you experience in yourself will make you feel uneasy, but they will be good for you and for all of us," she promised her students.

Giovanni encouraged students to see and hear the spirituals through the eyes and ears of the original singers and their progeny. She not only raised questions to the class, but she often provided her own answers. In one instance, she asked students to think about why people in the midst of suffering and trauma would want to sing. She believes we must sit with the idea that the singers were simply proud of their work in spite of it being imposed on them. They sang as an expression of that pride. This forced all of us, especially students, to discard the common image of enslaved people as victims in favor of an image of them as intact human beings in all times and places throughout centuries.

Her work encourages us to consider the multiple layers of injustice they experienced and their desperate but powerful response to it, as captured in their moans and, eventually, their songs. Through her work, she introduces us to the genius of the singers, seen in so many ways, including their decision to escape from slavery by day rather than night. The effectiveness of this strategy is reflected in the eagerness to pass fugitive slave laws and in the sheer number of escapes over the years—one hundred thousand, by the South's own estimate.

Nobody claims to know when or where particular spirituals were created and sung. Giovanni doesn't speculate; she simply points out the universal meanings of the songs and how they show the challenges that enslaved people faced in dealing with their captors. "Done Made My Vow to the Lord. And I never will turn back." This saying allows us to picture the horror experienced by the Africans thrown into the holds of slave ships during the Middle Passage. Giovanni helps us to understand the experience of people in bondage by immersing us in the lyrics, melodies, and rhythms of the songs they have passed down to us. Her approach lends new meanings to songs like "This Little Light of Mine," "Sometimes I Feel Like a Motherless Child," "All of God's Children Got Shoes," and many other spirituals that have previously been thought about in less creative ways.

If students follow the guidance of Giovanni, they are guaranteed to be touched by the infinite wisdom that comes through these songs we call spirituals. We need all the wisdom we can get!

All of that first semester wasn't always so alive and wonderful. During the Christmas holidays, I lost four male students from other classes. Two were killed in car accidents, one from alcohol poisoning, and one shot himself through the heart. We learned this when we came back for the second semester. I fell apart but knew I had to pull myself together; a new semester was about to begin.

"Oh, Ethel, this is horrible. I'm so sorry. Try and think about it like this, you probably won't lose another student for a long time. This is a big place with so many students; statistics are against them," Giovanni tried to comfort me.

The next day wasn't a teaching day; she called me at home "to check on me." I was still stunned, but listening to spirituals helped me to try and get through such a shocking and painful experience.

The Fisk University Years

The most important thing Giovanni ever did was to leave high school and go to college at Fisk University early. "That was a good thing, one more year of high school, and I'm sure I'd have been a secret alcoholic or something crazy like that." She blinked her eyes quickly, showing so much love and pride for Fisk. She was blinking toward tears. "Fisk is special to me because my Grandpa had graduated from there in 1905. I had hoped to follow in his footsteps. It was not to be. I had too much anger, too much hurt, and not enough of myself. I got kicked out."

Giovanni maintains that was a good thing too. She was allowed to recognize that the dean who kicked her out was wrong, but she was wrong too. She met Jackie Cowan and considers her to have been a lifeline. She allowed Giovanni to sit in her office for hours, reading a book or just sitting. "But the anger was leaving, and the love was coming through. She gave me responsibilities, and I would do anything to keep from letting her down. She might not have understood me, but we traveled the road together to my graduation and graduate school."

There were many others of her mother's friends: Theresa Elliot was always there for her. "My heart belonged to her." Her mother's friend, Lauretta, paid for college for one semester, and her mother paid for the next semester, then she received a scholarship.

"I didn't understand why they kept saying I had a bad attitude. I always thought I was a nice person. Imagine my surprise when 'bad attitude' was what I kept hearing about me." She shook her head. "Beats me. True, some people wondered why I learned to hate Theodore Currier since he had been was very kind to historian John Hope Franklin."

Franklin said this about Theodore S. Currier, "a professor of history at Fisk University in Nashville, Tennessee. He was the first 'white man' who treated me as his social and intellectual equal." Currier became his "mentor, major professor, and closest friend." Because of Currier's influence, Franklin decided not to follow his father into the law but instead chose an academic career in history.

By the time Giovanni encountered Currier, "he was old and, in my opinion, corrupt, and he wouldn't give me a recommendation for a Woodrow Wilson."

"Chicken," he said. He called everyone "Chicken" or "Chief." "Your hair is so rebellious."

"I wanted to tell him, go f**k your 'Chicken.'"

A Distant Star Called Possibility: The Sisters of Wintergreen

When Nikki Giovanni and Virginia Fowler invited me to Wintergreen, here's how Giovanni described Wintergreen to me. "Well, it's like, a distant star called possibility." I didn't know what that meant but knew that I would soon. Giovanni envied her mother's friends, although not always. When she was a little girl, she knew something extraordinary was going on. "Mommy had girlfriends, and they were always around. Flora was one of those friends. Mommy and Gus helped to send her to college. Gus (my father) talked to her parents and convinced them to let her go. Flora used to babysit my sister Gary and me. She hated it, especially me; I was such a whiney child." Giovanni laughed. "Imagine that, me whiney and crying all the time. Nobody I know would believe that." Giovanni went on to say girlfriends are the most precious gift on earth.

Her first time at Wintergreen was after she spoke at James Madison University in Harrisonburg, Virginia. There she met scholar Joanne Gabbin, and while they were dining with students, Giovanni mentioned she accepted an invitation from Virginia Tech to be a Visiting Professor. She was looking forward to their universities working together.

"We must get together to welcome you to Virginia," Gabbin said with glee. She invited Giovanni and about ten other women to Wintergreen, a resort between Lynchburg and Charlottesville. It was a weekend of girlfriends getting to know each other. Some of us are famous and some of us are not. It doesn't matter; what matters is that we've been gathering on the mountaintop for more than thirty years cheering each other on.

"We played cards, swam, walked in the woods (dodging bears), read poetry to the group, cooked, and ate." Giovanni recalled somebody saying, "let's do it again." They have been doing it again for thirty years. "Wintergreen is a haven where we cheer each other on. Not my mother's friends, for sure. But we ride in the night winds, our hearts skip across the clouds, coming to rest on a distant star call possibility; we arrive at Wintergreen."

Know Who's Playing the Music before You Dance

During the three years we taught together, Giovanni published: *Scared Cows and Other Edibles*, edited *Appalachian Elders: A Warm Hearth Sampler*, *Racism 101*, *Knoxville Tennessee*, *GrandMothers: A Multicultural Anthology of Poems, Reminiscences and Short Stores about the Keepers of Our Traditions*. Of course, I was thrilled when she asked me to contribute to *GrandMothers*.

Nikki Giovanni

I reread *Gemini: An Extended Autobiographical Statement My First Twenty-Five Years of Being a Black Poet*. It had been more than twenty years since I first read it. The title comes from the zodiac sign that Giovanni was born under (June 7, 1943).

"I almost entitled *Gemini* 'Rejected Writings,'" Giovanni said.

"That's a great title that all writers can identify. Why didn't you stay in the genre of nonfiction since you're such a great storyteller?" I asked.

"I think poetry is a more natural medium for me because you get so many dissimilarities that you blend. Poetry is kind of like soup, or a stew, or something you keep adding spices until you get the flavor right. But I enjoyed writing *Gemini*."

Gemini is not a strictly chronological autobiography in the usual sense (which I appreciate); rather, it is a collection of selected and arranged recollections and reflections that helped her develop into the black revolutionary poet that she was at the time of its writing. Some readers even call it a collection of essays. Giovanni was twenty-eight when she published *Gemini*. Most of the pieces had indeed been written several years earlier when she reflected on having turned twenty-five.

The book is divided into thirteen sections and covers everything from a history of her grandparents, John Brown and Louvenia Watson, to an appreciation of actress, singer, and black icon Lena Horne to an appraisal of the early black novelist and short-story writer Charles Waddell Chesnutt to a review of a book on black music by black writer Phyllis Garland which Giovanni found severely limited. Through these comments, and especially in the last section, *"Gemini—A Prolonged Autobiographical Statement on Why,"* Giovanni grapples with various aspects of her thoughts and feelings in an attempt to explain and justify her stance as a revolutionary. She is never apologetic; rather, she speaks her mind very matter-of-factly in the characteristic Giovanni manner, as she does today and, I am sure, always will. Readers learn something about Giovanni's life but more about her ideas.

One reviewer wrote the following: "All of the essays involve personal observations mingled with political concerns, as the final lines of the essay '400 Mulvaney Street' illustrate: 'They had come to say, "Welcome Home." And I thought Tommy, my son, must know about this. He must know we come from somewhere. That we belong.'"

Family and belonging, identity, and one's relationship to the world are a capsule of Giovanni's major themes. As the people of Knoxville come to

229

hear her, Giovanni realizes her connection to a place and people. Sharing this with her son underscores the importance of family and passing on legacies, a lesson for not only him but for all black people. "To know that they come from somewhere and therefore belong is part of the message in this work," she said of *Gemini*.

Giovanni came to New York City in the 1960s to attend graduate school at Columbia University. So many magazines and people would invite her to submit articles. She learned the game very early on. "You have to pay or play. Otherwise, you'll go broke because you're doing speculative work, and you can't get paid for that." Giovanni could always write the article that was wanted, but if it was rejected, she still got seventy-five percent of the pay. That's how she ended up with essays that became *Gemini*.

"Do you remember when you became a poet?"

"Not a lot. I am not a big fan of that; I mean, even now, people will say, 'I have a ten-year-old who writes poetry.' For me, it's like oh please, leave me alone. I've been writing all my life because I enjoy writing. When I was growing up, writing was not a subject. A subject is something that made sense, like history, science, and math, or arithmetic. It took me the longest to get used to; all of a sudden, there was a new idea of writing being a subject. And so, I've been writing all my life, first and second grades, as long as I can remember."

Giovanni's eighth-grade English teacher Ms. Alfreda DeLaney was the last person who called her Yolande, which is also her mother's name. She helped Giovanni not to just see some her limitations but offered solutions, always with love.

"Yolande, you have to take typing because your handwriting is so poor." She was born Yolande Cornelia Giovanni Jr., in Knoxville, Tennessee.

Giovanni answered, "Yes, Ms. Delaney."

"Did you learn to type?" I asked.

"If you call what I do typing. I'm still not good. At least it's readable. Ms. Delaney was honest. I like that. But in terms of being a poet, I am not a fan of that language, just because I have friends that are like, 'oh, I want to be a poet.' Why would you want to be a poet? Why wouldn't you tell your story? Content is what's important, not context."

Giovanni continued, "If someone said, 'I want to be a singer.' No, you want to sing these songs. Kathleen Battle would never say, 'Oh, I always wanted to be a singer' because it wouldn't make sense. I know it wouldn't make sense for Leontyne [Price] or Jessye [Norman] because they have always sang; the question was, do they sing opera, in which case you have a trained voice? Or do they just continue with that sort of raw talent that they have and sing spirituals? But they would never have approached it as the bigger picture but simply as 'this is what I do.' And do writing is what I do, and the fact that we are in a genre, we call it poetry, it's good, but I've never tried to not write other things," Giovanni explains.

She offers another example, "It's like you have to move around; one must move around. And if you have a car, if you make lots of money, you have a Lexus or whatever. If you're born to royalty like Prince Charles, you have a Maserati, or you write lots of books like David Baldacci, and then you drive your Maserati, or you have a Volkswagen, but it's all a car. And you don't even think about anything other than I need transportation."

Giovanni was influenced by many great teachers. Sister Althea, a black Episcopalian nun. I remember Sister Althea well. We used to visit Giovanni at the same time. One Thanksgiving, I drove from Morgantown, and Sister Althea drove from Cincinnati. She had driven one hundred miles more than me. My car was covered in mud and salt, but Sister Althea's car was clean and shiny as a freshly mopped floor. "She has a direct line to God," Giovanni said. They remained friends until Sister Althea joined the ancestors. She loved Tiger Woods. I used to watch golf with her while Giovanni and Fowler prepared lunch or dinner.

Another good fortune Giovanni had with teachers was Ms. Alfreda DeLaney, who, in a less segregated world, would've taught at a college or university. Of course, segregation was wrong, and a bad idea, but good things came out of it. Ms. DeLaney couldn't get another job but teaching high school. That's how Giovanni learned about Langston Hughes; Ms. DeLaney loved him. Giovanni did a book report on him and drew a picture of him with a bad nose. "I think Mr. Hughes would like this nose," Ms. DeLaney wrote. "That's why I always loved Hughes."

Giovanni laughed when I asked her about influences on her writing. Coming of age in the 1950s, she said you could "name black writers on one hand." She opened her left hand like a book. "We all knew and loved [Paul Laurence] Dunbar. That's what church was about; Children's Day and Mother's Day, everybody was going to recite Dunbar since he felt, to us anyway, like a home boy. He was born in Dayton, Ohio, and I was raised in Cincinnati."

I was thinking about brown baby Little brown baby wif spa'klin' eyes,
Come to yo' pappy an' set on his knee.
What you been doin', suh—makin' san' pies?
Look at dat bib—you's es du'ty ez me.
Look at dat mouf—dat's merlasses, I bet;
Come hyeah, Maria, an' wipe off his han's.
Bees gwine to ketch you an' eat you up yit,
Bein' so sticky an sweet—goodness lan's!
Little brown baby wif spa'klin' eyes,
Who's pappy's darlin' an' who's pappy's chile?
Who is it all de day nevah once tries
Fu' to be cross, er once loses dat smile?
Whah did you git dem teef? My, you's a scamp! . . .

She recited the whole poem and smiled after every word. "I can recite that poem in my sleep. My generation ended up complaining about Dunbar's plantation time. Of course, that's ridiculous because if he hadn't captured that, the only person that would've done anything with it would have been the minstrels." Giovanni slaps her hands on her desk. "And it was Dunbar speaking to that particular point. Black children would've been called picka-ninnies, but it was nice that he called black children little brown babies."

As a child, she also knew the works of Gwendolyn Brooks "whom I got to know as a friend. James Weldon Johnson. Somebody was always reciting 'God's Trombones.'" Giovanni stood up from her desk and raised her hands to the heavens. "God stepped out on space, and He looked around and said: I'm lonely—I'll make me a world." She laughed. "My grandfather was a Latin scholar, so he would read the Greek dramas."

Early on, Giovanni read a reference to Walt Whitman's *Leaves of Grass*, which seemed so enchanting to her, the idea of "leaves of grass." She went to the Carnegie Library (the black library) and asked to check the book out. "Well, we don't have it," the librarian said. "I'll have to go and get it." The memory stayed with Giovanni. She had no idea what Ms. Long had to go through to get the book. She had to go to Lawson McGee (the white library) and ask them permission to get that copy and bring it to Carnegie. She could imagine the white librarian asking, "Well, who wants to read it?"

The February before I left Virginia Tech for a tenure track position at West Virginia University, we experienced another deep blow. Arthur Ashe died from AIDS, which he contracted through a blood transfusion during his brain surgery. A big part of my relationship with Giovanni is that we love tennis. Her mother, Giovanni, used to play with the great Althea Gibson, the first African American to win grand slam titles, French Open, Wimbledon, and the US Nationals (which became the US Open). And she was the first black athlete to cross the color line of international tennis. Giovanni, Fowler, and I used to play on the courts at Virginia Tech. They always beat me until I finally improved my game by joining a tennis group in Roanoke. Even before the great Williams sisters arrived on the tennis scene, we were big fans. Every year Giovanni goes to the Cincinnati Open, where she has box seats, and a street is named in her honor. She has also gone to Wimbledon. I used to go to the US Open in NYC every year with a group of tennis fans from Pittsburgh. I miss those days.

You Must Invent Your Own Games and Teach Others How to Play

Living and finding my way around Morgantown, West Virginia, in a tenure-stressed environment was a challenge. Giovanni continued to be in my life; she wrote letters, talked on the phone, and, of course, there was Wintergreen. It was difficult to leave my new world, but the state of Virginia had a freeze on jobs. In fact, before I set foot in the classroom, my $20,000 became $500 less. I didn't see a future as an instructor. I was thankful to have health insurance and a retirement. With my son in college, I needed more dependable employment.

Even though I was sad about leaving my new world, there was much to celebrate: Toni Morrison shook the literary world by receiving the Noble Prize for Literature; William Jefferson Clinton became the forty-second president of the United States. Progress was on the rise. We believed that the arch of social justice was bending in our direction.

But our hearts were broken too. We lost so many great ones, including and surely not all: Marion Anderson, Alice Childress, Billy Eckstine, Ralph Ellison, Dizzy Gillespie, Audrey Hepburn, Thurgood Marshall, Carmen McRae, Richard Nixon (didn't break our hearts), Jacqueline Kennedy Onassis, and Wilma Rudolph.

Hip-Hop Is a Cultural Expression—It's Embracing

Spirituals aren't the only music that Giovanni loves. She has always been a jazz, blues, and rhythm and blues fan. She loves opera, too, if it's by Leontyne Price, Kathleen Battle, or Jessye Norman. Two decades before rap music burst on the scene, Giovanni made soul-stirring recordings of her poems backed by some of the nation's most acclaimed gospel choirs. Giovanni is an unwavering supporter of black youth, including Black Lives Matter. She is a fan of hip-hop and artists like Queen Latifah. She was devastated by the assassination of rap singer Tupac Shakur. She sports a tattoo on her left forearm that reads "Thug Life" to honor Shakur. A huge poster of him greets you when you enter Giovanni's office.

"Tupac was a great man. That was a serious loss. When I look at a kid like Tupac, I know he was cut down before he blossomed because somebody could see there was another one of those lights coming and wanted to get rid of it." She wipes away tears. "If the kid had lived, he would have a combination of Martin Luther King and Malcolm X. You didn't have to be smart to see that the boy was dangerous."

Giovanni dedicated her book *Love Poems* to Tupac:

a lover whose love was often deliberately misunderstood
but who will live in the sun and the rain and whose name
will echo through all the winds whose spirit will flower and
who like Emmett Till and Malcolm X will be remembered
by his people for the great man he could have become and
most especially for the beautiful boy he was

Students often ask about her love of Tupac and who killed him, and why? "It's the same questions as who killed Malcolm X, Martin, JFK, or Bobby Kennedy." Bobby Kennedy had been a close friend of hers. "We have a whole list of assassinations. When you look at the great men of this century. It's the same forces. They are killed because of their politics." She pulled her hand through her short, curly afro. "People keep asking me how come black folks are sticking with Clinton. I say, hell, we know a lynching when we see one."

When I met Giovanni in the late 1980s, I thought she was so cool sporting her tattoo Thug Life to honor him. This was, of course, before the popularity of tattoos. She believes that rap music has been around for a long time in the form of poetry, whether you read Langston Hughes, Paul Laurence, or Gwendolyn Brooks.

She had the pleasure of meeting blues singer Alberta Hunter. Giovanni recalled her saying, "People always talking about the late blues saying it's slow. The blues ain't slow; the blues is truth-telling." Hunter inspired Giovanni's book *Blues: For All the Change.* That meeting made Giovanni think she wanted her next book to "deal with some of her blues—I still want to be free, I don't want to be intimidated." She thought of the writer Chester Himes, "I've had a stroke and a heart attack, but nothing put me back as much as bad reviews."

Once Giovanni told Toni Morrison, a good friend of hers, "I couldn't make it if I had to believe what people said about my work. I'd be depressed. But in the book *Blues: For All the Change,* the blues are saying, 'She ain't scared or intimidated.'"

In 1994 Giovanni published a revolutionary book *Racism 101,* hailed by critics as profoundly personal and blisteringly political, angry, and funny, lyrical, and blunt. But critics thought that Giovanni was indicting higher education for the inequities it perpetuates, contemplates the legacy of the 1960s by providing a survival guide on predominantly white campuses, complete with razor-sharp comebacks to the dumb questions consistently asked of black students.

Giovanni reminds us that we must keep raising the consciousness since there are a lot of black people who don't accept that we've been victims. "I really do intensely dislike such people as Shelby Steele or Clarence Thomas who say we aren't victims."

In addressing affirmative action, Giovanni believes that's the very least they [white folks] can do for us [Black folks]. "I am tired of Negroes saying, 'We don't need affirmative action.' Maybe we don't, but I do. Nobody considered five hundred years of segregation affirmative action for white people, but that's what it was."

Further in the text, Giovanni also excoriates Spike Lee while offering her own ideas for a film about Malcolm X. She writes about W. E. B. Du Bois, gardening, her friend Toni Morrison, *Star Trek,* affirmative action, space, exploration, President John F. Kennedy, the role of griots, and the rape and neglect of urban schools. Professor Virginia Fowler writes in her Foreword, "These pieces are artistic expressions of a particular way of looking at the world, feathering a performing voice capable of dizzying displays of virtuosity."

Nikki Giovanni.

Unlike the critics, I believe *Racism 101* should be required reading for all races and ethnicities of students. It's a teaching guide. Not only that, it should be required reading for every faculty and staff member of every college or university.

Cancer Diagnosis

When asked how she got to be Nikki Giovanni, admired for being a fierce and independent black woman, she said: "I'm not trying to do anything but be myself and survive. I went blonde a couple years ago; folks had a fit. What people didn't know, and what I don't mind talking about now, is that I'd done it because I had lung cancer and had to have my left lung removed. I needed to make myself feel better; I went blonde."

I'll never forget that phone call from her in February 1996. I thought it was a call to catch what we did over the holidays; what did I think about Mary Pearce winning the Australian Open and how exciting it was that Agassi beat Sampras in the men's final.

"I am calling to tell you I've been diagnosed with lung cancer."

I heard her, but I did not believe I heard correctly. "What?"

Giovanni repeated. I had no idea what questions to ask. But I did manage to ask how it was discovered. And what could I do? I knew that was a standard question when these things happened. "Well, I've lived a public life, and I will die a public death," she told me.

It was found during a routine checkup. I called a friend's husband, who specialized in black lung disease since it was a major disease in West Virginia. He gave me a list of questions to ask. Giovanni had the surgery in Cincinnati to remove one of her lungs along with two of her ribs. That was more than twenty years ago. Here's an excerpt from a poem, "Cancers," about her experience:

The blood vessels carry . . . cancerous cells . . . to all body
parts . . . cruising
would be the term . . . but this is not necessarily a love
poem . . .

Both Giovanni and I tried to raise Black boys to be Black men. She said when she had Thomas in 1969, there was no concept of single parents. They accused her of "setting a bad example because I wouldn't reveal the identity of my son's father." She said she wasn't a role model in that regard, "I just try to live my life and be a decent human being." She does not want to be defined by people since people want more than she can give. She's reconceptualizing family, even with her own son. "He's grown. I've done all I can do," she said wearily. "I want out of the mommy business. I want to go on a cruise. I want somebody to come by and say, 'Would you like another glass of wine.' I've earned that."

The mommy business is exhausting. We used to talk about what we were going to do with the extra money we'd have when our sons graduated from college, which was the same year. Thomas from Morehouse, where he had legacy, and Marcus from Wesleyan, where he was the cocaptain of the soccer team and graduated with honors.

"I called Thomas and said, I'm buying a dress and booking the hotel. We're good, right? I don't want no f**kups." I had a similar conversation with Marcus. But what Giovanni and I didn't realize was that law school and graduate school would zap all of that extra money we thought we'd have. Still, "Beautiful Black Men" conveys her profound love. "I wanta say just gotta say something / bout those beautiful beautiful / beautiful outasight / black men / with they afros walking down the street / in the same ol danger / but a brand new pleasure . . ."

Motherless Child

In 2004, scientist Robert Baker named a new species of bat for Giovanni: *Micronycteris giovanniae*. This is one of Giovanni's most treasured honors from one of her biggest fans. Early in 2005, Oprah Winfrey named her one of twenty-five Living Legends, a group that included Toni Morrison, Rosa Parks, Lena Horne, and Dorothy Height.

But heavy burdens were coming, and when they hit, it was hard and heavy. Early in December 2004, Giovanni's sister Gary was diagnosed with inoperable lung cancer, which had already metastasized in her liver. Doctors gave her less than a year to live. Six months later, her mother fell and was hospitalized. She hadn't been ill but died within two weeks. Her sister died two weeks later. Giovanni believes her mother died because she didn't want to bury her oldest daughter.

I recall talking to Giovanni while she sat with her dying mother. She was always writing; she never cried. I saved my crying for after the phone calls.

There were other heartbreaks that Giovanni had to put aside; she was too devastated, and her own grief had cut too deep. But she looked like she was coping when she lost Ossie Davis, Rosa Parks, her Auntie Annie, and Edna Lewis during that time.

My memory of the time is hazy; my own mother was suffering from dementia. I had just seen her in August before starting the new semester. She seemed her usual snappy self. I had planned to visit her again at Christmas. But the first week of October 2005, my sister called to tell me that our mother had been found walking down the road. A neighbor found her in her night-clothes, screaming, "She was gonna be late to work." My sister moved her in with her, but it was too much for her to handle. When my mother was moved into a nursing home, she stopped eating. By the first week of December, my eighty-four-year-old mother was gone.

For the New Year, I was looking for something that had to do with Wintergreen; I found a picture of Mrs. Giovanni. She was standing outside smiling and smoking a cigarette. She wore slack and a wind jacket. I sent the picture to Giovanni, who called and thanked me. She invited me to Easter dinner. "Bring pictures of your mother. And we'll just sit and talk, and cry, and laugh and eat."

ACKNOWLEDGMENTS

Creating and publishing a book is a lengthy, frustrating, and painful experience. One should never walk the journey alone. I didn't have to; I thank my generous and patient interviewees for their grace and goodwill—Louise Bruyn, John Canty, Deloris Pringle, Constance Curry, Sandra and Henry Ford, Virginia Blanche Franklin Moore, Nikki Giovanni, Andrea Lee, Gloria Naylor, Susan Perry Cole. I thank Ida Canty, the niece of John Canty, Wallace Hood, the nephew of Blanche Virginia Franklin Moore, Ann Curry, sister of Constance Curry, and Olivia Cole Welch, cousin of Ann Cole Lowe. Thank you all for making my world bigger and better.

I will always be grateful to University Press of Mississippi for taking a chance on me. Katie Keene, my first editor showed so much enthusiasm for the project and understood my vision immediately. I appreciate the hard work of Lisa McMurtray, who moved the work from manuscript to book. Jennifer Mixon knew just the right image to show my dreams, you're the best. Nell Lambdin, you had me when you told me how moved you were by my Big Mama character. I thank the nameless staff who worked hard in designing and creating this book. I especially thank Craig Gill.

I am so fortunate and thankful to my Wintergreen Sisters, who are always on the frontline with me. For this project, I received support from: an NEH fellowship at the Ernest Gaines Center, the University of Louisiana at Lafayette, PLAYA, Summer Lake, Oregon, and my friends, known as the Downtowners, who offered me a community and friendship when I first moved to Birmingham.

I thank my family: Marcus Bernard Smith, Lela Will Baker, Lila Mae Baker Kendrick, DeNekka Nicole Baker, Zerika Zinae Baker Stepter, Timothy Ferelle Stepter Jr., Timothy Ferelle Stepter, III, and Trenton Kade Stepter, Reginald Durand Baker, Nikki Nycole Baker, Amyah Baker, Tarvaris Marshun Greene, Tawana McLeod Greene, and Renia Breshon Greene.

No writer is better than her editors, Janice Eidus, Opal Moore, Dawn Raffel (the best in the business), and Joanne Sills, thank you for your thoughtful and honest critiques. Friends, you supported me and guided me toward the light. Mary Carter Bishop, Valerie Boyd, Beth Bradley, Mark Brazaitis, Ellen Brown, Jane Cardi, Mark Childress, Kim Connor, Daryl Dance, Janice Eidus, Patricia Elam, Anna Elfenbein, John Ernest, Virginia Fowler, LaWade Garris, Nikki Giovanni, Claudia Handler, Blair Hobbs, Jestina Howard-Crosby, Randall Kenan, Anna Lawson, Beth Macy, Donna Matern, Jeanetha Morris, Marilyn Moriarty, Greg Neimeyer, Mary and Rick Paynter, Christa Parravani, Lisa and Mike Perez, Fran Perkins, Deloris Pringle, Silvia Kunze-Ritter, Edwina Rogers, Pat Madison Saunders, and Georgia Tyson.

We all have had so many losses and so much pain during this extraordinary time. I honor all of those brave and courageous souls and hope they had a safe transition. May we all find peace.

NOTES

Chapter 1. An Army of God: Do What You Can Do—
Dr. Sandra Mathews Ford (1953-) and Henry Michael Ford (1953-)

I interviewed Dr. Sandra Ford and her husband, Henry Ford, at their home in Birmingham, Alabama, about their work in the Black Belt of Alabama, especially the Gees Bend area. Every first Saturday of the month, they and the army have provided medical services to the under-resourced and underserved citizens for nearly twenty years. We also talked on the telephone several times with most of my interviewees. Few used computers.

On the *Facing South* website, Junior Walter wrote an article about the poverty in the Black Belt of Alabama being compared to developing nations. This wasn't the article that Dr. Ford read. This article was written in 2018. Dr. Ford's article was published more than thirty-five years ago. She read this one and stated it was very similar to the one she read more than thirty years ago. There are many of these articles, including several from the United Nations. That article propelled Dr. Ford to become a physician and help the disadvantaged.

Chapter 2. A View of Grace from the Top—John Canty (1925-2019)

I interviewed John Canty in March 2014 in Summerton, South Carolina. Historian Delores Pringle introduced us and was present during the first interview.

Lee Daniels' The Butler was playing in theatres when I interviewed Canty, who did not care for the film. He said it was too violent and brought back too many bad memories of the time for him.

Canty didn't think the Civil Rights Act didn't change much for regular people. He thought the most improvement after the Civil Rights Act was the appointment of Thurgood Marshall to the Supreme Court and President Johnson's War on Poverty.

Canty graduated from high school in 1943. In fact, his high school was one of the five cases of *Brown v. Board of Education*. Other states included Virginia, Delaware, Kansas, and

Washington, DC. South Carolina was the first state, but Thurgood Marshall said it would never happen in the South; he chose Topeka, Kansas.

Chapter 3. An Unyielding Feminist: Shirley Chisholm—Susan Perry Cole (1948-)

Susan Perry Cole was a congressional aide for Congresswoman Shirley Chisholm and the first African American woman to run for president of the United States of America. Since the congresswoman was such a well-known figure, Cole provided many up close and personal moments of the woman who said, "she wanted to be remembered as someone with guts." I interviewed Perry in her office, where she is the CEO of the Legal Services Corporation in Rocky Mount, North Carolina.

Chapter 4. The Art of Activism—Constance Curry (1933-2020)

I interviewed Constance Curry at home in Atlanta, Georgia, in 2012. I've been talking to Curry all my life.

In August 1964 Curry went to Mississippi with SNCC (Student Nonviolent Coordinating Committee), led by Ella Baker and Julian Bond. That summer, the bodies of civil rights workers James Chaney, Andrew Goodman, and Michael Schwerner were found.

Southern Patriot, Ella Baker, the founder of SNCC from Shaw University, wrote a letter that was the beginning of SNNCC. Curry credits Baker for an important part of her education and experience.

Heart of Atlanta Motel, Inc. v. United States was a case worked on. The motel had violated the terms of the Civil Rights Act of 1964 by not allowing Blacks to stay there.

Chapter 5. What Color Is the World?—Blanche Virginia Franklin Moore (1917-2016)

I first interviewed Blanche Virginia Franklin Moore in a nursing home in Clarksburg, West Virginia; she was ninety-five years old. Moore maintained that she and her family have been discriminated all of her life, beginning when she was in the third grade and was sent home three times because she was too dark-skinned. The school only accepted *mulatto* students. Her other example of being discriminated was that West Virginia State University was supposed to be for our people (Black folks). According to Moore the College has no business calling itself a Historical Black College, with barely any Black students. Moore believed it was a wrong interpretation of *Brown v. Board of Education*. How could a white college call itself a HBCU?

Moore was reared by her grandfather Henry Franklin, who fought for education for Black children who often had no school for them, and equal rights for all; he was a smart businessman. But he was also known as an inventor; he even owned a patent for his machine that helped get coal out faster, but according to his granddaughter, his patent was stolen from the attorneys he hired to protect him.

The Black Diamond of 1918 stated that the Century Coal Company built two coal mines and first shipped coal from Century Coal Company in 1897. However, state records state it was 1916. By 1860–70, more than 1,000 African Americans moved to West Virginia to work. This increased the Black population from 0.1 percent in 1880 to 30.7 percent by 1910; by 1918,

Notes

it was at its highest at 115,000. This argument helped Franklin's argument for schools for Black children. Today about 60,000 African Americans live in the state of West Virginia.

Chapter 6. Designing Dreams—Ann Cole Lowe (1898–1981)

Ann Cole Lowe should have been famous for creating and designing the most photographed wedding dress in the world. She created and designed the wedding dress and the wedding party for Jacqueline Bouvier when she married Senator John Kennedy.

She was born in Clayton, Alabama, where I attended high school. Olivia Cole Welch was one of my best friends in high school . Her father and Ann Cole Lowe were first cousins. That's how I first learned of Lowe. I've always heard about this Annie who could make anybody and anything beautiful. Other than Lowe and her son, all of the family is buried in the Old Black Cemetery in Clayton. I interviewed five relatives who remembered her.

The *Tampa Tribune* published "There is much 'weeping and wailing and maybe gnashing of teeth,' to use the old expression, among Tampa society maids over the fact that Annie is going to New York . . . feminine society is wondering just how it will be able to survive the future events." It was 1917, and Lowe was on her way to the S.T. Taylor Design School in New York City.

Ladies Home Journal, April 1961 characterized Lowe as "a colored woman dressmaker" who designed and created Kennedy's wedding dress. Lowe wrote Kennedy and told her she was an haute couture. Kennedy's secretary telephoned Lowe and said Mrs. Kennedy didn't know anything about what to do with the article.

In 1917, eighteen-year-old Ann Cole Lowe enrolled at The S. T. Taylor Design School in NYC. They didn't know she was Black but allowed her to stay on, although she had to sit outside of the classroom. No white students would sit near her. She finished the two years and learned that the instructor had been stealing her designs.

Chapter 7. Walking Is Like a Prayer—Louise Bruyn (1931–)

I interviewed Bruyn about a book she had written more than thirty years about her one-woman walk from Boston to DC to protest the Vietnam War.

Chapter 8. Drinking from the Cup of Equality—Dr. Mary Emma Bruce (1910–2010)

I interviewed Bruce at least ten times. Her conversations and memories were like music. When I met her, she was eighty-two years old. She lived to receive an Honorary Degree from Hollins University, where not so long ago, her ancestors had been enslaved. And she lived to be one hundred years old.

Chapter 9. Another Other: White Negroes

During our first interview, Lee described this place of "White Negroes" as a "strange island." The Blacks were freed but lived together in isolation believing life was better there than on the outside. After slavery ended, freeing more than four million Blacks in the South, the younger "White Negroes" left and probably passed as white. The older ones died off. They had been prosperous and happy and lived in their own utopia.

Chapter 10. Two Ways of Seeing the World—Gloria Naylor (1950-2016)

I interviewed Gloria Naylor in 1997 on the mountain of Wintergreen, Virginia, where a group of Black scholars, artists, writers, and others have been gathering for more than thirty years to support and cheer each other on.

Chapter 11. We Reached out to the Arts and the Arts Said Yes—Nikki Giovanni (1943-)

By the time I met Giovanni, she had published: *Black Feeling, Black Talk* (1967) and *Black Judgment* (1969), both were reissued as a joint volume, *Recreation* (1970), *The Women and the Men, My House, Cotton Candy on a Rainy Day*, and so many others books and records. My approach to this conversation is her teaching. I've learned after thirty years how difficult it is. She is beloved over the globe. It took us three years to build the African American Studies Program at Virginia Tech. Giovanni is one of the most prominent poets in the world.

I can't begin to recall all of the artists, singers, you name it who came through our class those three years.

ABOUT THE AUTHOR

Ethel Morgan Smith is the author of two books: *From Whence Cometh My Help: The African American Community at Hollins College* and *Reflections of the Other: Being Black in Germany*. She's also professor emeritus at West Virginia University and has taught at Virginia Tech, Randolph College, Universität of Tübingen (Germany), and Monash University (Australia). She has been awarded grants and fellowships from Bread Loaf Conference, Virginia Center for Creative Arts, Fulbright-Universität Tübingen, Germany, Rockefeller Foundation (Bellagio, Italy), Brandeis University, a visiting artist at American Academy Rome, and two NEH fellowships.